Fridtjof
Nansen Land

Spitsbergen

New Siberian
Islands

A R C T I C

Greenland
Sea

Novaya
Zemlya

Kara Sea

North Cape

Barents
Sea

S i b e r i a

Iceland

CIRCLE

Yenisei
River

Lena
River

Sea of
Okhotsk

ISH
ES

North
Sea

Baltic Sea

Dvina R.

URAL MTS.

Ob
R.

River

A S I A

Sakhalin

E U R O P E

Dnieper R.

Volga R.

Irtish

Lake
Baikal

Amur
River

ALPS

Danube

Caspian Sea

Aral
Sea

Lake Balkhash

Hwang-ho
(Yellow R.)

Sea of
Japan

eira

Black Sea

Amu Darya

HIMALAYA
MTS.

Yangtze Kiang

JAPAN

Mediterranean - Sea

Euphrates R.

Indus R.

Brahmaputra

Salween R.

PACIFIC

ly

Suez Canal

Ganges R.

Mekong R.

Sahara
Desert

Nile

Red Sea

Arabian
Sea

Bay of
Bengal

South
China

Philippine
Islands

Guam

Niger R.

L. Chad

Irrawaddy River

Sea

OCEAN

A F R I C A

R.

Ceylon

Celebes

Gulf of
Guinea

L. Victoria

Borneo

Ascension I.

River Congo

L. Tan-
ganyika

Sumatra

New
Guinea

LANTIC

I N D I A N

Helena

Lake
Nyasa

Java

OCEAN

Zambesi R.

Madagascar

AUSTRALIA

Orange R.

O C E A N

Cape of Good Hope

Murray R.

Tasmania

A N T A R C T I C   O C E A N

A N T A R C T I C A

Lands and Peoples

THE WORLD IN COLOR

VOLUME V

THE GROLIER SOCIETY

NEW YORK   TORONTO

M

Volume V

TABLE OF CONTENTS

A BERBER FROM THE REMOTE ATLAS HIGHLANDS OF MOROCCO

A robed tribesman from the Atlas Mountains makes a strong point in what appears to be a heated argument. The Berbers are a proud people, fiercely jealous of their freedom.

Morocco and the Moors

A Glimpse of the Most Western Land of Islam

Known in the Arab world as "The Farthest West," Morocco sprawls over the Atlas Mountains between the Strait of Gibraltar and the western Sahara. In the Middle Ages it was a stronghold of the Moors who ruled over Spain. During this time and until the early nineteenth century, Morocco was one of the Barbary States, whose pirates were the terror of the Mediterranean. It finally came under European control and in 1912 was divided into three zones—the French, the Spanish and the International Zone of Tangier. The sultan of Morocco retains his title but has little actual power. Today, especially in French Morocco, there is a strong desire for complete independence.

LESS than two hundred years ago few travelers from the West had ever been to North Africa, and those who did go seldom returned to their native shores, for many of the seaports were the haunts of pirates and slave-traders, who liked nothing so much as the sight of a becalmed and heavily laden merchantman.

They were good seamen were these Corsairs and drove their long-oared galleys, rowed by slaves of all nations, even as far as the coasts of England, where they would land and attack some unfortunate Cornish hamlet at night, dragging off the inhabitants to hopeless slavery.

The lands along the coast of North Africa, whence these pirates came, were then known as the Barbary States from the original inhabitants, the Berbers who have probably existed there since the Stone Age. The Berbers, who are black in color but are really members of the white race whose skin has tanned and darkened through exposure to countless ages of African sun, were cut off from conquest to the south or from intermingling with the black race of Central and South Africa by the vast Sahara Desert, more impassable than any sea.

Walling off this "land of the Berbers" still more effectively is the snow-clad Atlas Mountain range, divided into the Great, Middle and Little Atlas, which stretches along the edge of the Sahara from Morocco in the west to Tunisia in the east. It was the sight of their great heights, lost in the clouds, that caused the Greek sailors to say that here Atlas was holding the world on his shoulders and the name has remained to this day.

The fertile, coastal strip was easily accessible, however, from the Mediterranean which washed its shores on the north and brought traders and conquerers alike. The Phoenicians and the Greeks came ; the Romans established colonies ; there were invasions of the Vandals, but the Berbers seemed little affected by the contact with other peoples.

In the seventh century came the Arabs enforcing Mohammedanism as they conquered even into the most inaccessible region, "The Farthest West," which came to be known as Morocco, and its inhabitants Moors, though this name only rightfully belongs to those who have Arab and Berber blood in their veins. The Moors became great conquerors. Their great military period was in the eighth century, when they sailed across the Strait of Gibraltar and seized upon the southern half of Spain. There, in Andalusia, they flourished for hundreds of years. At last they were driven from Spanish soil in the fifteenth century.

Morocco retained its independence for many centuries under various dynasties. It is still nominally independent; but to all practical purposes it has been divided up between France and Spain, which have set up protectorates. French Morocco continued to be governed by French colonial officials after the fall of France in World War II. In November, 1942, it was occupied by the Allies, and became a strong Allied base. The French Zone of Morocco is now governed by a resident general.

Morocco, like its Moorish inhabitants, is highly inconsistent. During the few

5

MORE HOMES FOR A BUSY AFRICAN CITY

Casablanca, a seaport on the Atlantic coast, is French Morocco's largest city and one of the most important ports of North Africa. Although it was founded in 1468 by the Portuguese, it is today a modern city. In this new housing development, the architects have adopted a style of architecture well suited to the hot weather and merciless sun of Africa.

weeks of spring, the land is a paradise of wild flowers and birds, but by July most of Morocco is once more a scorched and barren waste.

Though bitterness has often marked the relations of Morocco with the industrial and trading nations of Europe, there have been periods of co-operation that brought rewards to both sides. Railways and motor roads, irrigation systems and modern sections in the large cities attest to the hard work and technical ability of Euro-

peans and Moroccans alike. In the city of Casablanca the old and new rub shoulders. Camels and motor cars, Moors and French officers mix together in the wide streets and before the great hotels. Over the new white and yellow houses shines the fierce African sun, and behind is the tumbling Atlantic where the harbor bristles with the masts of ships.

Casablanca is the new Morocco; Marrakesh may be taken as an example of the old. It is an inland city built in a large oasis of palms, and behind it loom the great snow-clad peaks of the vast Atlas regions—the mountainous backbone of Morocco. The French military road to Marrakesh runs across desert where nothing grows and where the heat is intense. An occasional motor car flies past strings of laden camels which grimace as if in disgust.

The ancient rose-red walls of Marrakesh are seven miles around; from their ten gateways once marched the armies that carried fire and sword into Spain. Though a garage here and there shows the growth of European ideas of transport, the town is much the same as it was centuries ago.

In the streets, gray-eyed Berbers, in their cloaks of woven goats' hair, woolly haired men from the Sudan, Negro slaves, Jews and wild-looking nomad Arabs jostle together, for Marrakesh is a great center of the trading caravans, and here may be heard a hundred strange lan-

FRENCH EMBASSY—INFORMATION DIVISION

THE SULTAN'S GUARD LEADS THE WAY

At the head of a parade, the royal guard of the Sultan of Morocco passes under a triumphal arch in the old section of Rabat, the capital of French Morocco. The city is an important seaport on the Atlantic coast and it is here that the Sultan spends much of his time, in his palace southwest of the town. From the sea the 180-foot minaret of the Hasan Tower is visible.

guages. Camels and mules press through the crowds of gaping sightseers, merchants and beggars. Snake-charmers play on wooden flutes and allow their reptiles to bite their hands. As the serpents' poison glands have been removed, this is not so dangerous as it looks. Cake-sellers and venders of water and fruit cry their wares, and Negro jugglers and acrobats do their utmost to attract the people.

Cities That Are Truly Eastern

Here, as a living reproach to the memory of some bygone governor, stands an old Negro whose eyes have been put out for theft. He pleads monotonously for alms and he does not go unrewarded. The crowd is a mass of color, and the gaudy cloaks and scarves, yellow silks, silver girdles and gay turbans are dazzling to eyes that are accustomed only to the more sombrely dressed crowds in our country.

Marrakesh, once the capital of the old Moorish empire which included Spain, Tunis and the Sudan, is now only a shadow of its old self, but the Moors do not regret the departure of its glory. Under the shadow of its crumbling palaces and mosques, they quote their old proverb: "When a thing becomes perfect it soon fades." "What is to be will be," say the Moors and leave the magnificent, old buildings to decay, or to be restored by the French.

Fez, another old capital, also shows the old glory of Morocco. Here there are still holy men and story-tellers, mosques and shrines which no infidel may enter. The walls and ramparts are immense, and the town itself is a gigantic maze of minarets, green-tiled roofs and great Saracenic archways. Nowadays, the sultan usually resides at the coast city of Rabat.

A Glimpse of a Moorish Palace

Bou Jeloud is one such palace hidden away and seemingly forgotten. Its courtyards are set with Moorish fountains, and there are gardens within its walls where fig trees, roses and enormous masses of geraniums bloom in a setting of fairylike, Moorish architecture, with its wealth of colored tiles and carved cedar wood and its elaborate geometrical designs in plaster and stone.

The Moors are very superstitious. Some years ago a half-witted man in Fez used to remain in prayer for weeks at a time. This, added to his madness, which, in the East, is always taken as a sign of holiness, caused him to be regarded as a saint. He was thought too holy to be seen by common people, and a shrine was built for him wherein candles are kept burning night and day.

Though most people think of the Moors as one people, they are really composed of several distinct races. First, we have the true Arab, the descendant of the fierce Mohammedans from Arabia who conquered North Africa centuries ago. He inhabits the plains and the great towns. The Berber, who lives in the hills and may be gray-eyed and fair in coloring, is the original inhabitant of the country. The Rifs who fought so long against Spain and France are of this race. Negroes there are in plenty.

In all the coastal towns there are many Jews. Most are the descendants of those who left Spain when Moorish power waned in that country. Others trace their roots to Jewish migrations of pre-Christian times. In Morocco, Jews have been forced to live as second-class citizens in overcrowded, ghettolike sections called *mellehs*. Most Moroccan Jews have few legal or property rights and their poverty is extreme. In an effort to better their lot, considerable numbers have migrated, since 1948, to the Jewish state of Israel, in Palestine.

In Spanish Morocco

Besides French Morocco and the Tangier Zone, which came under Spanish rule in 1940 and reverted to international control in 1945, there is Spanish Morocco. This is a much smaller protectorate, mountainous and sparsely settled by several tribes of Berbers. They are pastoral people, that is to say, they depend chiefly on their cattle, sheep and goats for food and clothing.

This mountainous district, which is north of the Atlas region, is known as

© E. N. A.

MOORISH WOMEN of the higher classes, according to Mohammedan tradition, are kept in strict seclusion. They are not allowed to leave their homes unless their faces are veiled and unless they cover themselves with a cloak that reaches almost to the ground. The houses are built with flat roofs where the women may sit and chat in the cool of the evening.

BRIGHTLY UNIFORMED GUARDS AT THE KHALIFA'S PALACE, TETUAN

Moorish arches, like giant keyholes, span the entrance way of the Khalifa's Palace. The guards
wear uniforms of dazzling white to protect them from the penetrating rays of the sun.

STRAW-THATCHED HUTS MARK A BERBER VILLAGE IN MOROCCO

Some Berbers live in villages of stone houses and maintain their own mines, flour mills and olive presses. But others farm with primitive implements and live in straw-roofed sod huts.

VEGETABLE SELLERS ARRANGING WARES IN THE MARKET PLACE

The international zone of Tangier attracts many visitors. One of its most colorful quarters is the market place. Fruit vendors cry their wares, and snake charmers play reeds.

IN A MOORISH DOORWAY, a minstrel of Morocco and his wife relax at the end of the day. Her colorful costume—bright silks, brocade and beads—the rich tapestries, the archway and the vase in the left foreground remind us of the fine decorative taste of the Moors. Their architecture alone has given the Moors a high place in the world of art.

ON A NEIGHBORLY CALL, the bearded gentleman with the cane interrupts a stroll through cobbled streets to sit and talk with a friend. The loose robes protect their wearers against the blaze of the sun and the harsh blast of arid winds. The sun, a great artist, colors everything in North Africa: the walls, yellow and pink; complexions, a ruddy tan.

13

"BLIND" HOUSES ON A STREET IN MAZAGAN, MOROCCO

The street is hardly more than an alley, without sidewalks and poorly paved. From it one would hardly guess that the town is a port on the Atlantic Ocean, a little distance southwest of Casablanca, important chiefly for the export of agricultural products from the fertile region of Doukkala. Mazagan was founded by the Portuguese in 1502.

CITY OF SNOW-CAPPED MOUNTAINS AND TROPICAL PALMS

Marrakech, southern capital and largest city of Morocco, lies in the shadow of the snow-covered Atlas Mountains. Part of the city wall shows in the foreground. The Mosque of Koutoubia, with its lofty tower rising at the left, is considered the most beautiful structure in the city. It is also known as the Mosque of the Scribes and dates back to the twelfth century.

the Rif, and the inhabitants are great fighters. Physically these Rifs, or Riffis, are a much finer race than the true Moors, and many of them are red-haired and gray-eyed. To account for this, some learned men say that the Rifs are descended from Scandinavians who landed in Africa in the twelfth century.

There may be some truth in this theory of a common ancestry with the Caucasian race; for the Rifs, though fierce, have not the Oriental ferocity of the other Moors but are warlike in a genial, hearty way, like the old German robber barons, or the early Saxons.

It is not surprising that these fighting races resented the Spanish occupation of their lands, and, at various times revolts started among certain tribes. An indecisive guerrilla warfare was carried on till 1921, when the Rifs captured 20,000 Spanish troops with all their artillery, transport and ammunition. This is known in history as the Melilla disaster.

Abd-el-Krim, the leader of the Rifs, reorganized his army on modern lines, and then attacked the Spaniards vigorously. For a time he was successful, and

the courage of the Rifs and the fanatical bravery of their allies (who regarded the campaign as a Jehad or Holy War) prevailed against the armies of Spain. Nevertheless, Spain, unwilling to lose the last vestige of her empire, refused to withdraw from the struggle.

Unfortunately for Abd-el-Krim, some of his allies made raids into the French protectorate. With Spain he could deal, but to challenge the greatest military power then in Europe was another thing. From the day France entered the war, Rif independence was doomed. Airplanes, tanks and heavy artillery proved too much for the tribesmen, and after a long and desperate war with the two European powers, Abd-el-Krim surrendered to the French in 1926.

For many years, affairs ran smoothly in French Morocco. Apparently the French were better able to gauge the temperament of the Moors, and they governed with a mixture of firmness and tact. When the great market place in Fez was destroyed by fire, Marshal Lyautey, the resident-general, caused a replica to be built, complete with all the shrines of Moslem saints.

THE CARPENTER'S FOUNTAIN in Fez shows the architectural skill of the old Moors, a skill their descendants do not seem to possess. The city gave its name "fez" to a certain kind of cap, which was originally made there and which is worn in some Mohammedan countries. Fez, the northern capital of Morocco, is divided into two portions by the River Pearl.

© E. N. A.

FEZ, A HOLY CITY of Islam, contains the shrine that we see here. It is that of Mulai Edris II, the founder of the city, and no infidel may set foot therein. Within the city walls are mosques and palaces and gardens, and the university, though formerly much larger, is famous as a centre for the study of the Mohammedan religion and law.

Like the Romans, who once occupied these regions, the French regarded roads as a great civilizing influence. Roads mean communication, and communication means the exchange of ideas. When the roads were constructed in 1916, the Moors would descend at night and destroy them, but the French doubled the guards and the work went on. Saleh, Rabat, Marrakech and all the other big towns are linked by excellent roads, and hundreds of miles of railways stretch across the sands.

Under French rule, Morocco developed rapidly save only in the lesser known Atlas regions where the great Berber feudal lords held sway.

As the twentieth century entered its second half, however, the temper of the people was changing. The strong spirit of nationalism that was sweeping Asia had spread to Africa, too, and the French were having their troubles. Skirmishes took place between Arab demonstrators and the French police and militia, and some blood was shed. Morocco supported Tunisia in her appeal to the UN for independence, and by 1952 French Morocco was also agitating for home rule.

MOROCCO: FACTS AND FIGURES

THE COUNTRY

Lies on the northwest coast of Africa; bounded on the north by the Mediterranean, on the east by Algeria, on the south (indefinitely) by the Sahara and on the west by the Atlantic. Tangier International Zone (area, 135 square miles; population, about 125,000 with 17,000 Europeans); the northern zone, a Spanish protectorate (area, 7,787 square miles; population, about 1,140,000); the remainder, a French protectorate (area, 161,500 square miles; population, 8,225,-000). Other Spanish possessions: Ifni, enclosed by the French Zone (area, 675 square miles; population, 42,000); Southern Protectorate (area, 10,036; population, 12,000); Saguia el Hamra (area, 31,652; population, 11,000); Rio de Oro (area, 71,564; population, 25,000).

GOVERNMENT

The French Zone is a French protectorate, dating from April 1912. The sultan is religious primate and chief-of-state under advice of the French Resident-General. Administration is in the hands of the French and a native organization. Local administration is in the hands of native pashas and French controllers. The Spanish Zone is under the control of the Spanish High Commissioner and a Calipha who is chosen by the sultan from 2 candidates named by the Spanish government. Tangier became by statute of 1923, which came into force in 1925, a neutral and demilitarized zone with an autonomous government. Legislative power was placed in the hands of an international assembly, the president of which was a native representative of the sultan. International administration of the Tangier Zone, allowed to lapse during Spanish occupation in World War II, was restored in 1945.

COMMERCE AND INDUSTRIES

French Zone—Agriculture is the most important industry, but is carried on by natives using primitive methods. Principal crops are cereals, beans, chickpeas, canary seed, olives, vines, fruits and almonds; considerable forests of cork, cedar, arar, argan and oak. Gums are produced. Phosphate is the principal mineral.

Fishing and livestock-raising are important. Miscellaneous industries include flour mills, breweries, soap, candle factories, cement factories. The exports are phosphates, cereals, preserved fish, ores, fruits and other livestock and agricultural products; imports are sugar, petroleum products and machinery.

Spanish Zone—Agriculture of most primitive fashion is the chief industry; iron ore is mined; tunny fishing is important. Exports are iron ore, goatskins, canned and dried fish and esparto grass; imports are flour, semolina, refined sugar, tea, seed oils and wines.

Tangier International Zone—The chief industries are cigarette-making and fishing. Exports are skins, eggs and tinned fish; imports are flour, sugar, candles, fabrics, tobacco, coffee and tea.

COMMUNICATIONS

Railways: French Zone, 1,184 miles; Spanish Zone, 58 miles; and Tangier, 11 miles. Motor roads: French Zone, 7,447 miles; Spanish Zone, 540 miles; and Tangier, 65 miles. Nine air lines serve the French Zone. Length of telegraph lines in the French Zone, 11,044 miles with connections to cities in the Spanish Zone. Telephone line mileage in French Zone, 103,847.

RELIGION AND EDUCATION

Mohammedans of the Sunni sect predominate; the Jewish population numbers more than 200,-000. Illiteracy is widespread. In the French Zone, Moslem and state schools of primary, secondary and higher levels have an enrollment of about 225,000. There are state and Hispano-Arabic schools in the Spanish Zone. In Tangier, schools under French and Spanish protectorate governments supplement Jewish and Moslem schools.

CHIEF TOWNS

French Zone—Rabat (French capital and principal residence of the sultan), population, 161,600; Casablanca, 569,500; Marrakech, 239,-200; Fez, 202,000; Meknes, 162,400.

Spanish Zone—Tetuan (capital), 93,658.

Tangier International Zone—Tangier, 60,000.

FROM SENEGAL TO SOMALILAND

France's Overseas Negro Territories in Africa

France's Arab and Moorish peoples in Africa are treated in other articles, as are Madagascar, Réunion and Mayotte. This article deals chiefly with those French overseas territories where the population is predominantly Negro. It includes a fringe of small coast holdings reaching into the interior, which varies from the aridity of the world's greatest desert to the dense forests of an equatorial belt where the rainfall is excessive. The heat and disease-bearing insects make it unhealthful for white men who are unaccustomed to such climate. The Belgian Congo is discussed in the article In the Heart of Africa. French West Africa, which lies between French Equatorial Africa and the Sahara, comprises Senegal, Mauretania, French Sudan, French Guinea, Ivory Coast, Dahomey, Niger and Upper Volta. The population is Negro, Hamitic (of Caucasian origin) and mixed, with the usual scattering of Europeans. Then, in our trek across the continent, we come to French Somaliland on the east coast.

AFRICA has been the scene of the most extensive French overseas expansion, which began as early as 1365 when the Norman sea-faring folk of Dieppe explored the west coast of the dark continent, establishing trading stations in Senegal and Guinea. These expeditions were not backed by national support, although they enriched a dozen ship-owners and these practically founded the French mercantile marine. For a period the foothold in Senegal was lost, but had been recovered by 1637, and the nineteenth century saw considerable further expansion. At the end of the first World War, France made some gains where Germany had lost. Other articles deal with the Arab and Moorish peoples of French North Africa, which, separated by desert and mountains, is Medi-

FRENCH EMBASSY—INFORMATION DIVISION

RIVAL FOR MEDUSA

This native of Ubangi-Shari (French Equatorial Africa) in his war paint and headdress of spears is no less fearful a sight than Medusa, who could turn men to stone.

terranean rather than African in its geography. Another article treats of Madagascar, with Mayotte and Réunion islands off its coast. This one will include French Somaliland on the east coast, the Sahara (mentioned in another volume as one of the world's great waste lands), and in particular, French West Africa. This was once known as French Sudan. When France drafted a new constitution in 1946, this area acquired the status of an overseas territory. It consists of eight small territories including Senegal, French Sudan, Niger, Upper Volta, Mauretania and the narrow coastal territories of French Guinea and the Ivory Coast, and also Dahomey which squares off a corner of Niger. The chapter will deal, too, with French Equatorial Africa. This was known until 1910 as

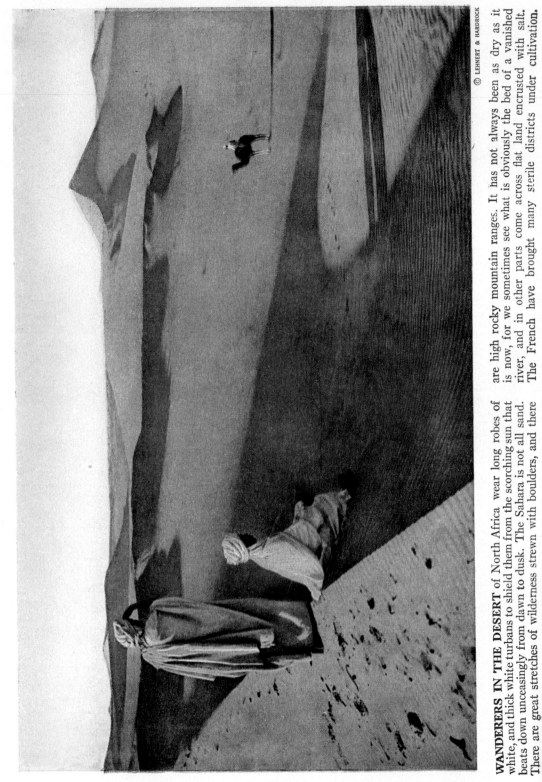

© LEHNERT & HARDROCK

WANDERERS IN THE DESERT of North Africa wear long robes of white, and thick white turbans to shield them from the scorching sun that beats down unceasingly from dawn to dusk. The Sahara is not all sand. There are great stretches of wilderness strewn with boulders, and there are high rocky mountain ranges. It has not always been as dry as it is now, for we sometimes see what is obviously the bed of a vanished river, and in other parts come across flat land encrusted with salt. The French have brought many sterile districts under cultivation.

AN OASIS IN THE SAHARA seems like paradise to one who has seen nothing but stretches of burning, shifting sand for days. Sometimes, when crossing these desert sands, a traveler sees a pool of water ruffled by the wind. This may be only a "mirage," or false picture, caused by the sand giving heat to the adjacent layers of air. This air becomes less dense, and possesses different properties of reflection than the cooler air above. This trick mirror may cause a far-away object to appear nearby, a scene to be upside-down or an image to seem double.

21

French Congo, a country not unlike the Belgian Congo described in In the Heart of Africa. The large block known as the Cameroons is a UN trusteeship under French and British supervision. In general this vast territory, shown on the map that follows, is an area too hot for white men. Either it presents the rock-strewn aridity of much of the Sahara, or the excessive wetness of the dense, vine-strangled forests to the south. There are but few hill regions so numerous in British Africa; yet it is populated, in places densely, by black tribes whose heavily pigmented skins protect them from the sun's ferocity.

Railways were late in coming to Africa, and some regions are as yet hundreds of miles from a rail line. There are hard-surface motor roads, but they, too, are scarce and poor in the interior. Long the principal means of travel in all of Africa, camel caravans are still important. Water travel has also been widespread, as central Africa has a generous share of long, navigable rivers. Air flights from Europe into Dakar and other important cities and towns are now regular occurrences, and airfields have been increasing in number throughout the territories. It is, therefore, rather simple to get a swift bird's-eye view of the continent.

The Rifts of Central Africa

As we fly over central Africa, we see below us the thick, tangled jungles that have made the airfield-builder's task so difficult. Moving on to the east we cross above two great Rift Valleys, cracks in the land mass filled with lakes and waterways from Lake Nyasa to the Nile and to the Red Sea. There are massive highlands through East and South Africa, and high country across Cameroon and northern Nigeria, but the Congo Basin lies in a great depression and the Sahara is in places (where it was once inundated) actually below sea level. Yet even this vast desert has the Ahaggar (Hoggar) Mountains, rising south of Algeria to as much as eight thousand feet and extending into the naked Tibesti or Tu Highlands, which in past

ages formed a bridge across the sands and stony wastes by which animals migrated from north to south. West Africa, however, has few mountains, though the Futa Jallon form the watershed of the Niger, the Senegal, the Gambia and other important rivers, and the Bauchi Plateau, Africa's great tin area, rises in northern Nigeria and Cameroon. The climate, so near the equator, varies rather in the amount of rainfall and the sharp change from noon to night rather than by seasons.

Oases and Camel Caravans

If we have flown from, say, Morocco across the Sahara, our first surprise will be to find, amid the stony red expanses and the white seas of sand dunes, occasional oases, green with date-palms, and inhabited by villagers, who offer succor to camel caravans en route to Timbuctoo and elsewhere. The oases are strung along the depressions where water rises to the surface, and these determine the great trade routes. A notable example of land reclamation is the Niger irrigation scheme of the French Sudan, which has turned the inland delta of the river into a productive cotton- and rice-farming area.

France controls most of the Sahara, some of which is still unexplored. That it has been in the main waterless for centuries is evident from the Arab name "Sahira," which itself means "desert." Yet ancient dry watercourses indicate that the region may not always have been so desolate as it is today. While the major portion of the French Sahara is rocky, in the western part there is sand which often piles up into dunes a thousand feet high; and when the swift hot winds come sweeping along, they carry this sand in clouds, burying the thorny dwarf plants—until another sandstorm shall uncover them— and stifling men and caravan animals.

Timbuctoo of Desperate Deeds

In the southern part of this desert not far from the Niger lies Timbuctoo (Timbuktu), a Negro town of mud walls and dwellings that was an important center of caravan routes from Morocco and Guinea.

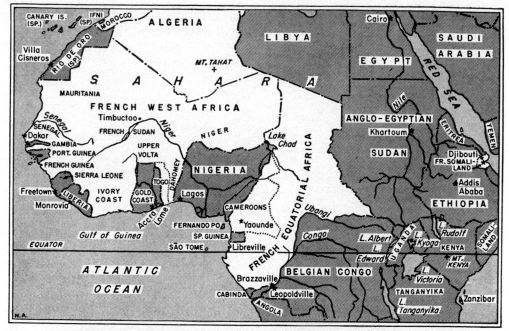

FRENCH AFRICA FROM THE ATLANTIC TO THE RED SEA

Though less important today with the decline of the caravan trade, it is accesible by
two motor routes. It can also be reached
from the coast by a railway from Dakar to
Koulikoro, from whence a steamboat service runs to Timbuctoo seven months a
year. The Negroes here are of different
stock from the Bantus south of the Cameroons, though both are primitive.

In the eleventh century the Tuaregs, a
nomadic people of Berber origin, occupied
Timbuctoo, and left a long record behind
them of oppression and slavery, robbery
and desperate deeds. Now there lived
along the Upper Niger a Sultan Samory,
a slave-raider who had formed a brigand
empire and sold probably a million and
a half Negro captives to the Tuaregs in
exchange for gold, ivory and cattle.
These Negro slaves were called black
ivory, and as the region abounded in the
big-eared African elephants, there was
much slaughtering of these beasts for
their tusks of white ivory, and proces-
sions of naked slaves used to be sent to
market carrying these tusks upon their
shoulders. In 1880 a French captain of
the marines, Joseph Simon Galliéni
(the same who distinguished himself in
World War I), was captured by Sultan

Samory and held prisoner until another
French force had overcome the many ferocious small tribes of mixed Berber and
Negro stock and imposed peace on the
region, rescuing Timbuctoo from the rule
of the Saharan Berbers. But by 1888
Galliéni had broken into Western Sudan
and defeated Sultan Samory, who was,
however, not captured until 1898. Timbuctoo is today a town in French Sudan,
the territory in the central section of
French West Africa.

Now let us view the parched and stony
(and in part mountainous) wastes of the
French Sudan. Circling above it, we see
to the eastward a shallow great expanse
gleaming like a steel mirror in a green
frame. That is Lake Chad, which during the rainy season may spread to twenty
thousand square miles in area, although
during the dry season it shrinks to half
that. Yet practically nowhere is it ever
more than fifteen feet deep. The silver
loops of two-thirds of the Niger River
and all of the Upper Senegal lead our
eye westward. These rivers grow with
the rains of July to October until the
Niger can accommodate small steamboats,
though for five months or more it is too
shallow. The lesser streams dry up, and

23

DATE PALMS are the chief trees of the Saharan oases, and they provide the staple food of the desert tribes. Sometimes an oasis is merely a grove of palms around a well; sometimes, when the water is supplied by a stream, it is larger and more luxuriant and fruit and grain may be grown. An oasis may include a permanent village or even a small town.

their beds become overgrown with shrubs that grow like wildfire in that equatorial climate. Anglo-Egyptian Sudan and what was formerly French Sudan (the word "Sudan" means Land of the Blacks) were for long a conquest of Turkey, which ruled it despotically through Egypt.

To turn southward for a short inspection, French merchants settled by the Gabun River above the Congo as early as 1839, and after the opening of the Belgian Congo, as described in the article In the Heart of Africa, the French secured a part of the Congo basin. Here it was that Du Chaillu discovered the gorilla. This and other parts of French Africa are amazingly rich in wild game—herds of elephants, with tusks heavy enough to employ four porters each, herds of vicious buffaloes, droves of vividly striped zebras, thick-skinned rhinoceri and clumsy hippopotami along the waterways, many varieties of the monkey tribe in the forests, herds of ostriches in the southern Sahara, to say nothing of the bright-striped zebras of the grasslands, lions, leopards, antelopes, giraffes and crocodiles.

Wild Berbers Tamed

Now if we are to continue our journey in logical order, we will fly from Timbuctoo across to the west coast of the Sahara to Mauritania, which is one of the eight territories that form French West Africa. Here live numbers of Moorish Mussulmans of Berber affiliations whose men-folk wear veils over their mouths and noses to protect them from the sand. Though caravans once feared their name, French influence under a colonial policy has been such that the natives look upon the French flag as their own. Their famous fighters have come forward in large numbers in both world wars to help their mother country against Germany—irony of fate, since it was Bismarck who had induced the French explorer, Jules Ferry, to go empire-building in Africa!

Proceeding southward along the coast to Senegal, we will find a new air base there, in the colony from which Ferry started to the Upper Niger when he claimed this valuable territory for the French. Senegal is a region of sandy soil where the natives cultivate groundnuts, corn, rice and millet. They weave and make pottery, as well as heavy jewelry of pure silver and gold, ivory and amber. There is a river service, during the rainy season, down the Senegal to the port of Dakar, one of the chief entries to French West Africa. It serves to carry the imports of the region and its exports, chiefly groundnuts (peanuts).

The Several Guinea Lands

Senegal is really the first of a series of coastal approaches (by means of either rivers or railroads) to the interior plateaus which are often called the Guinea Lands. Some of these belong to other European nations than the French: all have much the same character, whether in French Guinea, so-called, the Ivory Coast, Dahomey, Togoland, Gold Coast, Nigeria or the Cameroons. We find flat country frequently separated from the ocean by sand spit and marsh and infested by myriads of malaria-bearing mosquitoes and tsetse flies which cause sleeping sickness. The products are similar in all of these territories—groundnuts (peanuts), palm kernels and palm oils, coffee and cocoa. On the Futa Jallon plateau in the French Guinea interior, cattle-raising is an important activity. Diamonds and gold are mined in many parts of West Africa, particularly in the British territories of Sierra Leone and the Gold Coast, as the name of the latter indicates.

Many Enormous Swamps

All the way from the mouth of the Senegal to the mouth of the Congo, a region visited by heavy rains (at one place 390 inches in one year), there are large rivers rising in the hills and emptying into the Atlantic; and while these are at times broken by rapids, they are highways for native craft and small launches. But the coast is also characterized by mangrove swamps, and off the Bay of Biafra in the Gulf of Guinea is a colossal swamp into which more than twenty rivers discharge their silt. Here the oil-

THE HARP'S THE THING IN DJIBOUTI'S STREET ORCHESTRAS

The spectacular object in the foreground is neither a fan nor an ornate headdress. It is a native harp—standard equipment for street orchestras in the coastal town of French Somaliland.

26

MELONS AND PEANUTS FOR SALE OUTSIDE TIMBUKTU'S WALLS

Timbuktu, in the French Sudan, was once a market for slaves and gold. The city is still a trading center and a halting place for caravans bound across the Sahara to Algeria and Morocco.

SUN-BAKED DJIBOUTI, THE CITY ON A CORAL PENINSULA

Djibouti is on the Red Sea, facing the Gulf of Aden. This is one of the hottest regions in the world. The city is a free port and is linked by rail with Addis Ababa, capital of Ethiopia.

27

MAYUMBA'S BEACHES FRINGED WITH PALMS WHERE THE ATLANTIC THUNDERS ON THE SHORES OF THE FRENCH CONGO

Cape Mayumba, formed by the estuary of the Mayumba River, runs parallel to the coast of French Congo. At the mouth of the long stretch of water it encloses is the small port of Mayumba, which ships the ivory, gum and copper which form the chief products of the surrounding district. French Congo, or French Equatorial Africa, with which it has since been included, has a total area of some 912,000 square miles. There are great areas suited to stock-raising, while the enormous forests covering over 300,000 square miles are capable of wide exploitation.

palm flourishes, the coconut, palm, bamboo and rubber-bearing plants provide material for export, the extensive cultivation of cotton is a dream of the future. The forests are valuable for their mahogany, cedar, ebony and other rare trees, although these are usually linked together by lianas and difficult to lumber.

The Ivory Coast has two great lagoons connected with one another by a canal, Grand Lahou and the port of Grand Bassam, with a lagoon over one hundred miles long and twelve feet deep, with jetties built to avoid the sand-bar at the harbor entrance. This opens up a region of pineapple and cocoa plantations and wild inland mahogany forests.

Dahomey reaches inland from primeval forest across the great Lama swamp (now crossed by rails) to the rich grasslands or savannahs, interspersed by fresh-water swamp forests, where the huts are made of grass, and palm oil is extracted for market. On an inland plateau stands Abomey, the scene of the notorious "Customs" when, annually, scores of human victims were sacrificed to the ancestral spirits, that they might serve them in the beyond. The dominant people here are the polygamous Ffon (Fons, Jejs or Jefe), Negroes of the Ewe family, an offshoot of the Bantus, ranging from chestnut to a yellowish tinge and possessed of unusual keenness as traders. The lagoon port of Whydah (Hwedah), since annexed by France, was originally Portu-

J. R. Birtwistle

ART SERVES RELIGION: DAHOMIAN SCULPTOR CARVING A FETISH

Fetishism is not idolatry, but a belief that the services of a spirit may be appropriated by possessing its material embodiment, and a fetish thus is a useful spirit in its proper shrine. This devout Dahomian is making a clay image for presentation to his fetish priest, using the beak of a slain fowl to carve the features.

THIS PART OF THE SCHOOL DAY IS FUN

Little girls learn to sing a new song in the public school at Rufisque, a district in Senegal, one of the eight territories that make up French West Africa. Their teacher is showing them how to clap their hands in time with the singing. Although education became compulsory in 1949, inadequate school facilities can serve only a small part of the population.

CHEERFUL FISHERMEN HOPE FOR A BIG CATCH

Fishing is an important source of food for the natives in the African towns located along the Atlantic coast. These fishermen of the town of Thiès, in the territory of Senegal, are preparing their nets for the day's work. Thiès is forty miles east of Cape Vert, the most western part of Africa, where Dakar, the capital of French West Africa, is located.

30

PIX

FASHION DESIGN, A HIGHLY INDIVIDUALIZED AFFAIR IN DAKAR

Dakar, Senegal, is the Negro fashion center of Africa. Each woman is her own designer and brooks no dictation. Though garments vary with the woman, basically they are always long, full and flowing. Indeed, social status is measured by the amount of material that is used. Color is also important. Brilliant hues and striking contrasts are considered to be the most beautiful.

guese and Portuguese names are borne by many of the natives. Here the French built the first fort in 1671, at a time when the kings of Hwedah derived vast riches from the dues levied on the export of slaves and ivory. In 1777 Whydah was conquered by the king of Dahomey because the Whydahs, who were fetish worshipers, had placed nothing but their great fetish Dahn, a carved serpent, to guard a strategic ford, and it happened that the Dahomey leader feared only his own fetish, a panther. His king, Agaja Dosu,

has been called a Tamerlane in miniature. Dahomey's neighbor, Togo, rising to hills between three and four thousand feet in altitude, smelts iron as well as cultivates large plantations.

French Somaliland, finally, directly eastward of the Anglo-Egyptian portion of the Sudan, has hardly enough inhabitants all told to make a city, though they are a cosmopolitan assortment—Sudanese, Somali, Arabs, Ethiopians, Indians, Jews and others. There are salt mines, coast fisheries and some trade.

FRENCH AFRICA: FACTS AND FIGURES

French Somaliland and each of the 8 sections of French West Africa are Overseas Territories. Each is under a governor, a government council and an elective assembly, and each has representatives in the French Parliament and the Assembly of the French Union.

FRENCH SOMALILAND

On the Gulf of Aden, bounded by British Somaliland, Ethiopia and Eritrea. Area, 9,071 square miles; population, 55,770. Chief industry and export is salt; imports include cotton goods and cattle. Population of capital and chief town, Djibouti, 17,000.

FRENCH WEST AFRICA

Bounded on the north by Spanish Sahara, Algeria and Libya; on the east by French Equatorial Africa; on the south by Nigeria, Gulf of Guinea, Gold Coast, Liberia and Sierra Leone; and on the west by Portuguese Guinea, Gambia and the Atlantic Ocean. Area, 1,815,768 square miles; population, 16,607,000. A governor-general at Dakar is assisted by a government council and a grand council consisting of 40 delegates, 5 from each of the 8 territorial assemblies. Chief exports: peanuts, peanut oil, coffee and cocoa. Chief imports: textiles, fuel oil, machinery and foodstuffs. Railways, 2,350 miles; all-weather roads, 16,800 miles; telegraph lines, 27,080 miles; telephone lines, 11,523 miles. In 1,560 primary and secondary schools there were about 165,000 pupils.

Dahomey. Area, 44,660 square miles; population, 1,505,000. Chief products are corn, cotton, coffee and palm oil. Population of capital and chief town, Porto Novo, 30,800.

French Guinea. Area, 108,430 square miles; population, 2,262,000. Products include rice, palm kernels, bananas, rubber and coffee. Livestock, 850,000 head. There are deposits of gold, diamonds, bauxite and iron ore. Population of capital and chief town, Conakry, 43,420.

French Sudan. Area, 461,270 square miles; population, 3,350,000. Products include peanuts, rice, corn, millet and cotton. Livestock, 13,350,-000 head, including camels. Population of capital and chief town, Bamako, 101,650.

Ivory Coast. Area, 129,770 square miles; population, 2,064,000. Products include peanuts, coffee, cocoa, bananas, palm oils and kernels, and mahogany. Population of capital and chief town, Abidjan, 45,730.

Mauritania. Area, 364,000 square miles; population, 522,560. Products: cattle, gum, salt and prepared fish. Livestock, including camels, 2,920,000 head.

Niger. Area, 493,690 square miles; population, 2,041,000. Products include millet, peanuts, rice and cotton. Livestock, including camels, 6,172,000 head. Population of capital and chief town, Niamey, 5,750.

Senegal. Area, 81,050 square miles; population, 1,999,000. Livestock, 470,000 head; crops—peanuts, millet, corn and rice. Oceanic and river shipping is considerable. Population of chief towns: St. Louis (capital), 63,000; Dakar, 132,000; Kaolak, 33,000.

Upper Volta. Area, 121,860 square miles; population, 3,177,000. Products include corn, rice, yams, edible fats, sisal, and native manufactures. Livestock, 2,450,000 head. Population of chief towns: Ouagadougou (capital), 28,000; Bobo-Dioulasso, 52,000.

UNITED NATIONS TRUST TERRITORIES

Togo. On the Gulf of Guinea between Gold Coast and Dahomey. Area (French), 21,893 square miles; population, 999,000. Products include cocoa, cotton, coffee, corn, palm kernels and peanuts. Population of capital and chief town, Lomé, 33,000.

Cameroun. Bounded on east and south by French Equatorial Africa, southwest by Rio Muni and west by Bight of Biafra and Nigeria. Area (French), 166,489 square miles; population, 3,009,000. Products include cocoa, palm kernels, timber and coffee. Population of capital and chief town, Yaoundé, 50,000.

PORTUGUESE GUINEA

Bounded by Senegal, French Guinea and the Atlantic Ocean. Area, 13,944 square miles; population, 517,000. Products include rice, palm oil, seeds and hides. Population of capital and chief port, Bissau, 1,000.

TWIXT THE DESERT AND THE SEA

Algeria, Tunisia and Libya

The fringe of green that stretches from Gibraltar to the Nile between the Mediterranean and the Sahara is a dry land watered by scant winter rains and here and there by short streams that rise in a rim of coastal highlands. The Berbers who first settled this fringe and the desert oases beyond the hills and mountains have never had an easy time. They have been hosts to one invader after another. First came the Phoenicians, followed by the Romans and after them the Vandals. Next the Byzantine Empire held sway, only to be succeeded in the seventh century by the Arabs and in the sixteenth by the Ottoman Turks. From the start of Arab rule until the French gained control in the nineteenth century, Morocco, Algiers, Tunis and Tripoli were known as the Barbary States. They warred on one another and raided the fleets of Europe. Only very short periods of peace intervened, and the few natural resources were left barely touched. Within the past hundred years, especially since the end of World War II, a desire for a greater measure of national freedom has grown up in North Africa. Libya gained its independence in 1951, and French rule in Tunisia and Algeria has suffered many setbacks.

THE desert wastes of North Africa might be likened unto quicksands, for old civilizations, religions and cities have been engulfed by those fine, tawny particles that trickle through one's fingers like water. When an animal lies down to die in the desert, the wind-driven sand eddies over and about it, sometimes completely covering it and again leaving it exposed. And the sand has treated great cities and civilizations in the same way.

Nearly three thousand years ago, Phœnicians and exiles from Tyre founded the famous city of Carthage near modern Tunis. A race of merchant seamen, they united martial skill with a genius for trade. Their fleets returned laden with slaves and their caravans with gold, and their armies were recruited from every country bordering on the Mediterranean Sea. To-day, but little of their stronghold remains, and their gods, Moloch and Melkarth, are only half-forgotten names.

Out in the trackless desert, Roman cities lie buried. Their wharves are now a two days' journey from the sea, and their oil-presses are a hundred miles from the nearest olive grove. At Timgad, in central Algeria, there is a gaunt, ruined, sand-swept city which has been deserted for centuries, and broken columns are the only relics of a vanished civilization.

In the seventh century A.D. the Mohammedan conquerors swept across the Libyan Desert, through Tunisia and Algeria, and into Morocco. Carthaginians, Romans, Vandals and Byzantines—all had contributed something to the land that eventually became an Arab stronghold. About ninety miles from Carthage, the Arabs, or Saracens, built their mysterious, forbidden city of Kairawan. Then it was that Tunis once more became the centre of culture.

Arab genius kept alight the lamp of learning, while Europe yet awaited the passing of the dark ages. The courts of the North African potentates were filled with poets and musicians, and the colleges with learned men. Then the flame died. The books of the philosophers and chemists were burned in order that the Koran might remain unquestioned, and the golden age of Arab culture passed, as other civilizations have done.

For centuries these lands were in an almost continuous state of war with one or another of the European powers, because their ports sheltered swarms of pirates and slave-traders who boldly seized merchant ships or even small war vessels, confiscating all property and holding for ransom the captives. It came about that most of the nations of Europe were paying large tribute to these Barbary States in order to be free from their piratical attacks. After the American Revolution, when the United States, no

33

VEILED LADIES TAKE THE AIR IN CONSTANTINE

Constantine, which is southeast of Algiers, is one of the most important cities of Algeria. It was named for the Roman Emperor, Constantine the Great, who restored it in 313 A.D., after it had been destroyed in war. A large part of the city's population is composed of Mohammedans. The native section—the casbah—can be seen beyond the bridge.

THE BUSY HARBOR OF ALGIERS

Algiers, the capital of Algeria, is an interesting combination of the modern and the old. The modern part of the city, with handsome buildings and many open squares, stands on the lower slopes of the hills facing the Bay of Algiers. The older part, which is Oriental in character, is traversed by narrow, crooked streets and occupies the higher slopes.

LONG-ROBED BUYERS AND SELLERS OF CAMELS NEAR A VILLAGE THAT LOOKS OVER THE GREAT SAHARA

©E.N.A.

There are many streams running southward from the Atlas Mountains into the Sahara, but most of them flow underground and the others very soon dry up. The subterranean ones can be tapped by means of wells, and wherever there is such a well, the hardy palm trees will grow. That is why this view of the sandy desert into which southern Algeria merges is so checkered with clusters of dark foliage. In other places desert soil is rock or hard clay and is entirely barren. Sandhill districts are known as the areg, or erg; the other regions are the hammadas.

WELCOME SIGHT: AN OASIS WELL IN THE HEART OF THE SAHARA

The oasis well above with its coping of gypsum is in southern Algeria. Such little desert wells are
fed by underground streams and may reach a depth of between twenty and fifty feet.

longer under the protection afforded by Great Britain's tributes, sent a fleet to force the plunderers to peaceful ways, other nations did likewise and eventually the rulers promised to reform their countries. But the old Arab genius was lacking, and another country gradually assumed control in Algeria and Tunisia.

It was the French who seized this opportunity of acquiring a vast colonial empire, and they have done much of which to be proud. Their roads and railways in Algeria and Tunisia stretch from the Mediterranean into the desert, and all North Africa, save Libya, Egypt, and a small part of Morocco, is theirs. Time alone will show whether their work will be lasting or whether their roads, railways, irrigation systems and towns will disappear in turn.

Old Pirate-town of Algiers

Algeria, one of the old Barbary States, lies between Morocco and Tunisia, and its chief port and capital is Algiers, once notorious for its pirates. Algiers is an example of the renewed prosperity of North Africa. Its wharves are crowded with ships loading their cargoes of grain and tobacco; its palm-shaded streets echo with the rumbling of heavy lorries and tram-cars. Shops such as we might expect to find in Paris cater to wealthy citizens, and merchants and tourists of all nationalities may be found in its palatial hotels.

Algiers might be compared to a tumbledown house in which the drains have been repaired and the lower floors rebuilt, while the ancient attics remain the same. The attics of the town are the pirate town. Gleaming white against the blue of sky and water, it climbs above the mansions and the wharves of the intruders, and from a distance it looks like a pile of ivory dominoes. Each little flat-topped house seems to be peering over its neighbor, and at the summit is the Kasbah, the fort of the old Arab rulers.

Hidden Beauties of the City

Less than one hundred and fifty years ago the sight of a strange sail on the horizon would cause these roof-tops to be crowded with excited people. Was it a pirate ship returning laden with plunder and slaves? Or was it the fleet of Spain, France, Great Britain, or the United States coming to batter at the walls with shot and shell?

The old town is without a real street, and its winding alleys are closed to all save pedestrians and little, laden donkeys. Many of the houses are built over these alleys, up which climb white-clad Arabs with slippered feet. Blank, white-washed walls line these narrow ways, for the houses, like the Arab women, hide their beauty. Inside them we should find cool courtyards in which fountains play, and carved balconies overlooking the enclosures. Beautiful tiles cover the walls, and the plaster is molded into intricate patterns.

The bazaars of Algiers are fascinating places, in which the old life of the town can be seen. The shops are little booths raised from the ground, at which the owners sit cross-legged waiting for their customers. There are shoemakers' shops, where the wizened craftsmen sit stitching at heelless colored slippers. On all sides are piles of slippers of every hue, tasseled and embroidered in scarlet and green silk.

Fair People of the Algerian Hills

Here is a jeweler working with such tools as were used in Harun-al-Rashid's Bagdad. There are metal-workers, hammering brass into the most delightful bowls and boxes; and through the throng moves the itinerant water-seller, and the Maltese who has wandered up from the French town to sell picture postcards to tourists. With their usual instinct for commerce, the Jews have penetrated deeply into the business life of Algiers. They own many of the booths, but because they are not popular, they generally trade under Arab names.

From the old town can be seen the wooded slopes of the hills, where the Kabyles, or Berber Arabs, live. They are a distinct race of people and are the descendants of the original inhabitants.

37

HOPING TO LOOSEN PURSE-STRINGS BY MEANS OF PATHETIC AIRS

Just as people in this country play the fiddle or turn the handle of a hurdy-gurdy at the pavement's edge to get pennies from passers-by, so in the streets of Algeria we shall find Negro musicians strumming on curious instruments of home manufacture. Coin-decked dancing girls are there, too, who are called Ouled Nails, and travel from town to town dancing in the open street, in the pasha's harem or in the native cafés.

LITTLE ARAB WHO ONE DAY MAY LEAD A DESERT CARAVAN

This small son of the desert shows in his expression some of the dignity and aloofness that is characteristic of his race. His embroidered and tasseled cap, striped cloak and leather shoes prove him to be the son of a rich man. It is quite possible that his father is a trader, who has many times led a caravan on the arduous journey across the desert to Timbuktu, the terminus of one of the three great Sahara trade routes.

A BROAD WHITE BOULEVARD IN THE MODERN QUARTER OF ALGIERS

Large buildings that house business and government offices, department stores and hotels line the
Boulevard de la République, one of several fine streets in the heart of Algiers.

Many of them are fair. They are farmers and graziers, and on the hillsides are fields, pastures and orchards.

Agriculture is flourishing in Algeria, for the French encourage farming by developing irrigation schemes and many French farmers have settled there. Although the natives use the most primitive methods in working their farms, they produce large quantities of wheat, barley and oats, a variety of vegetables, tropical fruits and tobacco, most of which are shipped to France to keep the markets supplied during the winter months. From the grapes, which also grow luxuriantly, large quantities of wine are made. The fertile part of Algeria is a narrow strip of land bordering the sea; farther south and running parallel to the coast, there are the high plateaus of the Atlas Mountains, which extend to the waste of sand and rugged hills on the northern edge of the Sahara Desert.

Traveling through Algeria, we shall see orange groves, cornfields and the red-roofed farmhouses of settlers. In places

AN AGED SCHOLAR WITH AN ANCIENT TEXT FROM THE KORAN

A teacher at the Tlemcen, Algeria, mosque school instructs his class with a board, on which are printed, in Arabic, quotations from the Koran, sacred scripture of Mohammedans.

© LEHNERT & HARDROCK

IN KAIRAWAN (OR KAIROUAN), once a forbidden city to all "Unbelievers," we may now wander without hindrance. We may even go into the mosque, a thing we can do in no other Tunisian town. This is the most sacred city in the eyes of the Mohammedans. In 1881, the French forced an entry through one of the five gates in its walls and much of its sanctity was destroyed. Although now connected by railway with the coast, it has been little modernized and is still essentially Arabian.

42

© CRETE

ALGERIAN GIRLS are often quite beautiful, as witness this jewel-decked Kabyle who so proudly displays the charms of her person and raiment. The beauty of the women-folk—a beauty they lose very early—is not surprising considering the thousands of lovely girls who were captured by the Barbary corsairs and were brought back for the Algerian harems.

RUINS OF CUICUL AND THE TRIUMPHAL ARCH OF CARACALLA

At Djemila near Setif in Constantine Department are the ruins of ancient Cuicul, a Roman town.
It flourished in the third century A.D., during the reign of the Emperor Caracalla.

SPARKLING WATER FLOWS TO MAKE A THIRSTY LAND FLOURISH

A diesel engine turbine pump provides water to irrigate orchards and truck gardens in fertile valleys near Tunis that get little rain. The soil is well suited to the growing of fruit.

THE AFRICAN MECCA, the holy city of Kairawan, or Kairouan, is in Tunisia and stands in a plain once covered with gardens and olive and orange groves. It is now barren except for a scrub of sage, though the soil is very rich and tempting. When in 670, Sidi Okba, a great Moslem soldier, wished to found, in Africa, a city that would be the rallying point for the Mohammedans, he is said to have stuck the butt of his lance in the ground in the middle of what was then a forest, and said, "Here is your Kairawan" (resting-place), thus naming it.

© LEHNERT & HARDROCK

THE GATE OF THE DESERT towards which we are looking from the Saharan side, is very fitting, named, for the train that carries us to Biskra has been running for hours through narrow mountain gorges, and, by means of tunnels, through chain after chain of rugged desolate mountains. Suddenly it issues from a tunnel into the gorge of El Kantara—"the Gate of the Desert"—and nothing but flat desert lies before it. The palm trees, the crumbling wall and the mud house are in the oasis of El Kantara. The mountains belong to the Aures system.

47

we may see herds of camels grazing on the hillsides. The Arabian camel is used throughout North Africa, and without him commerce and travel would be almost impossible, though motor cars are being used more and more.

Situated on a rock over two thousand feet in height, which is cut off from the surrounding country on three sides by a beautiful ravine is the city of Constantine, aptly named by the Arabs "the city of the air." It is an ancient city rebuilt by Constantine the Great in the fourth century on the site of a Roman colony. Within the past one hundred years, new streets have been laid out and many fine buildings constructed, but the native quarter with its winding lanes and squalid flat-roofed houses, remains truly oriental.

Algeria's Largest Oasis

From Biskra, an oasis noted for its beauty, we can take a peep at the desert. The town is a great meeting place for the desert people, and if we stay there long enough we are almost certain to see representatives of all the tribes inhabiting the Sahara. Biskra is well-watered by underground springs, and hundreds of thousands of date-palms grow in the neighborhood. There are half a dozen Arab villages in the Biskra oasis, but the town itself is a curious mixture of ancient and modern, for its delightful winter climate has made it a popular resort with several fine, modern hotels.

In a shady corner we may come upon an old marabout, or holy man, tracing figures in the sand. He has charms and amulets—pink coral to avert the evil eye, the hair of a four-months-old baby for protection against scorpions, verses from the Koran sewed into leather bags, and many others. He earns his living by selling these charms to the superstitious Arabs. Past him hurry energetic tourists, equipped with guide-books and sunglasses, and accompanied by a Negro in a ragged goatskin cloak.

In the Tunis of To-day

When the Phœnician mariners first sailed into what is now known as the Gulf of Tunis they saw on the horizon the symbol of their deity Baal, the Horned God—a happy omen, which, we may be sure, was not lost upon the founders of Carthage and Tunis. And to-day the pine-clad pinnacle of Bou-Cornein, which in Arabic means "the Father of Two Horns," is the most conspicuous landmark on the coast. It is so called because the summit is curved, forming two horns.

Tunisia is a protectorate, but entirely under French control, and in many ways it resembles Algeria. The wealth of both lies in a comparatively narrow strip of fertile coastal land, which on the south is succeeded by mountainous country and desert. There are almost as many Italians as Frenchmen in Tunisia, and Mussolini hoped (though it proved in vain) to add the colony to the great colonial empire he was planning for Italy.

The white city of Tunis lies on the Bay of Tunis, across which, at sunset, the red flamingoes fly to their homes among the reeds. People of all nations rub shoulders in its streets and boulevards, and the flags of many nations fly upon the ships in the harbor.

In the Perfume Bazaar of Tunis

In Tunis there is a street as fragrant as a flower garden. This is the perfume bazaar, where the scent of thousands of roses is imprisoned in little crystal vials. Each perfumer sits in his little cupboard of a shop, which is raised several feet from the ground, and the air is heavy with the mingled perfumes of orange blossom, attar-of-roses and verbena.

These sellers of perfumes claim descent from the Moorish aristocrats who were driven from Spain in the fifteenth century. Often their most treasured heirloom is the key of their ancient castle in Spain, which, it is to be feared, is sometimes as legendary as the proverbial ones.

The Arab shopkeeper is a man of leisure. His booth is his bed and there he dozes, drinks coffee and prays occasionally. He seems indifferent to custom and puts more faith in Allah than in

DATE PICKERS IN LIBYA, NORTH AFRICA, SCRAMBLE UP THE PALM TRUNKS

Much of Libya is desert country. Along the coast, however, bordering on the Mediterranean, are oases where groves of date palms and olive, orange, lemon and almond trees flourish.

THE DATE HARVEST is of great importance to the oasis-dweller, for dates are his chief food and his chief article of commerce while the branches are used for thatching his buildings. The golden-brown fruit, hanging in heavy clusters is cut down in the autumn, and the sorting, storing and packing them keep men, women and children busy for weeks.

WHITE TUNIS—Tunis la Blanche—lies spread out below the muezzin, who, from the gallery of the minaret, turns his face to the east and calls the Faithful to prayer. Tunis is a beautiful city lying beside a shallow lake that is connected by a strait with an inlet of the Mediterranean. The ruins of ancient Carthage lie only a few miles away.

© E. N. A.

IN CONSTANTINE, third city in Algeria, we shall find many wonderful examples of Moorish architecture, but none will please us more than the building that was formerly the palace of the beys of Constantine, with its sunny galleries, graceful arches and colored tiles. This is one of the historic buildings of the old town. Parts of it date from **1232.**

TELEGRAPH WIRES LOOK OUT OF PLACE IN ANCIENT TRIPOLI

Slender minarets break the monotony of flat-roofed, whitewashed houses in the native quarter of Tripoli, the capital of the colony, now called Libya. This cobbled street, lined with dilapidated-looking shops, is the Strada della Marina. The Mediterranean Sea washes the city walls on the north; the sands of the Sahara almost touch them on the west.

advertising or salesmanship.

Kairawan (or Kairouan), in Tunisia, is considered by Mohammedans to be one of the holiest cities in Africa, being sometimes known as the "African Mecca." It is visited by many pilgrims. Roman cities fell that Kairawan might rise, for, as it was built soon after the Arab conquest, it was largely constructed of pillaged Roman masonry. Cornices from temples to Roman gods are built into the city walls, and some of its foundation stones are the altars where pagan sacrifices were once performed.

Tripolitania, Cyrenaica and part of the Sahara area known as the Fezzan make up the Arab kingdom of Libya. The independent kingdom came into being on December 24, 1951, with the proclamation of the newly chosen king, Idris I. The United Nations had a friendly part in the making of Libya, and several richer, older nations have promised to aid the new country in its growing years.

The Fezzan, in central and southern Libya, is sparsely settled, with only about 4.3 inhabitants per square mile. The land is largely desert, with few good roads. There are fertile oases, however, where date palms are grown. Transportation is largely by camel caravan.

Cyrenaica, in the northeast, is rapidly becoming modernized, and the people are clamoring for education. Bengasi, chief port, is the seat of the regional government. There is an airfield near by, and short railroads and good highways are centered here.

Archaeologists have uncovered in Cyrenaica a wealth of Greek and Roman remains, buildings, sculptures, ceramics and other ancient treasures.

Tripolitania forms the western portion of Libya. It is largely farming country, where citrus fruits and olive trees flourish, and fields of barley ripen under the

TRANS WORLD AIRLINES

LETTERS WRITTEN AL FRESCO

A familiar street-corner stand in Algeria is that of the letter writer, who, for a fee, will take dictation or will compose for you any sort of missive you desire. Illiteracy among the Moslems is still high, perhaps up to 90 per cent. Comparatively few Moslem children in Algeria go to school. The picture above was photographed in the city of Constantine.

AT THE JOURNEY'S END both man and beast, though hardened to desert life, are glad to see before them the walls and minarets of a town and to know that soon they will find plenty of water for their refreshment. While the Arab on the left bathes his weary feet, the camels come to drink, still wearing over their humps the basket "coats" that prevent their backs and sides from being chafed by saddle or pannier. Two of the camels are not yet unloaded. The presence of a horse shows that this city is only on the fringe of the desert.

A BEDUIN WOMAN of Tunis admires silver ornaments—earrings, brooches and jeweled necklaces,—and she likes to wear many at one time. Often she wears a large part of her husband's capital, and as his wealth increases so will the number of silver chains, supporting coins or charms, that she fastens to her necklace. Chains may dangle from her brooches as well.

soft Mediterranean airs.

The capital and chief city is Tripoli, called "the white city" by the Arabs, who built there a number of beautiful, gleaming mosques, a palace for the pasha and other handsome structures. Tripoli was once the center of a great slave trade, and it was one of the chief ports from which the Barbary pirates sailed out to prey on European and American shipping, around 1800, capturing hostages for ransom as well as treasure. United States Marines put an end to those bad old days; and their accomplishment is remembered in the Marine Corps anthem: "From the halls of Montezuma to the shores of Tripoli."

Tripoli is very close to the desert, and one feels the presence of the immense Sahara, even when wandering through the city streets. From some convenient vantage point we may glimpse a string of camels afar off, bringing loads of ivory or other merchandise to market.

The Arabs who inhabit the desert are from a hardy race of nomads, descendants of the fanatical warriors who overwhelmed Roman Africa centuries ago. They count their wealth in horses, camels and sheep and move from one oasis to another under the guidance of a sheik.

ALGERIA, TUNISIA AND LIBYA: FACTS AND FIGURES

ALGERIA

Bounded on the north by the Mediterranean Sea, on the east by Tunisia and Libya, on the south by French West Africa and on the west by Spanish Sahara and Morocco, it is a Government-General within the French Union. There is an Algerian Assembly. There are three departments, Oran, Algiers and Constantine, that send delegates to the French Parliament, and four Southern Territories. Total area, 845,905 square miles; population, 8,830,000. Agriculture is important but restricted to the coast; 1/3 of farm acreage is owned by Europeans. Chief crops are grains, potatoes, artichokes, beans, tobacco, flax and many kinds of fruit. Forests include cork and evergreen oak, pine, dwarf palms and cedar. Livestock, 8,170,000 head, more than half of which are sheep and goats. Fishery products include sardines, anchovies, tuna and shellfish. Leading mineral products are iron ore, phosphates, iron pyrites, coal, zinc and lead. Electric-power production, 586,000,-000 kilowatt-hours in 1950. Chief exports are wines, alfa (esparto grass), phosphates and iron ore; leading imports are textiles, sugar, iron and steel, petroleum and cereals. Motor roads, 33,-200 miles and 6,960 miles of desert roads; railways, 2,780 miles; 73 airfields; number of telephones, 81,800. People are mostly Mohammedan; others, Jewish and Christian. Education: 332,000 pupils in 2,190 primary schools; 23,400 in 146 secondary schools; nearly 5,000 in university at Algiers; also professional and technical training schools as well as higher Moslem schools. Population of chief cities: Algiers (capital), 315,210; Oran, 256,661; Constantine, 118,774; Bône, 102,823.

TUNISIA

A protectorate within the French Union, it is bounded north and east by the Mediterranean Sea, on the east and south by Libya and on the south and west by Algeria; area, 60,150 square miles; and population, 3,470,000. The Bey of Tunisia exercises limited rule under the direction of a French Resident-General, who is assisted by a Cabinet of 5 French and 6 Tunisian ministers. Agriculture is the chief industry; principal farm products are wheat, barley, oats, olive oil, wine, dates, almonds, citrus fruits, alfa grass and cork; livestock, 3,979,000 head. Mineral products include phosphate, iron, lignite, lead and zinc. Electric-power production, about 141,000,000 kilowatt-hours in 1950. Exports: cereals, olive oil, dates and citrus fruits, phosphates and other mineral ores. Imports: textiles, machinery and manufactured goods. Roads, 5,445 miles; railways, 1,303 miles; telegraph lines, 2,327 miles; telephone lines, 29,800 miles. Religion: Moslems predominate. Education: a total enrollment of nearly 300,000 in 552 primary, 15 secondary and 61 technical schools, 2 normal colleges, 3 special schools and a Moslem university. Population of chief cities: Tunis (capital), 364,593; Sfax, 54,637.

LIBYA

Bounded on the north by the Mediterranean Sea, on the east by Egypt and Anglo-Egyptian Sudan, on the south by French Equatorial Africa and French West Africa and on the west by Algeria and Tunisia; area, 678,000 square miles; and population, 1,124,000. A former Italian colony, made up of Tripolitania, Cyrenaica and Fezzan, Libya enacted a constitution in October 1951 and became independent, December 24, 1951. Chief agricultural products are dates, olive oil, citrus fruits, grain and alfa grass; livestock, in Tripolitania and Cyrenaica, 1,404,000 head. Other important industries: sponge and tuna fishing and tobacco growing and processing. Exports: hides and skins, wheat, vegetable oils, esparto and sponges; imports—food, motor cars, machinery and building materials. Railways, 223 miles; roads, 2,200 miles; international telephone, telegraph and cable connections. Moslems predominate; Jewish population, 15,000. Education: 38,000 pupils in 317 schools of all kinds. Population of chief towns: Tripoli, 146,-000, and Bengazi, 60,000 (joint capitals).

EGYPT'S WONDERS OF THE PAST

Its Vast Temples and Palaces and Their Builders

The fertile valley of the Nile includes most of the cultivated land of Egypt. It is full of interest because of the daily scenes of its cities and villages and, to all who like to think about the things that men did in past ages, it is one of the most attractive places in all the world. We may have a glimpse of present-day Egypt in the chapters on Cairo and the Gift of the Nile. Here, we are to read of the Egyptians who lived thousands of years ago and of the wonderful tombs, temples and sculptures which they left and which reveal to us the very life of those ancient times.

ANCIENT Egypt was one of the most curiously shaped countries in the world. It consisted of two narrow strips of fertile land, one on each side of the Nile, beyond which stretched vast deserts. Thus, although it was several hundred miles in length, Egypt was only a few miles in breadth. The prosperity of the land depended upon the Nile. Along it ships brought trade to the towns; its annual floods enriched the fields with a coating of mud; from it the villagers obtained water for irrigation —as they do still.

This country was the home of one of the oldest civilizations. Even previous to the beginning of written history, which some historians say was seven thousand years ago, there were people living in Egypt whose flint implements and pottery indicate a civilization beyond that of any other pre-historic

Egyptian Antiquities, Cairo

MODEL OF AN UNKNOWN LADY

This graceful wooden statue, one of the most beautiful of ancient Egyptian statues in existence, was probably executed more than four thousand five hundred years ago.

people about whom we know. Paintings on vases show that they used boats with oars and even sails, and they cultivated grain. All these things have been found in the graves, for the Egyptians believed in a life hereafter and they thought it necessary to be buried with their possessions in order that all would be ready for them when they returned to another life on this earth.

History begins with the rule of Menes who lived, some believe, about 5500 B.C., though others think it was not until 3400 years before the birth of Christ. Menes united the two provinces of Lower and Upper Egypt into one nation and established the city of Memphis where he made his residence.

From his time on, there have been so many rulers of Egypt that historians have divided them into thirty dynasties or families

FAWCETT

QUEEN HATSHEPSUT built this terraced temple to the god Ammon beneath the cliffs at Deir-el-Bahri. Chapels were dedicated to the goddess Hathor and to Anubis, the god of the dead, and several chambers were also devoted to the worship of Hatshepsut herself. To secure myrrh and incense for the temple, an expedition was sent by the queen to Punt, "Land of the Gods," which was south of the Sudan and reached to the Red Sea. This was about 3,500 years ago but a carved record of the expedition can still be seen on the temple.

HEWN FROM SOLID ROCK, four immense statues of the Pharaoh Rameses II of Egypt stand outside the temple of the Rising Sun at Abu-Simbel, two on each side of the entrance. Here we see an Arab standing on the lap of one of these enormous figures. He seems an insignificant dwarf, indeed, compared with the statue of the long-dead ruler.

in each of which reigned many kings, known as Pharaohs. The names of these have been gleaned from tablets and papyri, for early Egyptians inscribed their deeds by means of pictures and marks which learned men have deciphered for us. This was the earliest form of writing.

Outstanding among the Pharaohs was Khufu, or Cheops, who organized the government so that the country was ready for the greatest period of its history. He built the Great Pyramid in 2900 B.C. and it far excels anything that has been constructed even to this day, but we shall read of that in the chapter on the Sphinx and the Pyramid.

At the height of its power, about 1560 B.C., ancient Egypt was an empire comprising not only the Nile Valley but Palestine and the greater part of Syria. Thothmes III was ruling then with the assistance of his step-mother, Hatshepsut, who seems to have been a very able woman and was undoubtedly the first feminist. She is often referred to as the "Queen Elizabeth of Egypt." Thothmes III, possibly the greatest ruler in Egyptian history, led his army in seventeen campaigns against the Syrians, crossed the Euphrates and received gifts from the Hittites in Asia Minor and from the king of Babylon. During his reign, the peoples of Punt and Ethiopia, just south of Egypt, acknowledged its supremacy and sent enormous quantities of ivory, gold and spices to its temples and courts. Ships and caravans traded with Babylon, Crete, Greece and various Syrian towns. Records of all these activities were chronicled on the walls of the great temple at Karnak.

Of the same dynasty but living a hundred and sixty years later was Amenhotep III, who is known as a great builder. The magnificent temple at Luxor, temple pylons and whole avenues of sculptured rams, though damaged by time, are still viewed by thousands of tourists each

THE COURT OF RAMESES II WITHIN THE RUINS OF LUXOR TEMPLE

The most famous ruin in Luxor is the temple, its sculpture still noble though battered by time. Built by Amenhotep III of the eighteenth dynasty, it occupies the site of an older sanctuary.

year. Cuneiform tablets of this period show that he carried on quite a correspondence with the king of Babylon and other monarchs in faraway lands.

His son, Amenhotep IV, stands out because he was a religious fanatic. Casting aside all deities, including Ammon and many others whom they worshiped and in whose honor they had built and decorated these vast temples, he forced the people to worship a universal god "Aten" who represented the sundisk. He even changed his name to Akhenaten which means "pious to Aten." While he was so busy with religious reforms, however, his country was having political troubles and he lost Syria and other territory in outlying districts. Although his son-in-law, Tutankhamen, restored Ammon and the former deities to their places as the objects of worship, he did nothing to get back the lost territory, and it was not until the next dynasty, about 1240 B.C., that Seti I and his son, Rameses II, regained it. Rameses II is supposed to have been the oppressor of the children of Israel who, we remember from the Bible, came to Egypt because of a famine in the land of Canaan. So prosperous did they become that the Pharaoh made it very hard for them and they finally went back to their own land. Rameses II may not have treated the Jewish tribes justly but he did a great deal for Egypt. Following his reign, however, there was a long period of decline and the country finally fell to the Persians who were themselves driven out by the Greeks in 332 B.C. under the generalship of Alexander the Great, famous king and conqueror.

TRANS WORLD AIRLINES

IN THE TOMB OF KING TUTANKHAMEN

At lower left can be seen the beautiful head of the richly ornamented golden coffin, the innermost of three, in which the boy king of the second millenium B.C. was entombed. The coffin was made in human shape and his face was painted upon it.

When, after Alexander's death, his dominions were divided up, Egypt fell to Ptolemy, his lieutenant, who founded a dynasty by that name which lasted about three hundred years. The last of his line was the famous Cleopatra, who killed herself by means of a poisonous snake, and her empire fell to the Romans.

But let us pay a visit to some of the ruins of ancient magnificence. Perhaps the most wonderful are the Pyramids and Sphinx, but we shall leave them for the time being and go on, not so very far, to the site of the ancient city of Memphis, the royal capital of Egypt five thousand years ago. Nothing remains to-day of this city, formerly so great, but the ruins of temples, palaces and dwelling-houses. Even the gigantic statues of the Pharaoh Rameses II, that once stood here, have fallen to the ground.

THIS STATUE OF TUTANKHAMEN, one of the two that stood in the ante-chamber of his tomb, like sentinels guarding the dead, is of carved wood, splendidly adorned with a head-dress and ornaments of beaten gold. It is seven feet in height, and the head-dress has the upraised serpent, the sign of loyalty. King Tutankhamen lived over 3000 years ago.

ROYAL TREASURE, including gold-plated furniture and rich gifts to the dead king, surround this statue of Tutankhamen, which is shown also on the opposite page. Here we see a beautifully decorated clothes chest, alabaster vases that once held spices and the remains of bunches of flowers. These were believed to be used by the dead in the other world.

HUNTING SCENES UPON THE TEMPLE WALLS AT MEDINET ABU

About half a mile from the Colossi of Memnon is the little village of Medinet Abu, where stand the ruins of two temples. On the outside of the walls of the larger building are pictured inscriptions showing Rameses III, who lived more than three thousand years ago, hunting wild bulls, mountain-goats and wild asses, and making war on the Libyans.

64

More interesting is Tell-el-Amarna, a town founded in 1340 B.C. by Pharaoh Akhenaten, the father-in-law of Tut-ankhamen. Here we can pace the ancient streets and alleys, and visit the palaces and mansions of the king and his great men. A few exquisitely beautiful paintings and sculptures remind us of past glories.

When we inspect the dilapidated little houses in the workmen's quarter we can easily imagine how the poor folk lived in the days of Akhenaten. Some of their food-bowls and water-jars are still in a perfect state of preservation and could well be used to-day. The Pharaoh himself had a wonderful pleasure palace with gardens, an artificial lake and many pools.

The Egyptians were famous for the immense size of most of their important temples and monuments, as well as for the magnificence of the decorations that they lavished on them. Let us go to Dendera and visit the huge temple of the goddess Hathor. This was built in comparatively modern times—about the beginning of the Christian era. The pillars of the temple, all of them covered with carvings and richly painted, are about forty feet high. On the outer walls is a figure of Cleopatra, one of the most famous queens in the world's history, that is almost three times the height of an ordinary man. The greatest pains were taken to make the temple beautiful, and although it is now in ruins, it has not entirely lost its magnificence.

TRANS WORLD AIRLINES

THE GLORY THAT WAS ANCIENT EGYPT

In the ruins of the great temple at Karnak, tall pillars bear the sculptured lotus and papyrus. The lotus pillar (foreground) was a symbol of Upper Egypt; the papyrus, of Lower Egypt. The lotus, a water-lily, was known as the sacred lily of the Nile.

Traveling up the Nile from Dendera, we presently arrive at Thebes. We shall not, for the moment, visit the city itself but the temples, and especially those of Karnak and Luxor. Among them all, the temple of Ammon first claims our attention, since it is the largest and one of the most splendid. Almost four hundred years were spent in building it; and as we look at the huge pillars in its famous Hypostyle Hall, at the enormous blocks of stone of which its walls and towers are built and at its gigantic statues, we wonder

ALABASTER VASES were among the many priceless treasures found in the tomb of Tutankhamen, who died about 1350 B. C. Their exquisite shapes and decorations show how artistic were the craftsmen of Egypt in those ancient days. The fragrance of the perfumed ointments that these vases contained was still perceptible when they were discovered in 1922-23.

BESIDE THIS SHRINE, which was placed in the ante-chamber of Tutankhamen's tomb, stands a wooden ushabti figure. On it is painted a charm to ensure that its soul shall obey the dead king in the other world. The shrine is covered with heavy sheets of gold, and on its doors, here shown open, are depicted incidents in the lives of Tutankhamen and his wife.

THE TEMPLE TO THE GODDESS HATHOR, BUILT BY THE PTOLEMIES

Dendera on the Nile has one of the finest of Egyptian relics, the Hathor temple. The twenty-four columns, six across and four deep, are fifty feet high and seven feet in diameter.

HIEROGLYPHICS AND BAS RELIEFS COVER THE GIGANTIC REAR WALL

Figures and inscriptions narrate the stories and rituals connected with Hathor, the Venus of Egypt. They also tell something of the history of Cleopatra and the Ptolemies.

A CROWNED BIRD IN STONE BY THE TEMPLE OF EDFU, DEDICATED TO HORUS

The hawk, or falcon, symbolized Horus. Sometimes he was shown as having a man's body and a hawk's head. Carvings such as those in the background decorated the temple walls.

THIS STRIKING CREATURE, with a long, slender body and legs like those of a cat, is one of the twin supports of the couch of King Tutankhamen, that was found in his tomb in the Valley of the Kings, a valley of rock-cut tombs, among the Theban Hills. The monster is made of wood, richly gilded, and its gleaming teeth and long, pink tongue are of ivory.

TWO WOODEN HANDMAIDENS, half life-size and beautifully carved, were found in the tomb of Mehenkwetre, a nobleman who lived about 2000 B. C. Models of servants were placed in the tombs of nobles and were called Ushabtis, or "Answerers," since their spirits were supposed to wait upon the nobles' spirits in the other world. They carry food in the baskets.

how it came to be built in an age long before cranes and other mechanical devices were known. Especially do we marvel at the genius of the ancient architects under whose care it was built, and at the patience and skill of the artists who adorned it with their carvings.

Very wonderful too are the temple of the moon-god, Khensu, the temple of Rameses III, in which the pillars are carved to represent the god Osiris and the long avenues with rows of sculptured sphinxes on each side of them, that lead to the various temples. We must not miss the temple of Amenhotep III, however, for it is very splendid. Its doorways were in his time studded with gold, and the forecourt, which was built by Amenhotep, was paved with silver. Round this court are seventy-four columns, each in the form of a papyrus-bud.

Where the Pharaohs Were Buried

Beyond the Theban temples we see a line of bleak hills against the deep blue of the sky. In them is the desolate Valley of the Kings, which contains the burial-places of many of the great Egyptian Pharaohs. They were hidden here so that their bodies might not be disturbed by thieves in search of the gold and jewels that were buried with them. In this valley was found, in 1922, the tomb of the young King Tutankhamen, with all his treasures, but he was a very unimportant monarch compared with some of the others who were buried near by.

The graves of mighty Rameses II, of Amenhotep III, of Thothmes III and many another ruler of Egypt have all been discovered here. Some of the tombs are marvelously decorated, and from the pictures and carvings in them we may learn much about the ancient Egyptians. Others have contained articles of furniture and personal belongings of the dead kings, and from these also the story of the past can be read.

Embalming the Royal Bodies

The bodies of the kings as well as of all who could afford it were prepared for burial by a long and costly process. Em-balmed first, the body was then wrapped tightly in fold after fold of linen which had been soaked in some kind of preservative and placed in a coffin made in the likeness of the person it contained. This statue-coffin was placed in still another coffin of stone or wood. Thus, the remains and all its possessions awaited the day when the immortal soul should return. In the Museum of Antiquities at Cairo, the mummies of some of the famous Egyptian kings are on view, while in our own museums we may see the mummies of less important persons. All this has served to make the Egypt of the past very real to us to-day.

There are many other temples and monuments in different parts of Egypt that we might visit, but we shall leave the lifeless statues and great empty buildings and turn to the people who erected them.

Let us imagine ourselves in Egypt about 1240 B.C., in the days of the great Pharaoh Rameses II. We are at Memphis, but we wish to visit friends at Thebes, and so hire a boat in which to travel up the Nile. Our voyage will be extremely comfortable, since our deck-cabin is not too small and is very airy and handsomely furnished. We embark. Luggage and stores are all aboard. The rowers bend to their oars and we begin to glide placidly up the river. Day after day we proceed, sitting when it is not too hot on the high platforms at the bow and the stern to watch all that happens on the banks. Sometimes a breeze springs up and the gaily-colored sails are hoisted.

We Are Welcomed by the Merchant

At last we see Thebes, the most magnificent city in all Egypt, and the temples of Karnak and Luxor with three bare grim hills beyond them. Our boat is moored to the stone-paved quay, and we go ashore to meet our friends. One of them, a merchant, comes forward to greet us. He is bareheaded in spite of the hot sun, wears a linen robe with a long skirt and carries a stout cane.

He limps a little, since his laced leather shoes are new and tight. His wife, our friend explains, is looking forward

MC LEISH

THIS SCULPTURED ARCH of Ptolemy III, at Karnak, stands on the site of ancient Thebes. It is in the avenue that leads to the temple of Khensu, the god of the moon. The arch has carved reliefs showing Ptolemy III, a warrior king of Egypt who lived in the third century B. C., offering sacrifices to the gods of Thebes. The architecture is typical.

TEMPLE OF ISIS AND PAVILION KNOWN AS "PHARAOH'S BED" ON THE SUBMERGED ISLAND OF PHILAE

When the Nile was dammed at Assuan, the island of Philae was submerged. At times even the buildings are completely under water, including the two cut-off pyramids (left) forming the entrance to the temple of Isis, and the pillared pavilion (right), never completed by its builders of old.

eagerly to our visit, but she is at present at her jeweler's waiting while he makes a bracelet for her from a bar of gold that she was given that morning. Our other friend, a captain of the Libyan soldiers, would also have been on the quay to meet us had he not been obliged to investigate a case of theft, for his detachment acts as a police force in the workmen's district. The merchant suggests that we should go to this district on our way to his home on the chance of seeing the captain.

In the Streets of Thebes 1240 B.C.

The streets are narrow and the little houses of sun-baked mud are mainly of one story although some have two. Since very few of the doors are closed we can easily look inside. There is little furniture to be seen—palm-leaf mats that serve as beds and couches, some earthenware dishes and jars containing water and oil and a small image of a god are usually all that a workman's family possesses. Sometimes there are also two or three wooden chests, and in some of the two-story houses a room on the ground floor serves as a stable for a donkey.

Scantily dressed children swarm everywhere, and in most of the houses we see women busy at household tasks. Here is one grinding corn; there one is baking bread, the chief food of the poorer people. Another, helped by a neighbor, weaves cloth at a rough loom. We see very few men, however. Most of them went to work at sunrise taking with them their dinner—bread soaked in oil and some fruit—and will not return home till sunset.

We see some of them at work as we draw near to the market. The clang of hammers attracts our attention to a metal-worker's shed. Two brawny fellows are fashioning harness for a pair of chariot horses. Our friend speaks to a carpenter who is making some very handsome chairs for him. When we resume our walk he tells us not to go too near a certain booth. It is the workshop of a dyer, he explains and adds, quoting from an Egyptian poem, that the dyes are "evil-smelling as bad fish." We hear the tramp of a party

of men, and our other friend, the captain of Libyans, appears with a file of his soldiers.

Negro Soldiers and Sailors

In front of the line is a trumpeter and behind him a dozen infantrymen carrying light shields and axes and with spears sloped over their right shoulders. They wear felt caps and waist-cloths, but no armor, and are a very well-disciplined body of men. Behind comes the captain, unarmed though he carries a decorated baton of command. He is an Egyptian, appointed to the Libyan legion by Pharaoh, but the soldiers are Negroes.

As we pass through the market, let us look at the crowds around us. There are artisans, dressed only in waist-cloths, with their wives, who wear simple smocks. Clerks and priests in short kilts pass by, and smart merchants like our friend. Sellers of perfumes and roast meats, bakers, shoemakers and toy-makers urge us to inspect their wares. A barber wishes to shave us. The slave attached to a little restaurant suggests that we should have our evening meal there.

Marketing without Money

Our friend waves them all away, but wishing to buy us a present, stops at a perfume stall. Several little jars of scent are shown to us and we smell them, finally choosing two. Our friend takes another and offers the saleswoman a small block of gold for them. She declares that it is not enough. After a quarter of an hour's bargaining she accepts the merchant's offer and tells us that she is extremely pleased to be paid in gold, since that morning she has taken a pearl necklace, a silver bracelet and a fan set with gems in exchange for perfumes. Our friend explains as we stroll away that this system of barter is the custom.

Presently we arrive at his house. It is quite an imposing mansion of three stories and has a large courtyard surrounded by a high wall. The large windows of the two upper stories overlook the street. Within we find magnificent furniture—chairs, carved and gilded, chests with little

FAWCETT

FROM THE THEBAN HILLS above the Valley of the Kings, a royal burial ground of ancient Egypt, we look across a flat, green plain to the Nile and the far-away heights on the other side of the river. Beyond the left-hand shoulder of the ridge in the foreground we see the columns of the ruined Ramesseum, a temple built by Rameses II, one of the greatest of the Pharaohs. Not much more than half of it remains to-day. To the right of it are seen—tiny, light specks on the broad plain— the two colossi shown on the opposite page.

MC LEISH

THE COLOSSI OF "MEMNON," each about sixty-five feet high, stand by the Nile near the ancient town of Thebes. The Greeks and Romans took the right hand statue to represent the god Memnon, which, it is said used to cry mournfully at sunrise. The figures are statues of Amenhotep III and his wife Tiyi, a king and queen who lived about 1400 B. C.

pictures painted on them, and rich hangings. The walls are painted with figures of gods and scenes of everyday life.

The food that we are offered is excellent. We have roast meats in abundance, baked fish, stuffed duck and pickled fowl, fruit, bread and cakes. While we eat we hear news of the merchant's two eldest sons. One is an officer in the celebrated legion of Ammon—all the regiments are named after gods. He is going to take us to hunt wild fowl the next day on the estate of a noble. The other son is a scribe. This profession, it appears, becomes less and less confined to the middle classes for many of the working classes are educating their sons to become scribes.

When we retire for the night we find that we are to sleep on a mattress on the floor. Instead of having a pillow, we rest our necks on curved wooden supports. Everything is very clean, and the breezes that blow through our windows are cool and laden with the scent of flowers.

A Day of Hunting and Fishing

We go to the nobleman's estate the next day and, embarking on wooden canoes, proceed to a near-by marsh. We find plenty of wild fowl among the reeds, and our host soon kills three ducks with boomerangs. He has a pair of trained cats to retrieve the game for him. While he is throwing the boomerangs, slaves in two other canoes lower a net. This is soon drawn up filled with fish.

We dine with the noble and, while we eat, minstrels play on harps. Our host is a widely traveled man. As an army officer he has accompanied his regiment to Palestine and led a charge against the Hittites in his chariot. On another occasion he sailed down the Red Sea to Punt, on the East African coast, to obtain spices and gold for the Temple of Ammon. He is also well educated and in his library has books of tales and poetry, works on medicine and mathematics, all written on rolls of papyrus—sedge which was pressed to provide a flat writing surface.

By far the most interesting part of his life, so the noble tells us, was the period when he was at court in attendance upon the Pharaoh Rameses II. He describes an audience to us. The monarch, seated on his golden throne, wore a double crown, to show that he was king both of Lower and Upper Egypt. On his forehead was the royal golden cobra, the uræus. Near him was his eldest son Khamuast, an able statesman, a priest, and, so it is said, a great magician. His Majesty's Libyan guards, armed with their double-edged swords, were posted about the palace.

Attending the Great Pharaoh

A messenger from Palestine arrived and was admitted to the audience chamber. He and the councilors assumed attitudes of worship when they came into the king's presence since they regarded him as the descendant of a god and himself a demigod. Kneeling, with their faces close to the floor, they gave him their news and heard his answer. Another messenger came to tell Rameses that there was a famine in some distant province; yet another brought word of a convoy of gold that was on its way from Ethiopia.

We ask the noble to tell us more of Rameses II and he agrees willingly. Rameses, while still a boy, had been associated with his father Seti I in the government of Egypt. When only ten years old, he was sent to the wars in Syria and a little later went to subdue the turbulent tribes of the lands watered by the upper Nile This he did successfully. Rameses was a great warrior and after he became Pharaoh led an army against the Hittites in Syria. The chariots were under his own command, and by his bravery he succeeded in turning the battle of Kadesh from a defeat into a victory.

Prosperous Reign of Rameses II

Much of his vast wealth was spent on building operations. As well as raising huge temples, he had the irrigation canals of the Nile delta repaired and extended and established caravan stations along the route to Ethiopia. Rameses was one of the greatest of the Pharaohs. Egypt was peaceable under him; the people were prosperous and the police efficient.

THE SPHINX AND THE PYRAMID

Two Mighty Monuments of Bygone Ages

In the preceding chapter we tell of the marvels of ancient Egypt with the exception of two that are perhaps the most fascinating—the Great Pyramid and the Sphinx. The oldest example of a sphinx is the Great Sphinx at Gizeh, which is 150 feet long. But the sphinx was not peculiar to Egypt for, as we shall read in this chapter, there were also Greek and Assyrian sphinxes which, however, differed greatly from those of Egypt. The pyramids also are not confined to Egypt for gigantic monuments of this type are to be found in the Sudan, in Algeria and even in Mexico. The largest of these monumental structures is the Great Pyramid of Gizeh which is the sole survivor of the "Seven Wonders of the World."

FROM the Nile at Gizeh we may see dark against the cloudless sky of Egypt, three immense tombs like shapely mountain peaks built in the desert by man. If we approach them, we find nearby a huge battered monster of stone. It is to this group of remains that we usually refer when we speak of the Pyramids and the Sphinx. But there are other pyramids and other sphinxes which, though perhaps less famous, are not less interesting. These are to be found not only in Egypt, but also in lands thousands of miles across the seas.

"Sphinx" is a Greek word which means the "throttler." It was used to designate a terrible being which had, so it was said, the head of a woman, the body of a lioness and wings. According to the ancient legend, she originally lived in Africa, but was sent by the gods to Thebes in Greece to punish the sins of a Theban ruler. Taking a rock near the city for her abode, she asked every passer-by a riddle. "What walks on four legs in the morning," she would demand, "on two at noon and on three in the evening?"

All who could not guess were devoured, and everyone failed until Oedipus came. He was able to tell the Sphinx that the answer was, "A man"; because, as a baby, he crawls on hands and knees, in the prime of life he walks upright, and when old age makes him feeble he can only progress with the help of a stick or crutch. Since her riddle had been solved, the Sphinx threw herself from her rock and the Thebans were never troubled by her again.

Thus we see that the Greeks believed their Sphinx to be an evil monster preying upon mankind. When they came to Egypt and there saw huge carved figures that were half-beast and half-human, they called these sphinxes too. But although it was at one time thought by the Egyptians that sphinxes roamed the deserts, they were more generally accepted as symbols of the grandeur and power of the Pharaohs. Their most notable characteristic was their superhuman dignity. Their bodies, made like those of lions, represent might and nobility, and their heads are usually portraits of ancient kings. Sometimes, instead of having a man's head, they had that of a ram like those at Karnak, and there are some that were made with the head of a hawk. To the Egyptian this did not detract from their dignity for a ram was emblematic of the great god Ammon, whom they worshiped, and a hawk was symbolical of the king as a warrior.

It might be asked here, What is a sphinx, since it had all these forms? It is not merely a monster with a body that is partly beast and partly man. A mermaid is not a sphinx, for example; nor are the winged bulls with the heads of bearded men that we find in Mesopotamia; nor is the Hindu god Ganesha, who is represented as having a man's body but an elephant's head. We may take it as definite that true sphinxes have a lion's or a lioness's body and a head which is either a portrait or symbol of a human being or god. Whatever other character-

79

THE GREAT SPHINX at Gizeh is the oldest and most famous of all sphinxes. It is probably the oldest statue in the world, but no one knows exactly when it was carved, or which Pharaoh the huge head represents. To-day one may see the mammoth paws of the sphinx, for recent excavations have uncovered them. The statue has also been repaired and strengthened.

AN ALABASTER SPHINX, almost perfectly preserved, was discovered in 1912 on the site of the ancient city of Memphis. It was probably carved about 1240 B. C. during the reign of Rameses II. The sphinxes were given their name by the Greeks, quite incorrectly as it happens for the Greek sphinx is a demon and not, like the Egyptian, an emblem of majesty.

THE GREEK SPHINX HAS WINGS AND A WOMAN'S HEAD

The Egyptian sphinx is always male and wingless; the Greek sphinx is female with the body of a lion and the wings of a bird. According to an old Greek legend the Muses had taught her a riddle which the Thebans must answer. All who could not solve it were carried off to be eaten. When Œdipus gave the correct answer, she killed herself by falling from a rock.

istics they may have are purely incidental. So we would not consider the kneeling rams found in Egypt as sphinxes, although in appearance they closely resemble them.

The great sphinx at Gizeh, which has been mentioned already, is the most celebrated of its kind. For centuries it has been considered a thing of awful mystery. Indeed, it was once thought, quite wrongly, to be an idol of such importance that Arab invaders, in their desire to spread Mohammedanism and to do away with all other kinds of worship, deliberately disfigured it. But in spite of their fanatical efforts at destruction and of the ravages of time, the sphinx is still beautiful, and its size makes it extremely impressive.

At Karnak we may see long avenues

THE SPHINX IS A SYMBOL OF KINGLY POWER

A true sphinx, with the body of a lion and the head of a Pharaoh, was, in the ancient myths of the Egyptians, a symbol of the sun god with whom the Pharaoh was identified. These figures were placed at the entrance of the temples. The sphinx shown here has the conventional lion body and the head of King Sesostris III, of the 12th Egyptian dynasty, 2000–1788 B.C.

AT MEDUM, on the desert's edge, forty miles south of Cairo, is the queerly shaped pyramid of King Sneferu. It rises in three tiers from a mound that is really another tier covered with debris. Most likely it was once a true pyramid in shape. King Sneferu built for himself another pyramid at Dashur, but it was probably in this one that he was buried.

MC LEISH

THE GREAT PYRAMID, most famous of the group at Giza, covers nearly thirteen acres and rises to a height of 450 feet. From a narrow opening in the northern face a passage leads to several rooms. One contains a stone box, which most experts think is the sarcophagus, or tomb, of Khufu, or Cheops, an Egyptian king who reigned in the twenty-ninth century B.C.

Gaddis & Self

ROWS OF SPHINXES THAT LINE THE APPROACH TO THE GREAT TEMPLE OF AMMON AT KARNAK

On page 65 we read about the great ruined temples at Karnak, in Egypt. Here we see one of the avenues of sphinxes that lead to them. It is two hundred feet long and once led to the riverside. The Nile now flows, however. some distance away, for it has changed its course since then.

The Egyptian sphinx is a crouching lion, usually with the head of a man. These have rams' heads, because they line the approach to the Temple of Ammon, a great god who in primitive times was worshiped in the form of a ram. Some sphinxes have hawks' heads.

lined with sphinxes. Some, as we have already said, have the heads of rams; others are like representations in miniature of the sphinx at Gizeh. All are wonderfully wrought. Splendid indeed must have been the effect when the rows were complete and the shapely figures were yet unspoiled by weather and hard treatment. One of the most beautiful sphinxes ever discovered is that which stands on the site of the old city of Memphis. It is of alabaster and is extraordinarily well preserved, so that we may study the grace of its lines and the serene and kingly expression on its face.

Sphinxes of Other Lands

The ancient Assyrians also had sphinxes, but like the Greeks represented them as having wings and considered them to be demons. Although they have lions' bodies, these creatures are far from being noble or stately. Their faces are incredibly foolish for they have great staring eyes and are usually smirking. Those of the Hittites, who lived in Asia Minor, are more ferocious in appearance but are stiff and conventional. Some have two heads, and they resemble an ordinary lion to which a human head has been given in addition to its own.

In Central America, among the carvings of the ancient Maya peoples, are some monsters that are not unlike sphinxes. We see, therefore, in how many different lands the conception of this strange type of imaginary creature met with acceptance.

Let us now turn to the Pyramids. Pyramids were usually erected to glorify the dead. In prehistoric times, the people undoubtedly marked the graves of their dead with poles and brushwood and possibly a covering of loose stones. Later, these rude constructions developed into the Pyramids, which were elaborate monuments built over burial places. In the majority of cases, the bodies were placed deep in the earth beneath them and not in the heart of the structure as one might suppose. Some of the chambers above were used as a storehouse for things the deceased might need hereafter.

The Famous Pyramids of Egypt

The Egyptian pyramids are the most famous. They were the tombs of kings and sometimes of queens and other important persons. Most have the perfect, symmetrical form of those at Gizeh. In others we see a series of great "steps" ascending to the summit. This type is constructed of several lofty tiers of masonry, each of which is smaller than the one immediately below it. The most interesting example is the pyramid of King Zoser at Sakkara, which is especially worthy of note, because it is probably the earliest that still survives. It is almost six thousand years old. Another very ancient tomb, the pyramid of Sneferu at Medum, which we see on page 84, is constructed on a somewhat similar plan.

The pyramids were usually of stone, though a few built of bricks are still to be seen. These are generally of comparatively recent date and, like that at Dashur, are in a ruinous condition. The sizes of the pyramids vary. There are examples small enough to be almost insignificant, and there are immense structures like those at Gizeh.

Everyone has heard of these three wonderful monuments, and an infinite variety of fantastic theories as to their purpose has been advanced. Actually, however, the smallest is the burial place of King Menkaura, the medium-sized one that of King Khafra and the largest that of King Khufu. The smallest is also the most modern, but it is nearly five thousand years old.

Within the Great Pyramid

Let us visit the pyramid of Khufu—the Great Pyramid, as it is called to distinguish it from its neighbors. Although from a distance its sides appear even and unbroken, when we approach it we see that it is composed of vast blocks of stone, most of them higher than a man and some weighing many tons. Imagine the work it must have been to bring over two million blocks by boat across the Nile, then to have transported them, probably along greased roads, and to have placed

THE PYRAMIDS OF GIZEH, it has long been thought, were built by thousands of wretched slaves, driven to perform a stupendous task by their tyrannical rulers. It is now considered more likely that the Pharaohs who ordered their construction were conferring a great bene- fit upon their subjects. The three months of the year during which the Nile was in flood were a time of great hardship, for no agricultural work could be done. Then the peasants were set to work upon the pyra- mids, and were fed and housed at the king's expense.

them in position by means of pulleys and ropes. And so accurately was it done that the base lacks but a fraction of an inch of being a perfect square. Such was the engineering skill of the early Egyptians. Each of its sides measures about 755 feet, and its height is about 451 feet. But these bare measurements give little idea of its majesty—it is one of the most magnificent tombs in the world.

Now, as has been stated, the burial chamber was usually underground, beneath the pyramid. There is such an apartment below the Great Pyramid, but it is unfinished, and the real burial place is within the colossal mass of masonry. If we enter the passage which opens upon the north face of the pyramid, we ascend for some distance before we come to the grand gallery, from which, turning southward, we can reach the so-called Queen's chamber. If instead we continue to climb, however, we reach an antechamber and then the King's chamber.

In it is a huge empty sarcophagus, carved from a solid block of granite. Indeed, one of the few disappointing features of the Great Pyramid is the fact that it contains so little. It was entered ages ago by tomb robbers. The King's chamber is ventilated by channels leading to the open air.

Other ancient peoples must have been profoundly impressed with the desirability of pyramids as tombs. In the Sudan, as we show on page 89, small varieties are found, while in Algeria there are large tombs which have obviously been evolved from Egyptian pyramids.

In America there are also many pyramids, but these were constructed for entirely different purposes. The Mayas set temples upon them, and thus gave an appearance of importance and stateliness to their religious buildings. In Mexico there is one massive structure, the pyramid of the Sun at San Juan Teotihuacan, that almost equals those of Egypt in size. It is built of adobe and is faced with stone and stucco. There are also many that are smaller, but very elaborately finished. All are more squat than the Egyptian pyramids and have steps to their summits.

© E. N. A.

SMALL FLAT-TOPPED PYRAMIDS THAT MARK THE BURIAL GROUND OF EGYPT'S ETHIOPIAN IMITATORS

That the ancient Egyptians had their imitators we can see from this photograph of a burial ground in ruined Meroe, an ancient Nubian town that was once the capital of Ethiopia. It is in the Sudan and contains about 200 small pyramids, dating from about 150 B.C.

BACK-BREAKING LABOR IN COTTON FIELDS IN THE NILE VALLEY

In an age when acres of crops are dusted with insecticides by airplane in a matter of minutes, there
are still areas where children work all day hand-picking boll weevils from cotton plants.

THE GIFT OF THE NILE

How Men Live Today in Fertile Egypt

Of the marvels of ancient Egypt we have already learned in an earlier chapter. Now we are to read of the modern Egyptians. Like most fertile lands, Egypt has suffered from many invasions. During the 5,500 years in which we can trace its history, a number of periods of foreign domination have occurred, yet many of the native inhabitants of the Nile delta and valley are of the same stock as those who were the subjects of the Pharaohs. The country became a British protectorate in 1914 and remained so until 1922, when it again became an independent state. Today the country is torn by political unrest. Its king is in exile, and a military leader rules the nation.

IF we look at a map we shall see that the wonderful country of Egypt is an oblong piece of land with the Nile River running through its centre like a backbone. We shall see that the Mediterranean forms the northern boundary and the Arabian desert and the Red Sea the eastern, while on the south is the Sudan and on the west the Libyan desert. The Nile, most famous of rivers, flows northward in a narrow valley which, in the course of ages, it has carved for itself in the rock of the desert.

The White Nile brings down mud and silt while the Blue Nile, which joins it at Khartum in the Anglo-Egyptian Sudan, brings down so much water at one time of the year that it causes the united rivers to overflow their valley. When the waters subside, however, there is left a covering of rich black mud. The mud which has been deposited at the mouth of the Nile where it runs into the still waters of the Mediterranean, has gradually formed the Delta, known as Lower Egypt, and the narrow valley of the Nile is known as Upper Egypt. These two constitute the Egypt of history—the land which has been called the Gift of the Nile. They form only about one-twenty-sixth of the whole area that is modern Egypt. The rest is desert and, save for a few oases, uninhabitable and useless.

We have read of ancient Egypt and know that the country fell into the hands of the Romans in 30 B.C. There it remained for nearly seven hundred years when the Arabs invaded Egypt in the interests of Islam. This land became a part of their territory and it so prospered that

the magnificence of court life rivaled even that of the Pharaohs. In 1517, however, Selim I, ruler of the Ottoman Empire, having conquered Syria and Palestine, came down into Egypt and had himself declared sultan.

Egypt was from then governed as a Turkish province directly under the Mamelukes, who, although subject to the Ottoman Empire, had considerable power. They lived most extravagantly so that there was little revenue for the improvement of the country and naturally it suffered exceedingly.

Impoverished, indeed, Napoleon found it when in 1798 he invaded it for the purpose of using it as a base for the conquest of India. His occupation of Egypt was not of long duration, however, for in 1801 he was forced to surrender to the British, and the British themselves stayed but two years longer.

There came to power about this time an Albanian, Mehemet Ali, who had come to Egypt originally to help the Turks against Napoleon. After the evacuation of the foreign armies, he sought to strengthen his power by siding first with the Turks and then with the Mamelukes. The Turks appointed him ruler of Egypt whereupon he rid the country of the Mamelukes by one of the most treacherous massacres known to history. The wily Mehemet Ali then consolidated his army and invaded Arabia, Palestine, Syria and portions of Asia Minor. The defeat of the Turks resulted in his being given hereditary authority over Egypt, under the suzerainty of the Ottoman Empire, however. Then he set about

ALL THE WORLD NEEDS SALT

In the sunny open market places of many Egyptian towns, the vendors sit beside their produce which is spread out on the ground. This cheerful merchant of Luxor is weighing salt for a customer from his large supply on the mat; he holds his not very delicately balanced scales in his hand. Many Egyptian natives wear the traditional dress of their ancestors.

MOST OF EGYPT'S CITIES ARE ALONG THE NILE

improving the condition of his newly-won domain and did a great deal toward bringing it back to prosperity.

Egypt again fell into troublous times under Ismail, grandson of Mehemet Ali, for he was very extravagant. To pay for his luxurious tastes, he sold a large number of Suez Canal shares to the British government and incurred such a large public debt that foreign governments were obliged to take a hand. Egypt was found to be in a state bordering on bankruptcy. Taking advantage of this state of affairs, the sultan of Turkey decided to oust Ismail and to appoint Tewfik, his son, as "khedive," although Ismail had paid a very large sum for this very title.

In 1882, Egypt had more difficulties for an Arab revolt, seemingly directed against foreigners, broke out. As the sultan seemed unwilling to interfere, Great Britain took a leading part in the organization of a government.

Of the people who made history in this land we already know, but what manner of people inherit it to-day? Are they the descendants of the Egyptians of old or have successive invasions wiped out that mighty race? The answer is that while the kings, priests and nobles disappeared, the peasantry remained, almost as slaves, to till the fruitful soil whose crops made the country so rich. Of the sixteen millions inhabiting Egypt to-day, most are "fellahin," or agriculturists. Some, like the Copts, are descendants of the old Egyptian race.

Christianity spread early to Egypt, but when the Saracens conquered the land in

93

the seventh century A.D., most of the Egyptians were converted to the new Mohammedan religion, so the fellahin are almost entirely Mohammedans. Those remaining Christians formed a small body which now numbers about a million the members of which are known as Copts. The Copts live mostly in the towns, and are skilled goldsmiths, watchmakers and tailors. Unlike the Mohammedans, a Copt has only one wife. Coptic women usually appear in the streets in flowing garments, with gold necklaces, bracelets and long black silk veils, although the veils are not worn over the face in Moslem fashion.

A railway now runs south as far as Assuan, but by far the most interesting way to see Upper Egypt is to go by the old highway—the river. The water of the Nile is brown. Brown, too, are the slender

well-formed fellahin whom we may see working in the fields all along the valley, using plows such as their forefathers had four thousand years ago and raising the water by means of the shaduf, as they did at the time of the Exodus, when the Jews left Egypt.

Another way of raising water is by means of a wheel turned by a blindfolded buffalo, camel or donkey in charge of a small boy, for among the fellahin even the children must work in order that the land, wherever possible, shall bear three crops a year. Clover is grown to feed the animals, and corn and wheat to feed the people. Cotton is cultivated for export; sugar-making is also a big industry, and beyond Minia, about 170 miles south of Cairo, fields of the greenish-purple sugar-cane extend for miles and miles.

In every town in Egypt we may see

© E. N. A.

LOW-LYING FIELDS OF THE NILE DELTA ARE EASILY WATERED

The Nile delta produces great crops of cotton and rice, and is watered all the year round by means of numerous canals which are filled by the river. To raise water to fields that are not more than five feet above the level of the river, the fellah uses the Archimedean screw. This device is believed to have been invented by the Greek, Archimedes.

EGYPT IS A LAND OF FARMERS

Although Egypt is primarily an agricultural country, with more than half of its people engaged in farming, the methods used are frequently very primitive. In the threshing scene above, the oxen are drawing a heavy sledge around. Its weight separates the grain from the chaff and the stalks. The man in the center rakes the stalks of grain toward the sledge.

NO MODERN FARM MACHINERY HERE!

The method of threshing with heavy flails is probably as old as the art of farming itself. These Egyptian farmers must put a lot of energy into their work, as they beat the harvested crop with their stout palm sticks. Among Egypt's most important crops are cotton, grains, corn, sorghum, potatoes, beans, sugar-cane, flax, sesame, Indian hemp and sugar beets.

PORT SAID AND THE MEDITERRANEAN END OF THE SUEZ CANAL

Work was begun on the Suez Canal in 1859 and the offices of the Suez Canal Co. were established in Port Said, which was then only a little village. A Frenchman, Ferdinand de Lesseps, who later unsuccessfully attempted to construct the Panamá Canal, was the builder of this waterway which joins the Mediterranean with the Red Sea. When the canal was opened to traffic in 1869 Port Said quickly grew into a busy port with a splendid harbor, as can be seen in this aerial photograph. On the opposite side of the canal is Port Fuad.

men sitting at the street corners beside a stack of sugar-canes which are broken off and sold as candy. Many other crops are grown besides excellent fruit and vegetables, and graceful feathery-leaved date-palms, with their bunches of golden dates, are to be seen everywhere.

Houses of the Villagers

Dotted here and there are the villages with the white domes of the mosques towering above the houses. These dwellings are built of either mud and wattle or of mud bricks, as wood is scarce. Each little house—they often contain only one or two rooms—has a tiny courtyard in front where the animals are kept and where the cooking is done. At the entrance to many of the villages are two mud towers which are shaped like temple pylons. These are for the pigeons, which are kept as much for their dung as for their flesh, for cakes of dried dung are used to keep the fires burning.

Inside the courtyard we can see something that looks like a high, wide font made of mud. This serves many purposes. It is used to keep fodder out of the reach of the animals, to keep the babies out of the reach of scorpions when the mother is busy and, in the hottest weather, it may serve as a sleeping place for the family. In cool weather the whole family and the animals sleep together in the dark airless house.

Along the Nile to the Great Dam

The towns on the Nile are all interesting places. In Assiut (Asyût) is the American College established by Presbyterian missionaries, the graduates of which are in great demand as government employees, and also we may see here the famous shawls made by clipping pieces of gold or silver tape to black or white netting. Kena, farther south, is a centre for the manufacture of pottery.

Many of the Nile towns owe their prosperity to the fact that they are favorite stopping places for tourists. Luxor is large and flourishing, not only because it is a sunny health resort, but because of its situation in the heart of ancient Egypt.

Here, where the valley broadens out, once stood Thebes, the city with a hundred gates, the metropolis of Egypt for four centuries, about which we read in the chapter Egypt's Wonders of the Past.

Assuan (Aswan), situated close to the First Cataract on the Nile, has always been important. Here started the caravans that traveled over the Libyan Desert and right across North Africa; here, too, was quarried the red stone which was used by the ancient Egyptians for their statues and temples. Now Assuan is a health resort with fashionable hotels, but its principal interest lies in the Great Dam. This dam is a solid piece of masonry a mile and a quarter in length, which extends across the river. By closing its 180 water gates as required, the waters are held back until they form a great lake, thus saving the land from disastrous floods, while the opening of the gates later on prevents drought and famine.

People of Upper Egypt

The people become darker-complexioned as we go farther south, and from Assuan to the border of Egypt at Wadi Halfa, the people vary from light coffee color to black. In the extreme south we shall find the dark negro-like Nubians. Their little villages and towns are better built and cleaner than those lower down the river, and the people themselves are intelligent and very interesting. The men wear the "galabeah," a long dark blue cotton gown, and usually a white turban. The women are fond of adorning themselves with elaborate silver jewelry.

Owing to the fact that for hundreds of miles it receives no tributary, and that it is being used throughout for irrigating the land, the Nile, which is a mile wide at Khartum, has shrunk considerably by the time it reaches Cairo. Below the city it enters the Delta, where the water is diverted into three large canals which feed a network of smaller ones.

The Delta is the most fertile part of Egypt and, in order to give as much land as possible to the cultivation of the cotton plant, the teeming population is terribly

STEP ONE: BRICK-MAKING FOR A HOUSING PROJECT

A workman at Gorna, the site of a government housing project, marking drying bricks with his personal symbol. Since the workmen are paid by the piece, each must identify his own work.

STEP TWO: BRICKLAYERS AT WORK ON A BUILDING IN GORNA

The materials used in the houses are made of little else than local mud. However, in the warm dry climate of Egypt, buildings of similar construction have lasted over four thousand years.

PIX

A STRIKING STUDY IN POINTED ARCHES AND LIGHT AND SHADE
Though this gallery has an air of the long ago, it is actually part of a modern market at Gorna.
When the market is open, traders' stalls are set up here. It is easily swept out afterward.

McLeish

ASSUAN (ASWAN), A TRADING CENTRE FOR THE SUDAN AND ETHIOPIA

Assuan is situated on the right bank of the Nile near the First Cataract, and not far from the town are the quarries whence the Egyptians obtained material for their temples and monuments. Three miles to the south of Assuan is the great dam across the Nile, by means of which the supply of water can be regulated according to need in the growing seasons.

crowded together. The villages are so packed with people that often the goats and the chickens spend their time amid the refuse on the roofs. In September and October, when the cotton is ready for picking, all the people work in the fields. The pickers stuff the cotton into the neck of their outer garment, which they have made into a pouch by tying it tightly at the waist. When the pouch is absolutely full they walk to the collecting ground, untie the waist cord and let the cotton fall to the ground.

All the cotton is exported by way of Alexandria. This city, with its large harbor and fine new buildings, is about half the size of Cairo, but it is less Eastern in appearance. Modern hotels, as well equipped as those of New York, help to make the tourists comfortable while street cars, automobiles, electric lights and theaters make it seem hardly possible

PIX

A MODERN MOSQUE ON THE SITE OF AN ANCIENT TEMPLE

The graceful minaret stands out sharply against a vivid blue sky, and the whole mosque gleams in brilliant sunlight. In drab contrast below are the crumbled ruins of an ancient temple to Ra, in Luxor. The temple was dug out after the mosque was built and without disturbing it. Thus do Moslem Egyptians worship on the spot where ancient Egyptians kneeled to a pagan god.

that such a modern looking place could have been founded more than two thousand years ago. A great many Europeans live there, especially Greeks, Armenians, Italians and others from southern Europe. There are Frenchmen and British, too, and numbers of Turks go to swell the mixed population.

If you visit Egypt as a tourist, you may go to Cairo by air; or you may take ship to Alexandria or to Port Said on the eastern point of the Nile delta. Port Said is the third largest city of Egypt, due to the fact that it stands at the entrance to the Suez Canal.

This canal, which unites the Mediterra-

nean with the Red Sea, was built by French engineers under Ferdinand de Lesseps and was formally opened in 1869 with grand ceremony. Representatives from all the great rulers of the earth attended the festivities. The Khedive of Egypt provided lavish hospitality.

The canal is about 104 miles long, thirty feet deep and 300 feet wide at the top. The idea of connecting the Mediterranean and Red seas did not originate with the people of the modern era, as one might suppose, since it was completed in rather recent times. An inscription on the temple at Karnak shows that a canal existed between the Nile and the Red Sea probably

KOSTICH

AGE-OLD DEVICE WATERS THE THIRSTY LAND

A patient ox, walking a treadmill, powers this old-fashioned device by which water, brought up in buckets from a well, pours into an irrigating channel leading through a field. The picture was taken near Luxor, site of ancient Thebes, on the right bank of the Nile. Modern methods of irrigation have been brought to many parts of Egypt, however.

ARAB WOMEN BRINGING PRODUCE TO MARKET

In many Mohammedan countries today men and women have given up their traditional garb and dress in the Western manner. Yet you will still find in North Africa Arab women dressed in long shapeless robes and wearing the face veil. These women bringing merchandise to market walk with easy grace, their burdens easily balanced on head cushions.

WELL-LADEN FELUCCAS ON THE NILE

The cargoes of pottery are carefully built up on these Nile River feluccas. A picturesque sight the flat-bottomed boats make, even when tied at the dock, their sails furled. In olden times they were used for transportation of passengers as well as freight; and long, narrow speedy feluccas were often seen on the Mediterranean, their two sails supplemented by oars.

103

as early as 1380 B.C. If it was important then, how much more important it is to-day, for without it the ships that ply between the western and eastern ports would have to make their way around the vast continent of Africa, thus adding several thousand miles to the voyage.

According to an Anglo-Egyptian treaty signed in 1936, Britain was given the right to guard the canal for a period of 20 years. In 1951 Egypt announced that the treaty was no longer binding and that British troops must withdraw from the Suez. Britain, France, Turkey and the United States tried to persuade Egypt to join an alliance that would replace the 1936 treaty. Egypt refused and the problem, in early 1952, was yet to be solved.

The desert, which forms so large a part of Egypt, lies on both sides of the Nile Valley. That part to the east is a rocky waste and was once famed for its minerals. It was there that the ancient Egyptians got much of their gold. The Sinai Peninsula is another mineral-bearing region.

The western, or Libyan, desert is a rocky plateau, where the winds are forever shifting the sands. Beduins roam these deserts, but as time passes more and more of these people are ceasing to be nomadic, and are settling down with their tents and their animals on the outskirts of the Nile Valley. In the western desert are several oases. That of Kharga grows enough food to support its inhabitants and is noted for its grapes and oranges.

Egypt may be compared in shape with a wineglass, mostly stem. The Nile forms the life-supporting stem while the triangular-shaped delta is the cup. This narrow stem and cup form the arable land of Egypt. From an airplane it appears as a ribbon of green—Nile green—in a sea of yellow sand. The green strip of fertility, stretching a thousand miles, goes close to the walls of the desert, where it stops as abruptly as though it were cut off by a gardener. Through the ages Egypt has had one long drink every year from "Nature's wineglass."

EGYPT: FACTS AND FIGURES

THE COUNTRY

Bounded on the north by the Mediterranean Sea, on the east by Israel, the Gulf of Aqaba and the Red Sea, on the south by the Sudan and on the west by Libya. The area including the Libyan Desert, the region between the Nile and the Red Sea and the Sinai Peninsula is 386,198 square miles; the population is 20,439,-000; cultivated and settled area of Nile valley, delta and oases is only 13,500 square miles.

GOVERNMENT

Independent sovereign state and hereditary constitutional monarchy. In 1952, General Mohammed Naguib ousted King Farouk and took over as Premier. A Regency Council was appointed to act for Farouk's son, Ahmed Fuad II, until he comes of age. The council is responsible to Parliament which consists of a 147-member Senate and a 264-member Chamber of Deputies. Members are elected by popular male suffrage.

COMMERCE AND INDUSTRIES

About 62% of the population are engaged in agriculture which is almost entirely dependent on irrigation. Grain, cotton, beans and sugar are the important products. Mineral products include phosphate rock, petroleum, asbestos and chromite. Other mineral deposits are salt, gypsum, cement, building stones and sulfur. Leading exports are cotton, cottonseed, onions, rice and petroleum. Leading imports are textiles, fertilizers, minerals, metals, machinery, electrical equipment and autos.

COMMUNICATIONS

The Nile is the great highway and much traveling is done by boat. The railways, state-owned, have a mileage of 4,188; private companies own over 862 miles of light railways. Length of surface roads, 8,870 miles; of telephone lines, 491,000 miles; of telegraph wires, 12,290 miles. There are international wire and cable connections, about 6,400 post offices and stations and regular air-mail service. The Suez Canal, 103 miles long, connects the Mediterranean and Red seas.

RELIGION AND EDUCATION

Moslems form over 91% of the population. In addition to Moslem mosques and universities at Cairo, Tanta, Damietta, Dessuqi, Assiut, Zagazig and Alexandria under the control of the Council of the University of El Azhar at Cairo, there are primary, secondary and special schools. There are also 2 state universities.

CHIEF TOWNS

Population: Cairo (capital), 2,100,000; Alexandria, 925,000; Port Said, 178,000; Tanta, 140,-000; Mahalla el Kubra, 116,000; Suez, 108,000; Mansura, 103,000; Asyût, 90,000.

THE COLOR OF CAIRO

Life and Glamour of Egypt's Historic Capital

THERE is a thrill in our first sight of Egypt. We know what an ancient country it is and we are anxious to set foot upon the land which has seen so many thousands of years of interesting life. A glistening white city first meets our gaze. That is Alexandria.

We shall not loiter at Alexandria. Somewhere beyond, on the banks of the Nile, lies the city of a thousand dreams, where from a cloudless sky the sun shines down upon all the races of mankind—for Cairo is a Tower of Babel if ever there was one—and upon such strange build-

ings as are only to be found in Eastern cities.

Already, gazing from the windows of the train that takes us from Alexandria to Cairo, we feel the spell of Egypt. Here are the palms, the green plains, the groups of dusky Egyptians, the string of camels and the sad, mouse-colored donkeys.

We are eager for the sight of Cairo, but when at last we really do see it—well, it is at first rather disappointing. A railway station is usually a sad affair, even such an attractive railway station as Cairo's, and the way thence to the

CAIRO, A MIXTURE OF OLD AND NEW

A white-clad police officer, wearing the typical Egyptian fez and holding his police whistle in his right hand, directs traffic from the control tower in Cairo's El Mahatta Square. Cairo is a city of striking variety; modern buildings and sections contrast with the ancient Oriental quarters and bazaars where, externally, little has changed for hundreds of years.

hotel is not as a rule very much better. So it is with Cairo. We must wait a little while before we find the city for the fulfillment of our dreams.

While we are waiting let us glance at Cairo's history. It is not so ancient a history as many people think. The Pharaohs, Egypt's ancient rulers, had been dead many years and the pyramids were very old when the site of Cairo was merely waste land and sown fields extending from the Nile to the Mokattam hills. As far as it is possible to judge there were no buildings there except a couple of fortresses up to the year 641, when the Commander-in-Chief of the armies of

THE DAZZLING ALABASTER MOSQUE WITHIN THE CITADEL

The Citadel (El-Kala), built by Saladin about 1177, is a landmark in Old Cairo. It stands on several hills. Within the walls are five mosques. This one takes its name from the gleaming stone of which it is built. Besides the mosques, the Citadel contains an extensive palace and an extraordinary well that has been bored down through solid rock for 270 feet.

the victorious Caliph Omar captured the Roman fortresses and built a town, which he called Al Fustât. This was the first Mohammedan capital of Egypt.

Fustât, in Arabic, means "tent," and this is the story the Arabs tell as to how the name came about. When the victorious general marched north to capture

Alexandria he left his tent standing because he refused to disturb the doves that had commenced building there. On his return from the conquest of Alexandria he commanded his army to build their quarters around his tent which was still standing. From that fact the new settlement, which was the first Arab city of

© E. A. A.

CAIRO ON THE NILE is a great river port. We are here looking across the branch of the Nile between the island of Roda, on which we are standing, and that part of the city called Old Cairo. The craft moored along the farther bank are feluccas with their short masts and long, slender spars. The stone wall on the right is part of an embankment protecting a garden. Along the top of the wall visitors walk to see the famous Nilometer. This is a large stone well with a graduated pillar in the centre to indicate the rise and fall of the river.

DONALD MC LEISH

THE WATER SELLER with his goat skin bottle and brass cup is one of the commonest sights although waterworks now supply most houses, and here and there one can see a public drinking pipe jutting from a wall. The people still continue the old way of doing things. A squeeze from the water seller's elbow sends a jet of cool water from the shining nozzle.

KOSTICH

A HOLY CARPET RETURNS FROM MECCA

Each year thousands of devout Mohammedans make the pilgrimage from Cairo to the holy city of Mecca, in Arabia. It is the duty of every follower of Mohammed to go there at least once in his lifetime. The most sacred shrine at Mecca, the Kaaba, is always covered with a carpet, which is renewed annually. Here we see a carpet and its honor guard on the return journey.

A LION STANDS GUARD BY THE NILE

Majestic and dignified as a Pharaoh, a gigantic sculptured lion keeps a calm vigil above the restless color and noise of a typical Egyptian crowd. Near the entrance to Cairo's bridge over the Nile, Egyptians mingle, old-style and new-style. Some wear Western dress; others wear fezzes and Egyptian garb. Burdens are carried either on the head or in baskets.

© E. N. A.

IN CAIRO BAZAARS the way is blocked by donkeys and mules, carts and carriages, besides the crowds of Egyptians, Arabs, Jews, Syrians and a sprinkling of European tourists. There is always a pandemonium caused by the shouting of the coachmen and camel drivers, as they try to clear the way, and by the haggling in the shops. Awnings above the crowd give shade.

MOSQUE EL AZHAR, known as "the splendid," which can be seen at the end of the street, was converted into a university nearly a thousand years ago. Students come from all parts of the Moslem world to gain knowledge of the Koran. The enrollment is over ten thousand. Their ages range from fifteen to seventy-five for, indeed, some spend their lives here.

MINARETS ABOVE ONE OF THE OLD CITY GATEWAYS

In this street a row of tumbledown houses hides one of Cairo's most beautiful mosques, the Mosque of El Muayyad. It was completed in 1422. The two tall minarets are seen rising above the southern gate of the old Fatimate city, called the Bab Zuweila. Fatima was one of Mohammed's daughters, and the caliphs descended from her are called Fatimate.

Egypt, came to be known as Al Fustât, "The Tent."

Fustât soon became quite an important settlement with mosques, palaces, barracks and the dwellings of an Eastern capital. The summer palace, where the emirs of Egypt often resorted to enjoy the cool breeze, stood on a spur of the Mokattam hills where the Citadel now stands, and another magnificent palace had been built by Ibn Tulun in the Royal suburb of Al-Katâ'i.

In 969 a new Arab conqueror came down into Egypt. He captured Fustât and laid the foundations of a new city. It is said that on a clear August night he marked out the boundaries of his new city on the sandy waste which stretched north-

east of Fustât, and a square about a mile each way was pegged out with poles. Each pole was joined by a rope on which bells were hung, and it was arranged that at the moment when the astrologers gave the signal that the lucky moment had arrived, the first sods were to be turned.

While the workmen were awaiting the signal a raven perched on one of the ropes and set the bells tinkling merrily. Straightway every workman thrust his spade in the earth and began to dig. At this moment the planet Mars, which the Arabs call Al-Kâhir, was above the horizon, and although this was looked upon as a bad omen, the raven's signal could not be ignored. The new city was called after the planet Mars, "Kâhirah"—mean-

Donald McLeish

AN EXAMINATION IN THE MOSQUE OF EL MERDANI

Moslem students are chiefly concerned with learning all their work by heart. In this photograph a number of them are working at an examination. Everyone sits with seeming discomfort on the floor, for there are no chairs, and each has his pot of ink in front of him. This mosque was built by the cup-bearer to the Sultan En-Nasir about 1340.

BLUE PORCELAIN fashioned into tiles makes this one of the loveliest of mosques and has given it the name of "the Blue." The tiles are arranged on the eastern wall of the Liwan, or sanctuary, which the visitor sees from the palm court. There are patterns of exquisite design. "Blue Mosque," or Ibrahim Agha Mosque, is situated near the Wezir Gate

TALL MINARETS, standing up against the sky, surround us on all sides if we climb up to the flat roofs of any of the houses in the centre of the city. From the doorways opening out on the galleries of these towers, officials, called "muezzins", appear five times every day— at dawn, noon, four o'clock, sundown and midnight—to call the Faithful to prayer.

117

IN CAIRO, SWEET HERBS ARE HAWKED FROM DOOR TO DOOR

The man, in Egypt, who will bring round his goods to the door is sure to find customers, for there it is so hot that most housewives are glad to be saved a journey into the crowded market. The girl to whom this hawker is trying to sell sweet herbs is not a Mohammedan or she would not let a man see her unveiled. The sculptured doorway is typical of Cairo.

118

THE COLOR OF CAIRO

ing "the victorious"—and out of this we have derived the modern Cairo.

Thus was founded the great City of the Caliphs, of which it presently came to be written: "He who hath not seen Cairo hath not seen the world: its soil is gold, its Nile is a wonder, its houses are palaces, and its air is soft, its odors surpassing that of aloes-wood, and cheering the heart, and how can Cairo be otherwise when it is the mother of the world?"

Just one word more on Cairo's history. It was captured by the Turks in 1517, by the French in 1798, by the British who handed it back to the Turks, in 1801, and in 1882, it was again taken by the British.

Until the year 1883 Cairo was a very fair specimen of a large Oriental city, where Eastern life and character could be observed with delightful ease. It was just an Eastern city, and nothing else—decayed palaces, dusty streets, a considerable amount of filth and that endless variety of color of which no Western institutions may ever rob it.

The people were tolerant, and became more so as they mixed to a greater extent with Europeans. Railways, telegraphs and other inventions of the Frange, or European, had shown them that the "magic" of the West was more powerful, and probably more useful, than their own.

EWING GALLOWAY

SHARIA FUAD EL AWAL, A BUSY STREET OF DOWNTOWN CAIRO

Ciguerel department store is a gleaming white addition to tree-lined Sharia Fuad el Awal, one of many broad avenues in the modern quarter. The wide view of the intense blue sky chases away all the Oriental mystery that is so much a part of the older sections of Cairo where, in the shadow of magnificent mosques and palaces, tenements crowd narrow alleyways.

119

© E.N.A.

THE MOSQUE OF SULTAN HASAN —one of the finest in Egypt— stands on a shelving rock opposite the citadel. It covers more than two acres, and its loftiest minaret, 267 feet high, is the tallest in Cairo. This was built in 1357, so pleased the Sultan that he had the right hand of the architect cut off so that he could not design another. Next to it is the chief Liwan, or sanctuary, which is built on the side towards the holy city of Mecca. It is a madrasah, or school mosque, and classes for teaching Moslem religion and law are held there.

With these improvements the city began to develop rapidly. A person acquainted with the old Cairo, before its face was altered by Western influences, would see a great many striking changes. But in spite of improvements, much of Cairo preserves the air of an Eastern city.

The Mingling of East and West

Now these are matters of a more or less historical character. It is good to know something about them before setting out to explore and enjoy the wonders of the city. But even if we know nothing about them we shall be able to appreciate Cairo.

Impressions will crowd in upon us at such a furious rate that we shall hardly know how to sort them out afterward. This mingling of East and West, this jostling of strange and varied types of people and costumes, this jumbling together of buildings which seem like those only seen in dreams, this throb, throb, throb of one of the greatest cities in the East, will prove to be a source of endless delight.

But we shall not see much of all this in the European quarters—the Taufikia, the Ismailia and the Kasr-el-Dubara quarters, occupying the northwestern portion of the city. Here are the hotels, banks, ministerial offices, consulates, clubs and fine palaces of wealthy Egyptians and Levantines as well as of Europeans.

Where Aïda Was First Produced

In the center of Taufikia is the Esbekia Garden, a beautiful part, with Opera Square on the south. In the Opera House, which is now shabby and brown colored, was first produced Aïda to celebrate the opening of the Suez Canal, and the costumes are still used when that opera is given. The Khedive Ismail, who nearly bankrupted the government, paid Verdi $50,000 to write an opera for the occasion, but that was not his only method of celebrating, nor the only expense he incurred in connection with the great event.

Sharia Kamel is Taufikia's principal thoroughfare, its Fifth Avenue. Near the northern end of it once stood the luxurious Shepheard's Hotel, often called the most famous hotel in the world. Built in 1891, it was sacked and burned in 1952 during a savage riot. Sharia Kamel, at its southern end, becomes Sharia Abdin, which leads to the Midan Abdin, one of the city's royal palaces.

To the northwest of the European quarter is Bulak, the old part of Cairo, which is still kept very busy loading and unloading the produce carried up and down the Nile in strange ships. Like the rest of Cairo, the scene is bright and full of life.

Wonderful Palace on an Island

Bulak is easily reached by street car, and on the nights of popular festivals it is well worth seeing with its crowded streets, its gaiety and its curious customs. Just opposite is the Island of Bulak, commonly known as Gezira, where Ismail Pasha built a wonderful palace, such as those they used to build in the time of the Caliphs, and laid out a race course. The palace has now become a hotel, where the Khedival Sporting Club is always holding entertainments enjoyed both by Europeans and Egyptians. The island of Gezira is also the site of numerous foreign embassies and many of Cairo's wealthy citizens have villas there.

The fine Kasr-en-Nil Bridge, or Great Nile Bridge, connects the island with the east bank of the Nile. Most of the different types of people who live or work in the city can be seen by standing on this bridge between 6:30 and 9 A.M. when it is crowded with merchants, market-gardeners and peddlers, dressed in the oddest costumes, and bringing in their wares to the markets of the city. The brown water of the Nile flows beneath, dotted with the peculiar craft of Egypt. Tall-sailed painted boats, called feluccas, sway gently in the morning breeze and wait for the afternoon when the bridge is opened to allow such vessels to pass up or down the river.

Near the eastern end of the bridge is the Cairo Museum, which contains the most valuable collection of Egyptian antiquities in existence. The body of

FELUCCAS WAITING FOR THE SWING BRIDGE TO OPEN

Every afternoon the feluccas gather near the Great Nile Bridge to wait for its daily opening. The bridge is then closed to road traffic for about one and a half hours. So that all may be informed, the exact time is proclaimed by notices put up at each end. In the morning a crowd of country folk may be seen crossing the bridge to go into Cairo's markets.

122

Tutankhamen and the priceless articles, pictured with the chapter on Ancient Egypt, are on display here. We may see also the mummies of Egypt's mightiest Pharaohs so well preserved that one may even tell the color of the hair. The museum was started through the efforts of Auguste Mariette, a French Egyptologist, and a statue of him occupies a place in front of the museum.

Then we come back to the main streets. What do we notice? A visitor from the West will probably feel quite at home with the kodak shops and pharmacies but will be impressed by the way Cairo seems to live in the streets. The innumerable cafés of the Esbekia place their chairs and tables on the pavements, so that it is frequently necessary for a passer-by to step into the road, and run the risk of being knocked down by an arabiyeh, or carriage, dashing through the street at the absurd rate these Eastern drivers love so much.

Backgammon for a Cup of Coffee

These cafés are interesting, since in them will be found people from almost every quarter of the earth. Here are groups of Italians, Greeks and Levantines arguing noisily or drowsily smoking the bubbling nargileh (water-pipe), or playing a kind of backgammon for the price of a cup of coffee.

As we continue through the streets, every step will reveal a new and fascinating picture. Odd little shops, protected from the sun's glare by torn flapping awnings, catch the eye. Not that the goods displayed for sale are always particularly attractive but the dark interior has an air of mystery and the promise, not often fulfilled, of strange merchandise. Now comes a door with a bead curtain jingling in the breeze—probably a barber's shop. A mass of color piled among the shadows of a hole in the wall proves to be a fruiterer's. Next to it is a native café with pitch-black Ethiopians and tall Nubians and a dozen other varieties of modern Egypt's many races.

The streets, of course, are choked with a motley crowd in which only the camel or a lonely Arab from the desert seems able to maintain any dignity. The drivers of vehicles and beasts of burden keep up an incessant shouting as they thread their way through the crowd. "Make room, O my mother!" calls a shrill-voiced donkey-boy. "O Sheik, take care!" "You, good fellow, to your right!" "By your favor, effendi!" and so on.

A Street of Saladin's Days

There is even more bustle in Cairo's bazaars than in the streets. From the Ismailia quarter, the way down to the bazaars is through the Muski, an extremely long thoroughfare running toward the east. A tradition says that the Muski dates from the time of the famous Saladin, who was the Crusaders' chivalrous foe.

Its character has changed a good deal in recent years, and many of the native shops with their quaintness and smells and sleepiness have been replaced by large shops built on the French pattern with plate-glass windows. At one time practically the whole of the street was roofed in, and on very hot days it proved a cool, if crowded, retreat. On festival days one sees representatives of many lands, from Sweden in the north to the White Nile in the south, and from India in the east to Morocco in the west.

Motley Carnival of Cairo

It is one of the most characteristic parts of Cairo—a carnival in which the costumes of Europe, Asia and Africa mingle in a fascinating collection. At first it is a little confusing. Here are Turks, grinning Negroes from the Sudan, bored-looking fellahs, or peasants, in their bright rags, wily Levantines, green-turbaned Sherifs, or Moslem holy men, dignified Beduins, and people whose race it is often difficult to guess. All day long the street is packed with donkeys, strings of camels, loaded wagons, water-carriers with their tinkling glasses, sherbet and sweetmeat sellers, carriages and richly caparisoned horses, porters shaped like sickles, from the burdens they carry, gorgeously dressed women, beggar chil-

CUNNING CRAFTSMEN AT THEIR BEAUTIFUL WORK IN THE BAZAAR OF THE TENT-MAKERS Donald McLeish

Cairo's chief shopping district is situated round about the street called the Muski. The various bazaars lead off from this highway, which is itself bordered by shops. Merchants of the same trade are all found close together, and in the tent-makers' bazaar the visitor can see the goods being made. But much of the finely colored stuff sold here as native work comes from France and England. The ornamental work consists of wall-hangings, pillow-covers, tent-linings and awnings. The interesting patterns are copied from the old Egyptian models.

METAL WARE AND WEAPONS FOR THE SOUVENIR HUNTER

A shop of curiosities displays a great variety of goods before the visitor who happens to wander down this "souk," or bazaar. There are fly-whisks, shovel-headed spears, swords that the merchant will tell you were found on old Crusading battlefields and relics that he says were taken from the Pharaohs' tombs, but it is not wise to believe all he tells you.

125

A GAME OF CHECKERS IN A COURTYARD OF OLD CAIRO

It is known that a game very like checkers was played in ancient Egypt thousands of years ago, and so it is not surprising to find one of our own games played to-day as far away as Cairo. One of the men is holding the mouthpiece of a nargileh, or water-pipe, used for smoking tobacco in the Near East. The tobacco is burned in the canister at the top.

dren, closely veiled women and all the odds and ends of Cairo's astonishing medley. The ring of hammers is almost deafening in the bazaar of the Brass Workers; and a strong smell of perfume comes from the Scent-Sellers' bazaar. In the Spice Market men pound strange roots and herbs in metal mortars. Beautiful rugs from Damascus, Ispahan and Samarkand can be seen in the carpet shops.

The buildings of Cairo are as interesting as the people, and as full of color.

"Every step tells a story of the famous past. The stout remnant of a fortified wall, a dilapidated mosque, a carved door, a Kufic (Arabic) text—each has its history, which carries us back to the days when Saladin went forth from the gates of Cairo to meet Richard on the plain of Acre, or when Beibars, the Mameluke captain, rode at the head of his cavalry in the charge which trampled upon the Crusaders of Saint Louis."

In the old Fatimate city is the great

TRAYS, PLATTERS, GONGS, VASES—ALL IN GLEAMING BRASS

The shining array of wares could hardly fail to catch the eye of a passer-by, which is what it is meant to do. One of the delights of the visitor to Cairo is to stroll through its bazaars, where all the shops are open to the sidewalk. Many of the articles are only inexpensive souvenirs, but one may also find useful objects and genuine works of art.

MODERN ARCHITECTURE—FIFTEEN STORIES OF IT—BY THE NILE

The newer part of Cairo has wide, well-kept streets and twentieth-century buildings. The Immobilia Building above is among the tallest of scores of modern business structures. It is on Sharia Kasr El Nil, a wide, straight street designed for heavy automobile traffic. The awnings over the shop windows are a welcome relief from the glare of the sun.

HOW MOTHER USUALLY CARRIES BABY IN CAIRO

Walking about the native quarters one notices that mothers carry their babies either clasped to one hip or else astride their shoulders. The cloak of the woman is usually dark blue and the face veil is made of a coarse kind of black crepe kept free from nose and mouth by a little cylinder of gilt wood. Notice the Arabic writing on the door.

mosque-university of El Azhar, which was built by Gohar in 973. It is considered to be the most important Mohammedan university in the world, and students come to it from many different countries, but it is so arranged that those of the same nationality live and study together. There are over four hundred teachers, and sometimes the students number as many as ten thousand.

The Voice from the Minaret

Let us look at some of the other buildings. Every visitor to Cairo will remember the blue tiles of the Ibrahim Agha Mosque, the wonderful doorway of the Sultan Hasan Mosque, and the delicate ornamentation and graceful minaret of Kait Bey. The Arabs had a very fine taste in art, as we cannot help but notice as we go about the city. Then, there is the Arab Museum which has a valuable collection of Arabian art and a fine library, both of which have helped to make Cairo the premier city of Arab learning.

We shall now go up to the Citadel on the Mokattam hills and look out upon the wonderful panorama of Cairo which is spread before us. We see below us a forest of minarets, rising gracefully from the flat-roofed, yellowish buildings in which the streets are like pathways of darkness. From these slender minarets, rising from Cairo's 250 mosques, goes out the call to prayer, not, as with us, by the ringing of bells but by the human voice.

The Citadel, built, so some believe, from stones taken from the Pyramids, was once the key to fortified Cairo but now it is worthless as a military stronghold. Its greatest feature, apart from the view it offers, is the Mehemet Ali Mosque with its two wonderfully slim and beautiful minarets.

How the Mamelukes Were Betrayed

The most direct road to the Citadel used to be through the Gate al-'Azab, and then along a narrow track walled on each side. It was in this narrow way that the massacre of the Mamelukes, a ruling class of soldiers in Egypt and who were the descendants of slaves, took place on March 1, 1811. All the Mamelukes of any position or power were decoyed into the Citadel on the pretense that they were to assist in celebrating the appointment of Tusun, son of Mehemet Ali, to the command of the army.

Having taken coffee, they formed in a procession and marched down the narrow way with a body of the Turkish Pasha's troops in front and behind. As soon as they arrived at the exit gate, it was suddenly closed upon them. The Pasha's men at various vantage points then opened fire, and those Mamelukes who tried to escape were cut down by the sword.

It is said that of the 470 Mamelukes who entered the Citadel, only one came out alive, having made his horse leap through an opening in the wall to the moat below. The horse was killed by the fall, but the man escaped.

Revered Mosque of 'Amr Ibn al-'Asi

The first mosque to be built in Fustât was that raised by 'Amr Ibn al-'Asi, who conquered Egypt in 639 A.D. The present mosque of 'Amr stands on the same site, but has very little of the original building in it. It is not very attractive but the people hold it in special veneration. It is said that, after a long, disastrous drought (1825-28) Moslems, Christians and Jews went there together to pray for rain. On the next day it rained. The credulous believe that one of the pillars was made to fly through the air from Mecca to Cairo by a blow from Mohammed's whip.

All through this glittering city you will find strange monuments of the people—mosques in plenty, old Arabic gates, an endless medley of bazaars all hung with the brightly colored merchandise of Eastern lands, ancient churches founded by the Copts, which was the name given to the earliest native Christians, mysterious lattice windows—all the fascination associated with the Orient, piled up like the jewels in Aladdin's cave.

And just a stone's throw away, on the threshold of the Libyan desert, the Sphinx looks out unceasing to the dim minarets of the city, and the Pyramids rise like golden stairways to the blue of the sky.

ETHIOPIA AND LIBERIA

Two Independent Countries

Ethiopia, near the eastern coast of Africa, and Liberia, on the west coast, are two of the few independent countries on the continent. Ethiopia guarded its freedom jealously from the days of Homer until the Italians overran the country in 1936. When Britain drove the Italians out in 1941, Ethiopia regained its independence and in 1952 it joined in a federation with Eritrea, the former Italian colony on the Red Sea. Liberia began its life as a colony for freed American Negro slaves in the early nineteenth century. It became a republic in 1847 with a constitution much like that of the United States. A land of lush forests, rich mineral deposits and palm and rubber plantations, Liberia faces a future of great promise as its wealth of resources is developed.

THE kingdom of Ethiopia existed (with some changes of boundary) as far back as 1000 B. C., but little is really known about the country until comparatively modern times, though there are references to its wealth and power in many ancient writings. The tradition has been cherished that the rulers have descended from Solomon and the beautiful Queen of Sheba, who journeyed from her throne in Ethiopia to Jerusalem. The fabled Ophir of Solomon, the city of sparkling gold, was possibly in Ethiopia, and the rich country reigned over by Prester John, the fabulous adventurer of medieval times, has been identified by a few writers as Ethiopia. But "the glory has departed," long since.

Ethiopia, a land larger than France, owes its long integrity in large part to its situation upon a mountain stronghold. In 1896 it was recognized by the European Powers as the Kingdom of Abyssinia, after defeating an Italian army at Adowa. Forty years later the Italians, after an arduous campaign of several months' duration, conquered the country and annexed it as part of the Roman Empire. After the second World War broke out, the British successfully overcame the Italian armies in eastern Africa, and Haile Selassie, the emperor who had been in exile during Italian occupation, returned to the throne.

It is a land of potential wealth. Inland from the coast there is a stretch of mostly barren lowland, sometimes falling to below sea level. The climate here is inclement to white men. A good part of the country, however, is occupied by mountain ranges and fertile plateaus and valleys, where white men, once they become accustomed to the altitude, can live.

The mountain forests contain great drooping cedars and stately yews, as well as unusual specimens like the kosso (Hagenia), with pink flowers which hang like gigantic bunches of grapes. Everything is gigantic, even to the heather and the mountain thistle. Coffee is of particularly good quality, rubber, tobacco, bananas, rice, grapes and wheat are grown and flax may one day be an important item of export. To the south and west there is bamboo, which enables people to build better huts than the grass hives of the grazing regions, as well as bridges for the smaller streams. The larger rivers have to be forded or swum. Wild life includes leopards, monkeys and mountain hyenas. The birds are colorful, especially the flocks of little pink bee-eaters.

Near the centre of Ethiopia the Blue Nile (the Abbai) takes its rise, at Lake Tana. The river canyon has walls five thousand feet deep at one place.

The population is exceedingly varied, some seventy racial stocks being distinguished. These may be grouped in three major divisions: the original Hamitic peoples, the Semitic element and the Negro tribes. There is considerable intermarriage and the skin color varies from light chocolate to deepest black; nevertheless most Ethiopians fiercely resent being called colored.

Christianity probably reached Ethiopia in the fourth century. The form still practised is the same as the Coptic church of Alexandria. There are, however, many pagan tribes and a considerable number of Mohammedans, who scornfully called the Christians *habeshi* (mixed). From this the name Abyssinia arose. The people, however, have clung to the older name of Ethiopia for their country.

There are no large cities in our sense of the term. Addis Ababa, the capital, is but a rambling village, though it has 150,000 population. It has an elevation of over 8,000 feet and its cool nights make it very tolerable to white men. Down the roads come swaying camel caravans from the interior of Africa, jostled by automobiles. Cattle, sheep, dogs and chickens also make free of the main highways by day; at night the howling of hyenas shatters the silence.

As for Liberia, in 1822 a shipload of Christian Negroes embarked for the west coast of Africa and on arrival made a

BLACK STAR

RARE OLD MANUSCRIPTS FOR ETHIOPIA'S IMPERIAL LIBRARY

Librarians at the Imperial Library pore over old manuscripts that were found in the hinterlands of Ethiopia. Little remains of the literature of ancient Ethiopia before the time of Constantine the Great, but several hundred works written since his time are known to scholars. The manuscripts displayed above are probably about eight hundred years old.

MODERN OFFICE BUILDING IN ADDIS ABABA

The United States Reading Room in Addis Ababa, capital of Ethiopia, is in this pleasant, modern office building. Signs are in Amharic and English. The neat little pony drawing the rubber-wheeled trap is of the Ethiopian breed, peculiar to the country. These good-looking, intelligent horses resemble polo ponies in some respects, and they are good jumpers.

Major A. W. Bentin

A GREAT GATHERING AT THE BENEDICTION OF WATERS BY THE PATRIARCH OF THE SOUTHERN CHURCH

At the Feast of the Epiphany there is a large concourse of people at Addis Ababa, capital of Ethiopia, to see the Patriarch of the Shoa Church bless the waters. The rite is the same as that of the Greek Church, but the Southern Ethiopians, who are deeply tinged with Negro blood, regard their priests in the light of holy witch doctors, and to them the annual ceremony of the benediction of waters is a display of miraculous power. By probably as early as the fourth century Christianity reached Ethiopia from Egypt, and has persisted.

bargain with some native chiefs by which they exchanged twelve knives and other considerations for a strip of coast. The natives, when they saw that they had made a poor trade, tried to expel the newcomers, but the ex-slaves managed to hold their own; and in 1847 became the Free and Independent Republic of Liberia.

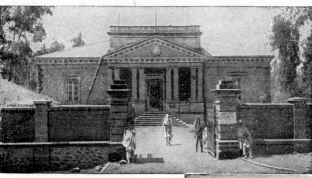

The republic now has fully 350 miles of coastline. It is a land of dense tropical forests in which a deep green twilight reigns and the huge tree trunks are swathed in creepers. The creeks are lined with mangroves, the roots of which writhe fantastically into the swamp. There are also high grasslands. Few people have penetrated into the interior of the republic. Even around Monrovia, the capital town, there are few roads, and as these approach the bush they degenerate into jungle tracks. Many of the tribes have a hearty dislike of roads, for experience has taught them that good roads mean a frequent appearance of the tax collector, backed up by a company of the Liberian Frontier Force, as Liberia's black army is called.

The Liberians—that is, the Negroes of American descent—form but a small part of the population and live only along the coast. Indeed, it is unsafe for them to go inland without an escort, as many of the inland tribes hate them as interlopers, and they are outnumbered by the aborigines.

These latter are composed of many tribes, such as the Krus, the Kpwesi and the Mandingos. Let us take the Krus first—also called Croos, Krev, Kroomen and Krooboys. For centuries they have hired themselves out as sailors to European ships. These Krus are Christians and speak English. They are an intelligent race.

The Mandingos live on the inland plateau. They have Arab blood in their veins and they dress picturesquely in flowing white robes and heelless slippers. They are Mohammedans and successful missionaries of their faith, and in this work they have done a good deal with those Liberian tribes which were cannibalistic,

E. E. Burgess

PUBLIC BUILDINGS IN ADDIS ABABA

Below is the Coptic Church of St. George; above is the principal bank of Addis Ababa. It is hard to imagine that the streets of the capital are thronged with camel caravans, as well as honking automobiles.

for in the remote depths of Liberia, cannibalism still exists, and the Mas tribes, who occupy the Grand Bassa country, were, until recently, openly addicted to dining off their fellows. Though they have now abandoned their degraded practice, most of the older people have devoured at least the flesh of captives of war.

The most powerful tribe of Liberia is

A PRETTY YOUNG WORKER IN A MATCH FACTORY IN ASMARA

The matches are held tight and separated in a framework so that the tips will not ignite accidentally. Asmara is the capital and chief town of Eritrea, which is joined to Ethiopia.

A PORTION OF THE VAST INLAND PLATEAU REGION OF ERITREA

The coastal area of Eritrea is hot and humid. The broad, inland plateau regions, however, have a temperate climate at 6,000 feet and are quite cold at their highest altitude of 9,000 feet.

MODERN TRANSPORTATION METHODS FIND THEIR WAY TO ERITREA

Busses are still a novelty in some parts of Eritrea, as the roadside audience would seem to indicate, but they are rapidly becoming the accepted means of transportation even in the hinterlands.

NURSERY FOR OIL PALMS NEAR MONROVIA

Oil palms grow well in the rich soil of Liberia, and palm oil finds a good market abroad. It is used for lubrication and in cosmetics and soap; and in some parts of the world in cooking. In this nursery young plants are grown from selected seed (the parent plants pollinated by hand). Each year several thousand baby palms are distributed to planters from the nursery.

A LESSON IN THE CABBAGE PATCH

A teacher from a United States economic mission shows the proper method of setting out cabbage plants to students who are being trained to serve with the Liberian Department of Agriculture's Extension Division. They will teach farmers better ways to work the land, explaining up-to-date, scientific methods such as diversification of crops to preserve fertility of the soil.

138

in recent years. In 1915 the Krus broke out in a rebellion which cost many lives before the Liberian Frontier Force, led by Negro officers borrowed from the United States Army, defeated the insurgents.

Monrovia, the capital of Liberia, is built on the shores of a lagoon. It is not a healthful town for white men and there is a scarcity of fresh food. The trying climate makes even trivial wounds and scratches dangerous, and malaria is prevalent. Monrovia possesses some fine buildings, but, generally speaking, it is a town of contrasts, for well-built houses are often scrappily finished off with galvanized iron streaked with rust. The houses are usually built with balconies and piazzas similar to those attached to

© E. N. A.

TWO SMART CITIZENS OF LIBERIA

Lengths of cotton cloth of vivid hue form the clothing of these two men. Their battered hats are considered nearly enough, save for gala occasions. Outside the coastal strip hats are superfluous.

the Kpwesi. They are hunters and warriors and, contrary to the usual native mode of waging war, they disdain ambuscades, but charge straight at their foes in mass formation. They use bows and arrows for hunting, but fight only with long knives. They are a musical race and, besides beating the inevitable tom-tom, play the harp and the flute. They are also expert in various crafts and show considerable taste in decorating their products.

The natives, as a whole, exhibit considerable hostility toward their Americo-Liberian overlords, and much desultory warfare has occurred

© E. N. A.

A KRU OF MONROVIA

In Monrovia, the capital of Liberia, people usually dress in gaudy colors and barbaric designs, fashioned in European style. This is a village belle.

139

houses in the southern states of America, and the gardens are gay with scarlet hibiscus blooms. Monrovia is the seat of the Liberian government. It is divided into five long streets which rise one above the other parallel to the waterfront.

On one side of Monrovia is a large colony of Krus, living in palm-thatched huts. There the Krus, or Krooboys, as they are called, stay during the short intervals between their voyages.

A rich American rubber company some few years ago acquired a huge tract of land in Liberia and has planted millions of rubber trees. Such an undertaking cannot but have a good effect on the financial condition of the country, and Liberia, already modeled politically on the United States of America, should derive further benefit from acquaintance with the enterprise of modern commerce. The above mentioned rubber company was not involved in the alleged forced labor conditions which an international commission was asked to investigate.

Except for rubber, which is increasing in importance, the development of the other products of Liberia's rich and productive soil has scarcely begun. There are vast tropical forests almost untouched and the same may be said of the mineral resources of which gold, copper, tin, zinc and iron are known to exist. The principal exports are coffee, cacao, palm oil, palm nuts and piassava fibre. There are no important manufacturing industries; however, a fishery has recently been established with facilities for canning.

Liberia's strategic location in Africa made it a valuable Ally in World War II. Air bases and harbors along its 350-mile coastline, facing the Brazilian bulge of South America across the narrowest stretch of the Atlantic assured a speedy flow of supplies during and after the war.

ETHIOPIA AND LIBERIA: FACTS AND FIGURES

LIBERIA

A Negro republic in West Africa, bounded on north by French Guinea, on the east by Ivory Coast, on the south by the Atlantic Ocean and on the west by Sierra Leone. Executive power is vested in a president and Cabinet; legislative power in a Senate and House of Representatives. Area, about 43,000 square miles; total population estimated at more than 1,500,000. Agricultural, mining and industrial development slight. Chief exports are rubber, palm kernels, palm oil and raw gold. Leading imports are textiles, foods and beverages, petroleum and coal, machinery and motor vehicles. Means of communication are poorly developed. Americo-Liberians are mostly Protestants. Government educational system supplemented by mission schools. Capital is Monrovia, population, about 10,000.

FORMER ITALIAN COLONIES

Ethiopia regained its independence in 1941. Following World War II Somaliland became a UN trust territory under Italian administration, and Eritrea was under a British Military Government, to be federated with Ethiopia in 1952.

ETHIOPIA (ABYSSINIA)

Country in northeastern Africa. Area, 409,160 square miles; population, about 15,000,000. Chief industries are agricultural and pastoral. Forests contain valuable trees. Iron, gold, platinum, coal, copper, sulfur and potash are found. Chief exports are hides and skins, coffee, wax, grain, civet and native butter; imports are salt, cotton yarns and fabrics, building materials and petroleum. Length of motor roads, 11,120 miles; of railways, 424 miles. The Coptic (Christian) Church predominates; there are also Moslems and Jews. In schools throughout the country there are 60,000 pupils. Population of chief towns: Addis Ababa (capital), 300,000; Dire Dawa, 30,000; Harrar, 25,000.

ITALIAN SOMALILAND

Bounded by Gulf of Aden, Indian Ocean, Kenya, Ethiopia and British Somaliland; area, 198,420 square miles, and population, 1,246,000. Chief industries are cattle-raising and farming; leading exports are skins, livestock and bananas. Roads, 425 miles; railways, 60 miles. Population of capital, Mogadiscio, 70,000.

ERITREA

It borders on northeastern Ethiopia; area, 48,000 square miles, and population, 1,104,000. Leading industries are stock-raising and salt production. Population of chief towns: Asmara (capital), 117,000; Massawa, 80,000.

BRITISH AFRICA FROM WEST TO EAST

Its Strangely Different Races

Since the end of World War II, Britain's African territories and possessions have assumed a new and greater importance in her scheme of life. East Africa, particularly, is destined to become the newest and strongest link in England's life-line of empire. Here we take a journey straight across the great continent to the Indian Ocean and then down to Northern Rhodesia. The map will show us that the territory under British control does not form the unbroken belt from west to east which it does from north to south. In these far-stretching lands we shall find that many and strangely different races of people are living under the protection of the Union Jack.

IF we look at a map of Africa fifty years old we shall see that the central zone appears to be inhabited only around the coast. The rest has very few names, and some parts are blank. The land is vast. The early explorers lost their way in tropical forests, died of disease, or were killed by savage beasts or still more savage natives. Therefore tropical Africa was thought of only as the land of Nature's splendor and cruelty, of gold and elephants, slaves and cannibals. The map of today shows us two groups of lands, west and east, lying between the tropics, under the British flag. The group to the west is the older, and we will therefore start with Gambia, the earliest of the British possessions on the continent.

Nearly five hundred years ago, Portuguese sailors exploring the coast found here a wide river with a few islands in its estuary. In 1618 James I granted a charter to a trading company called the Merchant Adventurers of London. These men built a fort on an island, which they named St. James Isle, and so started the first little settlement. Today the British colony has moved to St. Mary's Island, where there is a town, Bathurst, with the most modern comforts and enjoyments. On the mainland, on both sides of the river for over two hundred miles, lies a strip of country from perhaps six to forty miles wide, which, in 1888, became a British

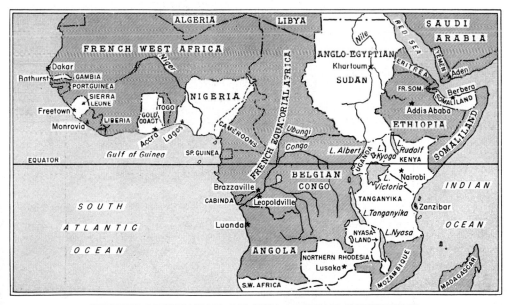

BRITISH POSSESSIONS ON THE AFRICAN CONTINENT

A STREET IN FREETOWN, SIERRA LEONE'S CAPITAL

Freetown, which was founded in 1788 as a home for freed slaves, is now a very busy city with a native population of about 86,000 and is the greatest seaport of Africa's west coast. It has a fine harbor and is also an important naval coaling station. For many years the inhabitants of Freetown have been known as keen and successful traders.

Protectorate—that is to say, it is a country occupied by natives under native rulers, but Great Britain is responsible for seeing that the native princes rule justly and for protecting the country from foreign attack.

Suppose we go by steamboat straight up the river. We shall pass first through dense forests of mangroves, a tree of the swamps. Then the mangrove forests thin out, and here and there in the swamps rise higher patches of cultivated land. Finally we come to fertile plains, over which roam great herds of cattle. The native counts his wealth by cattle, not by money, and Gambia exports hides and skins. We see other plains given up to the cultivation of the nut which we call the peanut. When the flower of this plant dies, the seed-pod pushes itself into the ground,

ripens there and has to be dug up; so it is also called the "groundnut." In olden days Gambia exported slaves, elephant tusks, wax, rubber and palm kernels; but now the natives are finding that growing the groundnut pays so well that, apart from millet and rice, they do not trouble much about other products.

The natives are real Negroes, with black skins, flat, broad noses, woolly hair and thick lips; they wear next to no clothing, and, apart from a few mission schools, and a few which are aided by the Government, have no education.

French territory separates the British West African settlements from each other, and we must sail along the coast to reach Sierra Leone, which is about 180 miles from north to south, though it does not extend far inland. The colony con-

McCann

MOHAMMEDAN SCHOOLMASTER OF BIMBUKU, A VILLAGE OF ASHANTI

Ashanti is the name given to the middle part of Gold Coast Colony, which lies between the Gold Coast proper and the Northern Territories. It is called after its fierce warlike people. Like their near relatives, the Fantis of the coastal districts, the Ashantis are mostly fetish worshipers; but some have been converted to Christianity, and some to Mohammedanism.

143

MAN'S WORK: TOTING MANGROVE TIMBER IN SIERRA LEONE

It takes powerful muscles to lift and carry the heavy logs, but these men seem to do it with effortless ease. The wood of mangrove trees, which grow so thick in swamps, is used as fuel in Sierra Leone. Chopping down the trees has other happy results. When a mangrove swamp is cleared, a fertile black soil is bared and mosquito breeding grounds can be controlled.

sists of one or two islands and a peninsula. All the West African coast was connected with the slave trade; for three centuries natives were captured or bought here and taken away into slavery by European nations, Britain included. About 150 years ago British people began to feel that this cruel trade was wrong, and in 1788 a British man bought land on the peninsula from the native king and made on it a settlement which he called Freetown, as a place of refuge for liberated slaves. Later on British merchants set-

tled here, and today Freetown, which is the capital of Sierra Leone, is a large, prosperous town, with schools and a university. Its harbor is the best on the West African coast.

The country inland became a British Protectorate in 1896. As the rivers are not navigable for any great distance, we shall have to go up country from Freetown by rail, and if it be December or January we shall be much bothered by the Harmattan, a dry dust-laden north wind blowing from the Sahara Desert.

We notice that the natives are not all black. Indeed, several of the tribes to the north and east are fairly light-skinned. Some of the northern tribes are Mohammedans, but the majority of the natives are pagans. We shall see them all very busily at work in the fields and forests, tending their cattle or their plantations of ground-nuts and rice, cassava and kola-nut trees, or collecting the natural products, mainly palm kernels, ginger and rubber. Diamonds and gold are mined.

From Sierra Leone the steamer must take us some distance south and east to the Gold Coast. This settlement was started with forts erected along the coast by various European nations; but Great Britain bought the land from Holland in 1871, and it became a British colony. Frequent quarrels with Ashanti to the north, particularly concerning human sacrifices, led at last to war with that country; and finally Prempeh, the king, was deported, and in 1901 Ashanti was annexed, while the country still farther north, which is now known as the Northern Territories, became a protectorate.

When the people found that the new

McCann

DRESSING-ROOM OF A YOUNG LADY OF THE GOLD COAST

The Fantis are said to be the most intelligent of all the Negro tribes. They are peace-loving, too, and are occupied in fishing from canoes and cultivating the ground. Their skin is chocolate colored, and they have the Negro's characteristic woolly hair. This young woman is arranging hers in the most popular fashion—in two stiff horns.

WATER FOR THE PEOPLE OF ACCRA ON THE AFRICAN GOLD COAST

The Weija waterworks, completely modern, are a boon to the seaport of Accra and its neighborhood, for the city is hardly more than five degrees north of the equator. During the dry season the plains of the coastal belt are parched and irrigation is necessary. The Gold Coast Colony is a British possession on the Gulf of Guinea in west-central Africa.

PHOTOS, BRITISH INFORMATION SERVICES

DRYING COCOA BEANS IN THE SUN, NEAR TAFE ON THE GOLD COAST

Much of the world's cocoa and chocolate come from the Gold Coast. The cacao tree will grow only in the tropics, in sites where it can have shade and plenty of moisture. These workmen are moving the beans around on their trays to speed the drying before the rainy season begins. The bean pods are green, but they turn a brown color when they are dried.

A GOLD COAST MINSTREL STRUMS A BEDECKED BANJO

The instrument is rather crudely fashioned but the music it provides is no less gay for all that. Gold Coast people have always loved to sing and dance, and today they have just as strong a yearning for education and modern comforts. Though the Gold Coast is a British colony, it has a large measure of self-government, with a prime minister chosen from among the people.

rulers were more just than their native kings, they settled down quietly. Even Kintampo, an important town farther north, which was one of the great slave markets of this part of the world, became peaceful and decided to trade in kola nuts instead of slaves.

The Ashanti are chiefly of a warm, dark brown color. Their land is a very promising one. In the western part are rich forests of cedar and mahogany, as well as a great number of trees yielding oil, rubber and fruits. In the east the forests are not so dense. Among the chief products of this part of the country are yams, bananas and plantains.

If we land at Sekondi we can take the railway to Kumasi, the old capital of Ashanti. Near here is found the gold which gave the Gold Coast its name.

In towns the people find employment making baskets, pottery and cloth and working in leather and metals. Most of the big towns are linked up by telegraph, and where the railway ceases, motor roads take its place. Gold, valuable timber (cedar and mahogany), kola nuts, grain, palm oil and palm kernels are exported, but about thirty years ago someone started growing cacao, and now the cacao industry is fast becoming the main source of the world's supply.

THEY SELL MATS MADE OF PALM FIBRE IN THE MARKETS OF BORNU, NORTHEASTERN NIGERIA

Bornu is another of the northern provinces of Nigeria, separated from Sokoto only by Kano. It is a very dry and very hot plain, but as water can generally be reached by boring wells, it is fertile, and yams, ground-nuts and beans, as well as fibre mats, are brought on the back of ox or donkey to its many markets. The mats are delicately plaited and are often ornamented with beautiful colored designs. The people of Bornu are such keen traders that they sometimes hold these great open-air markets at night, by the light of tiny oil lamps.

DRIVE-IT-YOURSELF, IN NORTHERN NIGERIA

A donkey can be hired from the "taxi" stand in the park, at Kano, Northern Nigeria. Lean back and relax in the specially designed easy-chair saddle, unfurl your umbrella and drive to your destination in comfort. When you get there, a gentle slap will send your steed jogging home by himself to his stand in the park. Kano is a market town serving a large district.

149

MINING VALUABLE COLUMBITE IN NORTHERN NIGERIA

These African workers descend into an excavation in Bauchi Province, to refill their headpans with the mineral that is needed to make special kinds of steel for building aircraft.

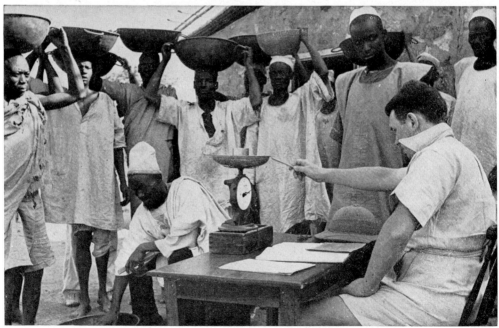

COLUMBITE ORE CAN BE ASSESSED ACCORDING TO ITS WEIGHT

The discovery of this mineral's importance in industry has meant that many abandoned mines could be reopened, and the people of northern Nigeria have found much-needed employment.

THATCHING THE ROOF OF A ROUND MUD HOUSE IN NUPE, NIGERIA

The tall roof of this circular house projects over the walls and makes a veranda upheld by carved posts. The Nigerians are clever thatchers and make perfectly water-tight grass roofs like this. They finish off the top with a plumy tuft. The Nupes, who live in central Nigeria, are an intelligent tribe, but were once slave raiders.

Rejoining the boat at Sekondi we will proceed eastward, passing Cape Coast Castle, the original British settlement, and Accra, the present capital, which now has a wireless station, and halt at Lome, just beyond the boundary. This is the entrance to Togoland, which before the first World War belonged to Germany. It is a narrow strip of country about the size of Ireland adjoining the Gold Coast. It is a fertile land, and in addition to palm oil and kernels—its chief exports— it grows cotton, corn, cacao, rubber and sisal hemp.

On the declaration of war in 1914 the British and French marched into Togoland, and the Germans, after blowing up their important wireless station at Kamina, surrendered unconditionally. In the final settlement the administration of Togoland was entrusted by the Allies to France and Great Britain together, Great Britain taking the northern part. We shall not stop in Lome or the little town of Togo farther inland, but will go on eastward till we come to Nigeria, the largest of all the British possessions in West Africa.

Nigeria is almost square-shaped, over four times as large as Great Britain, with a population two and a half times as large as that of London. Halfway up the western boundary it is entered by the River Niger, which flows along southeast until it is met by the Benue River coming from the eastern boundary. All Nigeria to the north of these two rivers is known as the Northern Provinces. The two rivers together form a stream two miles wide, which flows steadily south until about 140 miles from the coast, where it forms a delta, breaking into numbers of little rivers and lagoons.

At the extreme west is marshy and impenetrable Lagos. This, until Great Britain captured it in 1851, was a famous slave market, supplied by the province of Benin. To-day it is the capital and the greatest trade port of Nigeria. Apart from Lagos all Nigeria has been acquired by Great Britain during the last half century or so.

Dense Tropical Forests

We can travel up the river in a large steamer as far as Jebba, or we can go there from Lagos direct by rail, enter the Northern Provinces and continue north by rail as far as Zaria and Kano. Whichever way we go we shall pass through dense tropical forests where grow mahogany, ebony, cedar, rubber, cork, palm and kola-nut trees. Then come others, gum, locust bean, wild date palms and shea-nut trees. Shea-nuts yield a buttery fat which is used by the natives for food, and which is also exported to Europe for the manufacture of soap, candles and pomades. Presently the forests diminish and little clearings are seen where yams, maize, plantains, guinea corn and cacao are grown. The bread of the country is made from guinea corn. The Northern Provinces grow ground-nuts, shea-nuts, palms, rubber and gum trees and rear herds of sheep and cattle, keep dogs, goats and fowls, and, in the northernmost territory, use camels for transport, and Kano is an emporium for caravans from the Sahara and elsewhere. In this region the soil is poor, for the Sahara is drawing near. The natives of the north belong to the Hausa and Fulani tribes. The Fulani originally came from the eastern part of Africa. The Hausa, who once possessed all northern Nigeria from Lake Chad to Sokoto and beyond, are black, intelligent Negroes, Mohammedans by religion.

From Zaria we can, by means of a small mountain railway, climb the Bauchi plateau, a lofty tableland of granite, 150 miles long by 100 broad. The sides are sheer, and until the railway was built it was inaccessible except by three tiny and easily guarded passages.

A Modern Tower of Babel

The inhabitants are of many races, from jet black to light-colored people with almost European features. There are 164 different languages spoken on the plateau. The natives have mined iron, lead and tin for centuries. Although roads are being made in all directions,

there are places in Nigeria where no white man has ever traveled, and other districts, difficult of access, where slavery and cannibalism are still practiced. Near the Benue River there is a tribe, the Munshi, who are quite unconquered and are dreaded on account of their poisoned arrows. In the western part of the Southern Provinces we find the Yorubas, a brave, warlike Mohammedan people, but for the most part the Nigerian natives are black and pagan. Less than ten per cent of the children get any kind of education.

Adjoining Nigeria and running from the coast to Lake Chad on the east is a strip of country known as Cameroon. This, like Togoland, belonged to Germany before the war. It was surrendered in 1916, and later it was divided between France and Great Britain to administer. Some of the native tribes here are light colored, with almost European features and well shaped hands. They are a portion of the great Bantu family, a people of many races who speak practically the same tongue, found chiefly in East and South Africa. Near the coast Cameroon has plantations of rubber and cocoa laid out by the Germans, but apart from these the country, though fertile, is undeveloped. In Victoria, however, experiments are being made in the growing of vanilla and spices; there is trade in ivory, and ebony is abundant.

Arabian Stock in Somaliland

French and Belgian territories separate us from British East Africa. Suppose, therefore, we continue our journey by aeroplane. The countries adjoin each other with one exception, that of British Somaliland, a strip of land lying on the coast of the Gulf of Aden; and we will fly on over the Sudan and Ethiopia and visit this isolated country first. The natives here are not Negroes, but claim to be the descendants of Arabs. They are a tall, fine, active race, very dark, and in features they somewhat resemble the ancient Egyptians. They are a fierce, lawless people, many of them fanatical Mohammedans who have given Great Britain

© E. N. A.

A CHIEFTAIN OF GAMBIA presides over his court with the dignity and pomp of the kings of old. The crown, resembling the British crown, is of gold, studded with precious stones and mounted on ermine and velvet. By not wearing a shirt he reminds his people that he has the strong shoulders and arms of the hunter and fighter.

HELPING SCIENTISTS UNCOVER AN ANCIENT AND FORGOTTEN CITY

In Kenya, a British protectorate in eastern Africa, the ruins of Gedi have been discovered. Archaeologists believe it may have been built by Arabs who moved to East Africa seven hundred years or more ago. They have unearthed mosques and other buildings and a long protecting wall. Gedi is near Malindi, a small seaport not far from the equator.

much trouble since the protectorate was established in 1884. The trade of the country is in the hands of Arab and Indian merchants on the coast. The natives breed herds of camels, goats and sheep or grow crops of millet, coffee and indigo and collect the fragrant gums, myrrh and frankincense (the chief ingredient of incense), for which this land has always been famous. One of Somaliland's chief exports is ghee, a semi-liquid kind of butter used to a great extent in India.

Now suppose we fly back to Khartum, capital of the Sudan, a territory three times as large as Egypt. Most of the Sudanese are nomads, wandering from place to place with their cattle, sheep, goats and camels. In recent years there has grown among them a strong desire for their own

government, free of control by either Britain or Egypt. One step in this direction was their own election, in November 1948, of a legislative assembly.

For over fourteen hundred miles of its course the Nile flows through the Sudan and largely influences its cultivation. The northern provinces grow crops of millet, the chief food of the natives, also groundnuts, dates and cotton. In the three provinces of Halfa, Dongola and Berber there are well over a million date-palms. Moreover, the Sudan is rich in cattle, sheep and goats. Camels are in use throughout the greater part of the country.

Crossing to the White Nile, we journey south by steamer and pass through a fertile belt from which is obtained, among other things, the world's supply of gum

SUDANESE PATIENTLY WAIT OUTSIDE A TOWN CLERK'S OFFICE

The town clerk is an important person in the Sudan, handling most of the legal activities of the area he serves. Each morning throngs of villagers and traders gather outside his office to wait their turn for an audience with him. Among his various duties is the issuing of licenses. He also listens to all sorts of complaints and decides what should be done about each one.

IN KENYA COLONY, it is the custom for a man to buy his wife from her father. This Kikuyu man had to pay eight cows, ten goats and twenty jars of native beer for his bride.

THOMAS

NIGERIAN CHILDREN, like these little girls, wear few clothes, even when dressed in their best. Their heads were bound when they were babies and grew into this unnatural shape.

arabic. Presently the Nile is joined by the Bahr-el-Ghazal from the west, and here we enter a different kind of country. Low-lying and watered by many tributary rivers, its soil is the richest in the whole of the Sudan, but the natives are indolent, and content themselves with collecting timber from the tropical forests.

It is thought that the southern Sudan is the home of the true Negro race, and certainly the majority of the natives here today are pure black Negroes of the most primitive type. Some are even cannibals. They are a great contrast to the people dwelling in northern Sudan, who are mainly Arabs, Nubians or mixed tribes.

At Rejaf the Nile becomes unnavi-

gable. We must therefore march on foot to Numile, on the Uganda border. The distance is ninety-three miles, and we can walk only in the cool of the early morning. We cannot get even a donkey to carry our luggage, for the disease-bearing tsetse fly swarms in all parts of this district and kills off the transport animals. Uganda is in the region of the Great Lakes. A steamer will take us by river to Albert Nyanza. Thence by motor, steamer and railway we reach Victoria Nyanza, the second largest lake in the world, discovered by Captain Speke in 1858 to be the source of the Nile.

Uganda is as large as Great Britain. Of the natives, the most civilized are the

BRITISH INFORMATION SERVICES

RARE BIRD VIEWED WITH INTEREST BY NUBAS IN CENTRAL SUDAN

Drilling Airfield in the Nuba Mountains is an emergency air strip. It is only on rare occasions that it is used, so this visit of a Sudan Airways Dove calls for an inspection. The Nubas are a pure Negro tribe. The men paint their bodies with intricate patterns, while the women frequently adorn themselves by having a quartz ornament set in their upper lip.

Sign text:
WATER
POINT
MILE 1.

E·THIOPIA	SOMALIA·
MARSABIT · 156	GARBA TULA · 72
MEGA 333	HABAS WEIN 155
	WAJIR 225
ADDIS ABABA 752	EL WAK 30
	BARDERA 4
	MOGADISHU 6

ISIOLO

GUARDIANS OF THE LAW

Two Somali tribal policemen pose for their pictures at Isiolo, administrative headquarters of Kenya's Northern Frontier District, which comprises about half the area of the colony. Isiolo is just a small post consisting of government and police offices and a few shops. A sprinkling of Turkana tribesmen inhabit the area. The sign marks an important fork in the road.

SWAHILI WOMEN of Zanzibar take great pains with their appearance. They paint designs on their cheeks and foreheads and dress their hair elaborately. Their long toothed comb is like that used by the Fiji Islanders. Because these girls are a mixture of two races, Arab and negro, one sister may be dark with woolly hair, another lighter with straight hair.

LINCOLN

IN ZANZIBAR and on the neighboring mainland live the Swahilis or "coast people." They are the descendants of Arabs who generations ago came here as traders and married negro inhabitants. They speak archaic Bantu mixed with Arabic and use Persian, Hindu, Portuguese, German and English words besides. Their color varies and their features are often Semitic.

161

AFTER A RAIN IN DAR ES SALAAM, CAPITAL OF TANGANYIKA

The name of this port on the Indian Ocean—Dar es Salaam—is Arabic and means "haven of peace." Its harbor is almost landlocked, and there are deep-water berths for ocean vessels.

SURVEYING THE WORLD FROM ATOP BALES OF SISAL

Sisal is one of the chief crops of the low coastal lands of Tanganyika and one of the territory's main exports. From the tough sisal fiber, extremely strong twine is made.

KITCHEN ARRANGEMENT FOR COOKING LESSONS, IN THE CAMEROONS

An open wood fire is set at a convenient height, and there are "Dutch" ovens below. The girl is learning to cook at the Women's Domestic Science Center in Victoria, British Cameroons.

MC CANN

NANA PREMPEH ruled over the Ashanti, now part of the Gold Coast, until 1896, when he resisted British rule, was defeated and exiled. When the British established the Federation of the Ashanti in 1935, his nephew, Otuo Sir Osei Agyeman Prempeh II, was placed at its head.

HUNTER

A MASAI WOMAN should have the lobes of her ears stretched until they will meet over her shaved head. Her stone ear plugs, ear-rings and other ornaments, including many pounds of iron wire around her legs and arms, she may not remove during her husband's lifetime.

THIS WANDERING DERVISH of the Sudan carries a polished gourd as a begging-bowl.
Dervish is Persian for "seeking doors" or begging, and in Islam generally implies member-
ship in a religious fraternity. Of these, there are perhaps thirty, distinguished by their garb.
Each has its ritual, which may include whirlings and the self-torture of the howlers.

165

TWO LADIES OF KENYA SING AND DANCE

Kipsigis women in bright tribal attire and oddments of European dress—cotton prints and woolen stockings—sing to the rhythmic shuffle of their feet and the graceful waving of the fans in their hands. The Kipsigis, once a proud hunting and cattle-herding people, now farm the fertile land of their reservation; which is in the southwestern part of Kenya.

166

HOUSE IN THE ROUND—A NATIVE HUT IN NORTHERN RHODESIA

Building a home presents no problem in Northern Rhodesia. The forests provide the needed materials, and the native huts are easy to erect. The picture above shows one in the process of construction. The tree-trunk supports are in place, and slender branches are tied together for the roof. As soon as the roof is thatched and covered with mud, its owners can move in.

167

HIPPOPOTAMI comes from the Greek meaning "river horses." They may have been the behemoths of Scripture, although they are no longer found in the Jordan Valley. There is a pygmy variety about six feet in length, but these denizens of the Zambezi River are nearly as large as elephants. They spend most of their time under water with only their eyes and nostrils above the surface, or if they dive while foraging for plants, they come to the top every few minutes. Their teeth provide ivory, their hide makes whips and their flesh is eaten by the natives.

Batangas, who have been converted to Christianity. They are a tall, well-built race, and make clever iron-workers and carpenters. Many of them are musical.

New Guardian of Empire

The whole of British East Africa suddenly assumed a new and vast importance for Britain following the end of World War II. Her withdrawal from India and Palestine in 1948 left great gaps in the defense of the all-important life-line of empire; and her economic position in the world badly needed bolstering.

Military experts predicted that Kenya Colony would be turned into a huge military base for future defense of the life-line. (From here, for instance, the vital Suez Canal could be kept open.) In fact, in 1948, construction was begun on a gigantic storage depot near Mombasa.

East Africa also contains many natural resources necessary to England. Systematic geological surveys were begun to find out just how much mineral wealth is stored in these lands. Uganda is known to have rich copper and phosphate deposits; Tanganyika has large reserves of lead and gold and other minerals; and there is iron and chrome in Northern and Southern Rhodesia. The immense hydro-electric possibilities in Uganda are being exploited and a great dam at Owen Falls, on the Nile, is to help develop the basin of the Upper Nile.

Mohammedan Swahili

Mombasa has the finest harbor on the East African coast. Here we will take ship to the south for the island of Zanzibar, which, with the smaller island of Pemba, and formerly a strip along the mainland, has been the Protectorate of Zanzibar since 1890, and to obtain which Britain, among other concessions, gave Heligoland, an island in the North Sea, to Germany. The protectorate is ruled by a native sultan, subject to the British Government. His people, though comprising many races, are known as Swahili and speak one tongue. The Swahili of the islands depend for a living mainly on growing cloves for the spice markets of the world, though they are now starting to cultivate coconut palms. Once troublesome, these people, who are mainly Mohammedans, are now loyal subjects.

We now cross to the mainland strip at Dar-es-Salaam, the seat of government and main port of Tanganyika Territory, which includes the southern half of Lake Victoria Nyanza, where the tsetse-fly causes sleeping-sickness. The plantations are owned chiefly by Arabs. Ivory is a considerable source of wealth. Gold, mica and tin are found. The railway runs from the coast to Victoria Nyanza, and camel caravan routes are used. This region was formerly German East Africa, and is under UN trusteeship.

If we go south we strike Lake Nyasa and the Nyasaland Protectorate around its western and southern shores. This tiny country, with North Rhodesia and South Tanganyika, brings to memory the name of David Livingstone, the discoverer of Lake Nyasa and Victoria Falls.

In Honor of David Livingstone

Blantyre, the chief town of Nyasaland, is named after Livingstone's birthplace in Scotland. The natives, many of whom are Christians, are progressive people and value education. There are more than 195,000 students in the Mission schools. Tobacco-growing is the main industry of the country, but cotton, tea, rubber, coffee and corn are also cultivated.

Northern Rhodesia, to the west of Nyasaland, was not definitely taken over by the Crown till April, 1924. The unfinished Cape to Cairo Railway passes through it from south to north, and most of the population is settled along the railway line. In the high northwest, in spite of the trouble with the tsetse-fly, cattle are reared extensively, and exported, sometimes as many as twelve hundred head per month, to feed the natives working in the mines of the Belgian Congo.

The country has great mineral wealth. Here at Livingstone, in the extreme south, we will take our leave of British East Africa, with the thunder of the neighboring Victoria Falls in our ears.

v

A WITCH DOCTOR OF UGANDA IN HIS CEREMONIAL PAINT AND ROBES

To most of the primitive peoples of Africa the local witch doctor is an important figure in their lives. He is usually top man in the village, and he officiates at family functions such as marriages and funerals. He is supposed to keep evil spirits away from cattle and to exert a great deal of influence over such natural elements as the amount of rainfall.

BRITISH INFORMATION SERVICES

ONE STEP IN THE FIGHT AGAINST MALARIA IN SOUTHERN RHODESIA
Southern Rhodesia is waging an all-out war against disease. High up on the list of enemies is the dread killer, malaria, carried by mosquitoes. Here a member of the Health Department sprays an insecticide on a native hut in the Chikwakwa Reserve. In some sections of the country, much progress has been made in eliminating, or at least controlling, the disease.

BRITISH AFRICA FROM WEST TO EAST: FACTS AND FIGURES

GAMBIA

Crown Colony and Protectorate administered by a Governor and Executive and Legislative councils. Total area, 4,067 square miles, and population, 273,000. Chief export is peanuts. Population of capital, Bathurst, 21,150.

SIERRA LEONE

Colony and Protectorate under a Governor and Executive and Legislative councils. Total area, 27,920 square miles, and population, 1,975,-000. Leading exports are diamonds, palm oil and kernels, iron ore, kola nuts, ginger and piassava. Imports: textiles, tobacco, coal, bags and sacks. Railway mileage, 336; 2,000 miles of railway telegraph and telephone wires. Government and mission schools. Population of capital, Freetown, 87,000.

GOLD COAST

Comprised of Gold Coast and Ashanti colonies and Northern Territories Protectorate, it is administered by a Governor and Executive and Legislative councils. Total area, 78,799 square miles, and population, 3,869,000. Chief exports: cocoa, gold, manganese, diamonds and timber. Length of railways, 535 miles; of all-weather roads, 2,992 miles; of telegraph wires, 4,918 miles. Population of chief towns: Accra (capital), 136,000; Kumasi, 78,500.

NIGERIA (Colony and Protectorate)

Administered by a Governor and Executive and Legislative councils. There is also a House of Chiefs. Total area, 338,580 square miles; population, 24,000,000. Leading exports: cocoa and other food products, gold and other minerals, tobacco and rubber. Imports: cotton textiles, iron and steel products, salt and fish. Population of chief towns: Ibadan, 335,000; Lagos (capital), 230,000; Kano, 107,000.

SOMALILAND PROTECTORATE

Legislative and executive authority is vested in a Governor. Area, 68,000 square miles, and population, 700,000. Leading industry is stock raising. The chief towns are Hargeisa, the capital, and Berbera.

UGANDA PROTECTORATE

Administered by a Governor with assistance of Executive and Legislative councils. Area, 93,980 square miles, and population, 5,125,000. Leading exports are cotton, coffee, cottonseed and tobacco. Capital, Entebbe, 7,231.

ANGLO-EGYPTIAN SUDAN

A condominium, it is administered by a Governor-General appointed by Egypt with assent of Britain. There are also a Legislative Assembly and an Executive Council. Area, 967,500 square miles, and population, 8,350,000. Leading exports are cotton, cottonseed, gum arabic (most of the world's supply), camels, beans, corn, melon seed, hides and skins. Imports: cotton textiles, sugar, metals, metal goods, machinery and coffee. Shipping on the Nile and tributaries is considerable. Length of railways, 2,001 miles; of telephone and telegraph wires, 33,779 miles. Population of chief towns: Omdurman, 125,300; Khartoum (capital), 75,000.

KENYA COLONY AND PROTECTORATE

Administered by a Governor, assisted by Executive and Legislative councils. Total area, 224,952 square miles; population, 5,555,000. Leading exports are sisal, coffee, hides, skins, wattle extract and pyrethrum. Population of capital, Nairobi, 134,043.

NYASALAND PROTECTORATE

Administered by Governor with assistance of Executive and Legislative councils. Area, 47,-400 square miles; population, 2,407,000. Exports include tobacco, tea, cotton, pulse and tung oil. Population of chief towns: Zomba (capital), 7,526; Limbe, 12,608.

NORTHERN RHODESIA

Administered by Governor and Legislative and Executive councils. Area, 287,640 square miles, and population, 1,866,000. Production of copper, zinc and lead is considerable. Population of capital, Lusaka, 10,336.

SOUTHERN RHODESIA

Administered by a Governor and Executive and Legislative councils. Area, 150,327 square miles; population, about 2,101,000. Farming and dairying are profitable; gold and other mineral reserves are abundant. Population of chief towns: Salisbury (capital), 40,510; Bulawayo, 32,000.

ISLAND PROTECTORATES

Zanzibar and Pemba. Two major islands off the coast of Tanganyika. Total area, 1,020 square miles; population, 269,000.

Seychelles and dependencies. Comprising 92 islands, 1,000 miles from Kenya. Total area, 156 square miles; population, 36,000.

UNITED NATIONS TRUSTEESHIPS: FACTS AND FIGURES

TOGOLAND

Former German territory, now divided between France and Great Britain. British area, about 13,041 square miles; population, 397,000. Administered as part of the Gold Coast.

CAMEROONS

Former German territory now divided between France and Great Britain. British area, 34,080; population about 1,051,000. Adminis-

tered as part of Nigeria. The chief town of the British Cameroons is Buea.

TANGANYIKA

Former German possession, now administered by Governor and Executive and Legislative councils. Area, 362,675 square miles; population, 7,707,000. Leading products: sisal, cotton, gum and diamonds. Capital, Dar es Salaam, 70,000.

IN THE HEART OF AFRICA

Among the Forest Dwellers of the Congo

The Congo, Africa's second longest river, flows almost three thousand miles through the heart of the continent and, with its mighty tributaries, taps the vast territories of the French and Belgian Congo and Angola, Portugal's largest colony. Thick forests cover huge portions of the land drained by the Congo, and very little was known about these mysterious areas before the explorations of Livingstone and Stanley. Today, however, the Congo is no longer a region of mystery. Its wealth of resources has turned the eyes of the world upon it and upon the interesting people who inhabit it.

I N the year 1482 or 1483 a little fleet of galleons led by Diogo Cao went cruising along the west coast of Africa. The huge sails were emblazoned with large red crosses, and from the mastheads fluttered the banner of Portugal. For months the fleet had sailed slowly along that low coast, with its lines of palm trees and with the white surf breaking ceaselessly upon the yellow sand. The swampy mangrove thickets at the mouths of the Niger were passed; the vast Cameroon's volcano was sighted and the Equator crossed. Then the mouth of a wide river opened out before the adventurers.

From the natives, the adventurers learned that the river was called the "Kongo," and that the country just to the south of it was ruled by a great chief called M'wani Kongo ("Lord of the Kongo people"). The Portuguese then began to trade with him, and eventually established a Jesuit Mission among his people.

The Portuguese did not go far up the river because of the rapids which barred their progress, and also because of the savage tribes which attacked the expeditions. For four hundred years little was known of the river. In 1876, however, Henry M. Stanley, who had gained fame by his expedition in search of Dr.

IN THE COTTON FIELDS OF THE CONGO

Quick, careful hands remove bolls from a cotton plant in the lower plateaus of Kivu province, eastern Belgian Congo. In the higher reaches of Kivu are thriving plantations of cinchona, from which we get quinine, and coffee.

David Livingstone, the Scotch missionary-explorer, was again in Central Africa and came upon a river, called by the natives Lualaba (Great River), which he thought might be the Upper Nile and determined to explore it.

He came in from Zanzibar on the east coast in time to start in October from Nyangwe, a point on the Lualaba just west of the upper part of Lake Tangan-

173

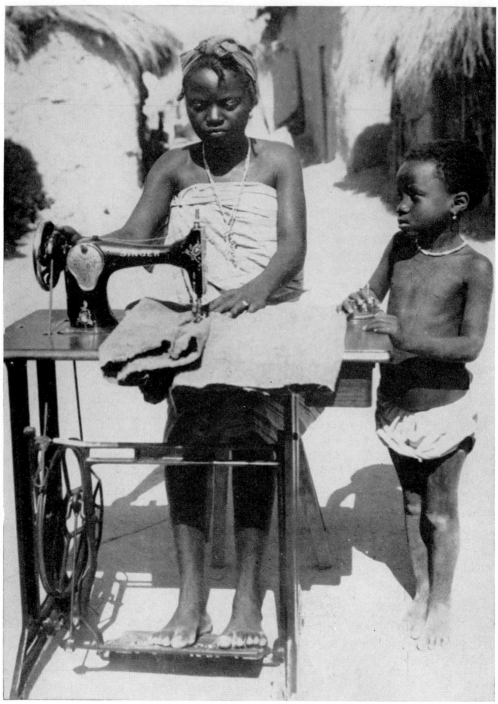

MOTHER AND SON AND A SEWING MACHINE IN AN ANGOLA VILLAGE

Like a busy housewife anywhere in the world, a woman of Angola welcomes the quickness and precision of a sewing machine. The Angolese perform many of their everyday tasks in the most primitive manner, but when they have the opportunity to use modern appliances and equipment, such as the sewing machine and trucks and tractors, they learn quickly and well.

HIGHEST SINGLE-LEAP FALLS IN AFRICA

The little-known Lofoi River, in the province of Katanga in Belgian Congo, sends its waters rushing down the steep side of the Kundelungu Mountain for a sheer drop of 1,260 feet into the valley below. It is said to be the highest single-leap falls on the African continent, exceeded only by the 2,810-foot drop of the Tugela River falls in Natal that makes several leaps.

EDUCATION AND PROGRESS GO HAND IN HAND IN AFRICA

The Marie-José Institute at Elizabethville, Belgian Congo, is an up-to-date junior high school for girls, operated by the Sisters of Charity of Ghent. Although the number of modern schools is steadily increasing in the Belgian Congo, only about one-twentieth of the colony's total population thus far has an opportunity to receive a scholastic education.

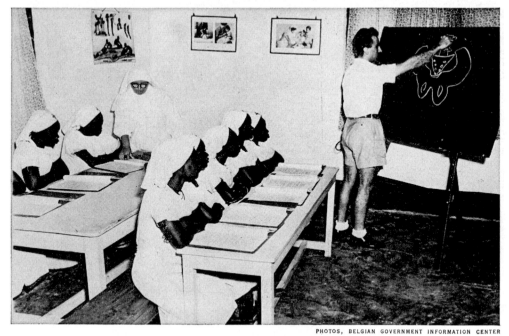

NATIVE NURSES LEARN ABOUT MODERN HEALTH PROTECTION

At this Red Cross school for nurses at Pawa in the Belgian Congo, white nurses and doctors instruct the native women in such things as first aid to the injured, hygiene and sanitation. These native women are eager to learn, and when they return to their villages, they will have the knowledge by which they can improve and protect the health of their people.

SABENA

EVERY INCH A KING

The king of a Ruandi tribe and a pygmy chieftain take each other's measure. Ruanda-Urundi is a United Nations trust territory in east-central Africa. It is united economically with Belgian Congo and administered by Belgium. Local law is in the hands of native chieftains invested with Belgian authority. The territory is densely populated and often faced with famine.

177

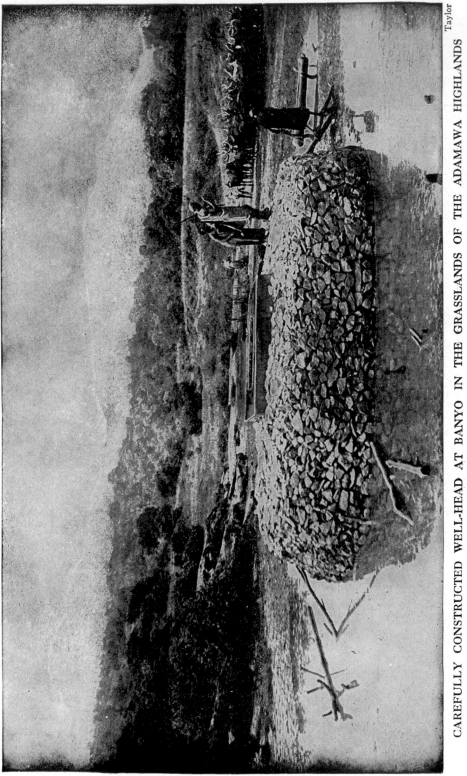

Taylor

CAREFULLY CONSTRUCTED WELL-HEAD AT BANYO IN THE GRASSLANDS OF THE ADAMAWA HIGHLANDS

The Adamawa district of Africa contains great tracts of upland savanna which afford excellent pasturage, and the herds of cattle kept by the Fulas and other tribesmen were at one time raised for export. The cement and rough stonework around this much frequented well was constructed by the Germans, for the Adamawa highlands were once part of German Cameroon. In 1919, however, it was divided between France and Great Britain. Banyo is now on the borderline between British and French Cameroon. Native cattle like those above were once exported.

A SINEWY DANCER OF THE WATUSI, DECKED IN TRIBAL REGALIA

The Watusi are among the tallest people on earth; it is not uncommon for a man to attain the stature of seven feet. They herd long-horned cattle among the highlands of Ruanda Urundi.

yika. It was a region of equatorial heat and heavy winter rains, where the waterways led through tangled jungle forest made terrifying at night by the howls of beasts and almost equally dangerous by day by reason of the myriad fever-breeding insects and the savage warriors who met them with flights of arrows. The heat was prostrating and food ran low, and the three white men who started with him died of the almost incredible hardships that met them all along the way. Stanley himself was prematurely aged by these experiences, but he was young and somehow managed to pull through.

After a few portages near the start where they had to pass some falls and rapids, the journey could be made entirely by canoe. At times the river widened into muddy swamp lands or lakes bordered by papyrus and other reeds and grasses; but for the most part it flowed through a tunnel of trees. For weeks of travel the Lualaba led them northward, then took a surprising sweep to the westward and southwestward as it became the Congo. The following spring they came to what is now Stanley Pool or Leopoldville, and here the river narrowed from three miles to perhaps three-quarters of a mile, to go leaping and thundering for 170 miles over rock-walled cataracts. Below that long detour, during which they had to hack their way through all but impenetrable underbrush, the stream was again navigable; and soon they reached Boma, a port some seventy miles inland. The Congo empties into an Atlantic stained red-brown with river silt, as the stream

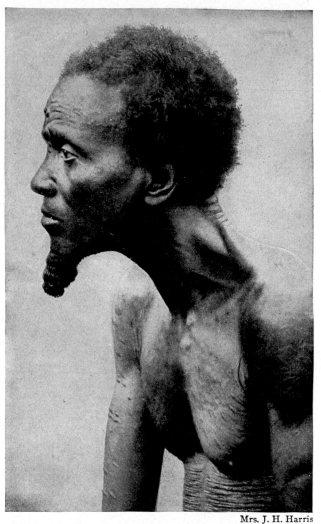

Mrs. J. H. Harris

THE MOST FAMOUS BEARD IN CONGOLAND

This man is chief of a troublesome folk, but they are proud of him, for plaited and coiled under his chin is his beard, rather thin, but many feet long. Only on state occasions does he uncoil it to the admiring public gaze.

widens over seven miles of delta fringed with mangrove swamp. Stanley had crossed the African continent from east to west and had traced nearly two thousand miles of navigable waterway. His dramatic published accounts of his adventures were translated into several languages.

A year after his discovery of what has proven to be one of the world's largest rivers, which drains a basin correspondingly vast, King Leopold II of Belgium formed an association for the opening of the Congo basin to commerce. To secure peace and further trade relations with the natives, he made hundreds of treaties with small independent African sovereigns. As a consequence, in 1885 the Congo Free State was founded with King Leopold as ruler. The state was ceded to Belgium, however, in 1908, and in 1927 its territory was increased by an exchange with Portugal which gave the latter country area for a port in the estuary of the Congo near Matadi.

EWING GALLOWAY

A GROTESQUE GROVE OF GRAIN CACHES IN PORTUGUESE ANGOLA

Looking every bit like giant mushrooms or, to the more fanciful, like an orchard of lollipops, are the grain caches of Angola. In order to keep the grain out of the reach of animals and vermin, the people weave coarse grasses and leaves into large nets. When they have filled the nets with grain they hoist them to the branches of trees or balance them on long stakes.

The main products of the Belgian Congo proved to be the ivory of elephant tusks and the products of the palm and rubber trees, together with resin, copal and certain vegetable fibers. The Belgians have made successful experiments in the growing of cotton.

Sands That Yield Diamonds

The sands of the Kasai River, a major tributary of the Congo, yield most of the world's diamond supply. Yet the value of South Africa's diamond production is far greater. A larger percentage of South African diamonds are of the quality best suited for jewelry. Most Congo diamonds are discolored or of an imperfect shape; less than 10 per cent can be ground and polished into precious stones.

Whether or not it is of gem quality, diamond is the hardest substance known to man. Oil-well drills tipped with industrial diamonds bore through shelves of rock that resist all other cutting tools. Granite is cut with saws that have diamonds set in their teeth. Diamonds expand only the tiniest fraction when they are heated and are therefore especially long-wearing and accurate when used as bearings in delicate instruments.

Another valuable mineral of the Belgian Congo is pitchblende, a heavy ore that takes its name from its lustrous, pitch-black sheen. The pitchblende of the Congo is concentrated in the southern district of Katanga near Shinkolobwe, a village seventy miles northwest of Elizabethville. For years (until the discovery of rich Canadian deposits) the Belgian Congo was the world's principal source of radium, a radioactive element highly valued in medicine for the treatment of tumors. Other elements in pitchblende include lead, the rare earths and, most important, thorium and uranium.

Uranium is the fuel of the atomic age, and the production of atomic energy has become one of the primary concerns of all the great nations of the world. There is a possibility that thorium, as well as uranium, can serve as a "breeder" of the isotopes that release atomic energy. Since the fields of Katanga yield both metals,

the Belgian Congo should, as she has done until now, continue to furnish a large portion of the raw materials that are needed for atomic research.

What of the people of the Congo? Let us journey up the river for perhaps a thousand miles. Here and there the native villages peep from amid the close green foliage. Our little steamer blows her whistle, and in a moment we see dusky figures gathering on the beach. Several dug-out canoes put out to meet us. The former warriors have become peaceable fisherfolk.

Our steamer slows down and drops its anchor. As we go ashore, the people crowd around us, moved by curiosity. The day has long passed when they feared the white man, but a chance visit never fails to create excitement. They wear little clothing, and their chocolate-brown bodies are tattooed. They have their teeth filed to points, like the teeth of a saw, and tribal marks are cut on their faces. These marks are cut deeply into the flesh of the cheeks and forehead with a sharp iron instrument. It is a painful process and not infrequently causes blood poisoning.

Large and small dugouts are drawn up on the beach, and fishing nets, attached to wooden frames, lie drying in the sun. Fish traps, too, made of split bamboo or of the cane called rattan, are in evidence. From one dugout the day's catch of fish is just being landed and carried up to the village market. Now the smell of the salt tide mingles with a welcome taint of wood smoke, for beyond the beach is the village with its two long rows of huts facing one another. The village's lower end opens on the shore, but the upper end is closed to enable the villagers to defend themselves in case of attack by neighboring tribes. Behind the village is the primeval forest, extending for hundreds of miles.

Homes of Bamboo and Thatch

The oblong huts are made of bamboo and thatch. It is interesting to watch the people building a hut. First a framework is erected—that is, long bamboo poles are driven into the ground and lashed to-

YOUTHS OF ANGOLA WEARING MASKS AND QUAINT COSTUMES

In most African tribes the initiation of young men who have "come of age" into the full rights of manhood is accompanied by much elaborate ceremony. In Angola, or Portuguese West Africa, the youths who take part in the rites of initiation wear white masks that are skillfully carven, however hideous, and ruffs and skirts of frayed leaves.

gether with cross-pieces and fibre. Then the big thatched roof of dry palm leaves is added, and last, the framework walls are covered with coconut matting.

Near the houses a space has been cleared in the forest to make gardens in which people grow yams, cassava and other vegetables; and there is likely to be a fragrant plantation of banana trees, their bright green leaves contrasting with those of the mango trees and the palms. The women cultivate the gardens and take the produce to the village, using big funnel-shaped baskets of split bamboo which they carry on their backs. Their task is not a little dangerous, for as a woman stoops to her work it is no uncommon thing for a leopard from the forest to spring murderously upon her.

One strange custom is that the boys, while still quite young, leave home and join in building a hut and keeping house for themselves. They provide food by

catching fish, trapping birds, squirrels and monkeys. They even stretch strings from the trees to catch bats. One of their chief delights is ratting, and many a nice plump field mouse finds its way into their cooking pot. Large hairy caterpillars, ants and beetles are also enjoyed.

There are two people in the village we must certainly visit—the chief and the witch doctor. We exchange greetings, then the chief leads us to his dwelling or the public "palaver house," where he holds a reception in our honor. Two or three European camp chairs may be brought out of the dark recesses of some hut and placed for us, while the chief takes his seat on a stool or in a hammock. We again exchange pleasantries, tell the chief why we have come to his village and make him a present—possibly a hatchet, a piece of cloth or even an alarm clock. In return, he gives us bananas, eggs, yams, coconuts, a couple of chickens or perhaps a goat.

IN A CONGO FISHING VILLAGE: A LONG, HORN-SHAPED BASKET MEANT FOR TRAPPING FISH IN THE RAPIDS

Before his hut—its walls of reinforced clay, its roof of thatch—the man of the family fastens a cane rod to his fishing basket, which serves as a weir when placed in a stream. The children watch their mother prepare the midday meal in a deep pottery mixing bowl.

The witch doctor is the priest of the village, and the people fear him because they believe he has power to command evil spirits; but he sells them charms to protect them from wild beasts, sickness, evil men and even those selfsame evil spirits. The people also think that he can bring dreadful diseases upon the village or cause a man to die. He is usually a cunning rogue, able to mix powerful poisons, and is certainly a man to be greatly feared where his enmity is incurred.

The Congo basin is inhabited by many tribes speaking different languages. Some villages are not at all like the one we have described.

To-day a belt of valuable mines two hundred miles long extends through the highlands. Lubambashi in Katanga gives Belgium a good supply of copper for world export, and the natives who are partly civilized are kept busy at the mines and smelting works. In the south and east highlands there are also gold, radium, diamonds, platinum and coal. Though the navigable waterways are still the important highways, short lengths of railroad connect them and there are more than 45,000 miles of roads. In addition there is regular air service between various districts.

For centuries there were rumors that a race of small black people existed in the heart of Africa, and many travelers and historians of past centuries had mentioned these dwarfs. In 1863-65 P. B. Du Chaillu came upon them. In 1887 Stanley, while passing through a vast forest between the Congo and Lake Albert, found numbers of these little people. Some of them were only three feet in height. They were so small that the explorer often thought his scouts had

Beale

NATIVE WIRELESS IN ANGOLA

Here we see the mondo or message-drum used in the Zombo highlands. By beating upon this wooden instrument the natives can send sonorous messages in code for long distances. News travels rapidly by this means.

caught children, until he perceived that they were full grown men and women. The women averaged but four feet in height and none of the men were over four feet six inches.

These tiny black folk live by hunting, and they are extraordinarily skillful at tracking game through the dark, swampy forests and killing it with their bows and arrows. They live in villages of small grass huts shaped like bee-hives. Stanley found one village of ninety-two huts. But the pigmies were very shy and always de-

A PEACEFUL HOME SCENE

Bandi natives, gathered before their hut in southeastern French Equatorial Africa, take their ease during the hottest part of the tropical day. The man in the foreground apparently finds the imported folding camp chair a rather doubtful luxury. Mangoes, a reddish yellow fruit that grows on a tree of the sumac family, can be seen hanging from above.

AN AFRICAN RIVER SCENE

Natives, balancing with no difficulty in their narrow dugout canoes, stand upright as they paddle along the Loange River in the Congo basin in central Africa. The river, which is over four hundred miles long, has its source in central Angola. It flows north to join the Kasai River, the most important southern tributary of the Congo River, in the Belgian Congo.

serted their villages as Stanley's men approached, although from time to time a few were captured and examined. These villages they abandon when they feel the need to move on, for a time, to where game is more plentiful. These forest dwarfs of the hidden recesses of the Congo are better termed Negrillos.

The vast basin of the Congo does not all belong to Belgium. Thirty - five years before Stanley unveiled the secrets of the river, the French had settlements on the Gabun River, some five hundred miles north of the mouth of the Congo, as we see in another article. Then in 1880 de Brazza placed under French protection a portion of the north bank of the Congo—from below Stanley Pool for four hundred miles to Ubangi. From here the whole northern bank of the Ubangi to the borders of the Anglo-Egyptian Sudan is French. It is therefore seen that almost all the northern tributaries of the Congo flow through French territory.

While many northern tributaries of the Congo water French possessions, some of the southern tributaries rise in Portuguese soil. In the fifteenth century, when the mariners and soldier-adventurers of Por-

© E. N. A.

WARRIOR SUBJECT OF FRANCE

This tall native of the French Congo lands, with his long, broad-bladed spear, is a born warrior. Fighting is the greatest pleasure of the wild tribesmen of this region.

tugal found the way up the main river blocked by rapids, they turned their attention to the country immediately to the south—the dominions of that King of Kongo above mentioned. Long years of exploration, conquest and colonization have resulted in the establishment of Portuguese rule over a vast tract known as Angola, the capital of which is the ancient port city of São Paulo de Loanda, founded in 1575. The highlands of Angola are adapted to the growing of sugar and coffee and the raising of oxen, but the territory is largely undeveloped.

In both the French and the Portuguese Congo the natives, with the exception of the pure Negrillos (pigmies), belong to the great Bantu family; and in times past supplied the slave traffic to a very large degree.

Though it is rumored that in certain tribes, rites involving human sacrifice are practiced, as when a man's wives are buried with him, little is really known. The word "Bantu" means "the people" and is applied to a large number of tribes speaking different dialects. The Bantus are of great interest to anthropologists, and several expeditions have been sent to Angola.

RATTLE-DRUMS, TOM-TOMS AND HORNS FOR THE TRIBAL DANCE

IN THE HEART OF AFRICA: FACTS AND FIGURES

BELGIAN CONGO

Belgian Colony in Equatorial Africa occupying the greater part of the basin of the Congo River. Administered by the Minister for the Colonies appointed by the King and the Colonial Council consisting of 14 members. Legislation for the Colony is vested in Parliament. The King is represented in the Colony by a Governor-General. For administrative purposes the Colony is divided into 16 districts grouped into 6 provinces, each with a governor. The estimated area of the colony is 902,082 square miles; the native population is about 11,073,300; the white population in 1950 was 52,113. The chief products are palm oil, copal, cotton, coffee and maize. Copper, diamonds, tin and uranium are mined. The Congo is the world's greatest producer of industrial diamonds, and its uranium ore furnishes a large percentage of the world's radium supply. Chief exports: copper (ore and crude), diamonds, uranium, palm oil, cotton, coffee, tin; chief imports: machinery, provisions, textiles. State steamship service on the Congo; railway mileage, 1949, 2,949. Length of telegraph line, 4,209 miles. International air service. Capital, Leopoldville.

FRENCH EQUATORIAL AFRICA (French Congo)

Consists of territories of Gabum, Middle Congo, Ubangi-Shari, and Chad, within the French Union. Each has a Governor; they have financial and administrative autonomy and each has an administrative council. The Lieutenant-Governors are under the Governor-General of French Equatorial Africa who is assisted by a Secretary-General and a Council of Government. Total area, 959,256 square miles; population in 1950 about 4,336,400. Resources largely undeveloped. About 300,000 square miles of tropical forest containing valuable timber. Large numbers of domestic animals are raised. Palm nuts, cacao, coffee and cotton are cultivated. Palm oil, cacao, cotton fiber and timber are exported. Seat of government, Brazzaville.

ANGOLA (Portuguese West Africa)

Portuguese colony administered by a Governor-General, stationed at Luanda. The colony is divided into 16 administrative districts. The area is 481,351 square miles and population in 1947 was estimated at 4,495,000. Chief products and exports are coffee, rubber, wax, oil seeds, sugar, sisal fiber and diamonds. Copper, gold, iron, manganese and salt are found. Half of the country's imports come from Portugal. Railway mileage, 1,442. There are 22,708 miles of highways, and external and internal air services. Capital, São Paulo de Loanda.

SPANISH GUINEA

Spanish colony on the Gulf of Guinea, composed of Fernando Po and several smaller islands, and Rio Muni on the African continent. A Governor administers the colony. Chief town, Bata. Area, 10,036 square miles.

TRUSTEESHIP IN CENTRAL AFRICA: FACTS AND FIGURES

RUANDA-URUNDI

Former German East Africa, now administered by Belgium as a United Nations trusteeship and as a part of Belgian Congo with a Vice-Governor at the head. Total area, about 19,536 square miles. Capital, Usumbura. Both districts are rich in cattle. Exports are livestock, hides and foodstuffs.

188

From Cape Town to the Zambezi

People of South Africa's Cities, Veld and Deserts

Zulus, Boers and the boundless veld are the three things of which we are most likely to think when our thoughts turn to South Africa. The Zulus, under their great leader Chaka, dominated this part of the African continent in the early part of the nineteenth century; the Dutch were the first settlers, and much of the agricultural prosperity of South Africa is due to their skillful farming. ("Boer" is the Dutch word for farmer, or peasant.) The veld is the open grasslands over which are scattered thousands of prosperous farms. But we shall also visit fine cities, gold and diamond mines, splendid orchards and sugar-cane plantations, and primitive peoples such as the Bushmen and the Herreros of the vast Southwest Africa Protectorate.

THE Union of South Africa, down at the tip of the continent where January is the hot month, is divided into four provinces—Cape of Good Hope, Natal, Transvaal and the Orange Free State. The population was estimated in 1946 to be more than eleven million, over half of whom are colored.

The Cape of Good Hope was discovered by the Portuguese navigator, Bartholomew Diaz in 1486, but the first attempt to colonize this pleasant pastoral region was made by the Dutch in 1652. The Cape really became a British colony in 1806, but up to 1820 the majority of the white population was of Dutch descent. Natal was settled by both English and Boers, beginning about 1824, and became a British colony in 1844-45. During 1835-38 many of the Dutch farmers, or Boers, were dissatisfied with the British administration which disapproved of their enslaving the Hottentots, and trekked north. Eventually they created the two Dutch republics of the Transvaal, north of the Vaal River, and the Orange Free State. Gold-mining began in the Transvaal in 1882, and the discovery of gold brought a great increase of prosperity to South Africa—until the outbreak of the South African War (1899-1902).

Later, strenuous efforts were made to develop the land more fully and to unite the different elements in the population, the English and the Boers of Dutch descent. These efforts were crowned with success in 1910, when the Union of South Africa was formed. Since the first World War the region that was once Ger-man Southwest Africa has also been administered by the Union government under a mandate from the League of Nations. Southern Rhodesia, that part of Rhodesia situated between the Transvaal and the River Zambezi, is also dealt with in this chapter.

We shall start our tour of South Africa from Cape Town, which is at the south-ernmost end of the African continent. It lies on Table Bay beneath the shadow of Table Mountain, part of which is, as its name suggests, flat-topped, and part of which looks, in the distance, like a lion's head. Cape Town is the oldest settlement in South Africa and an important port of call. In its streets we shall see not only British people and the Boers, with their large, wide-awake hats, but Kaffirs (the natives of the colony) and coolies from India and Malaya. Native boys and girls, dressed in all sorts of gaudy costumes, sell heather in the streets, for the heather that grows near Cape Town is famous for its beauty and variety of color.

Traveling northward from Cape Town, we pass through a region of rugged, barren mountains and fertile, well-watered valleys in which the earliest European settlers—the Dutch and French Huguenots—made their homes. This land is beautiful and fertile and produces fruit in abundance, particularly grapes.

North of this again we reach the great tableland of the Karroo, a vast plateau broken up by small hills called "kopjes." It is sparsely covered with small bushes of a dull olive green which are known as

JAN VAN RIEBEECK'S STATUE VIEWS THE CITY WHICH HE FOUNDED

Cape Town is South Africa's oldest city, founded in 1652 by the eighteen-year-old Dutch sea-
man and adventurer Van Riebeeck, who established it as a stopping place for ships as they rounded
the Cape of Good Hope. Today Cape Town is a modern, flourishing seaport, metropolis and
vacation resort. Flat-topped Table Mountain commands a magnificent view of the city.

South African Rlys.

FORDING THE BERG RIVER, WHICH HAS ONE OF THE MOST BEAUTIFUL VALLEYS IN CAPE PROVINCE

We cannot travel far in the Cape of Good Hope Province without being struck by the great natural beauty and variety of the landscape. Here, thirty-six miles from Cape Town, we see the Berg River, where, near the little town called the Paarl, it winds between wooded banks over-looked on one side by the peaks of the Drakenstein range and on the other by the Pearl Mountains. Much of the best South African wine is produced in the upper valley of the Berg, for the steep lower slopes of the rugged mountains are clad with fruitful vineyards.

191

ON A SOUTH AFRICAN FARM WHERE THE "CHICKENS" GROW EIGHT FEET HIGH

More ostriches are bred in the Cape of Good Hope than in any other part of South Africa, and especially in the valleys of the Breede River and its tributaries there are many thriving ostrich farms. The one shown above is at Montagu, a village near the pass of Cogman's Kloof.

The huge birds are kept in enclosures—those of the adults being about ten acres in extent, those of the chicks one hundred acres. We can tell the sex of these ostriches at a glance, for the males are black with white tail and wing plumes, while the females are a uniform gray.

CHILDREN OF THE MATABELES, A PEOPLE OF THE TRANSVAAL

Two Matabele youngsters get acquainted while big sister looks on, indifferent to the prattle. Clothes are hardly needed, but necklaces and armlets are worn from babyhood.

© E.N.A.

UNION GOVERNMENT BUILDINGS AT PRETORIA, ONE OF THE FINEST POSSIBLE SITES

Pretoria, which in 1860, five years after its foundation, became the capital of the Transvaal, is now the administrative capital of the Union of South Africa. It is a clean, well-built city, and of all its excellent buildings, this, the Union Government Building, made of native ma-terials and completed in 1915, is considered the finest. It stands on the flank of a hill with the city spread below. The avenues of Pretoria show as green lines, for they are planted with willows, palms and plane trees, oaks and Facarandas—large tropical trees with blue flowers.

194

Karroo bush. The air is clear, and we can consequently see very far. Indeed, rocks and big stones lying on hills several miles away stand out so boldly that we can almost count them. Occasionally we pass farms nestling among the hills, surrounded by small gardens and orchards, and here and there we cross a stream.

Most of the streams, however, dry up during the hot season; then water must be obtained from springs or by artificial means. In the early summer, if there has been a good rainfall, the Karroo becomes a wonderful flower garden, and it is possible to gather as many as sixty varieties of flowers; but this period does not last long. At the end of about two months the flowers are dead and the Karroo is again a desolate waste.

The Karroo is inhabited chiefly by British and Boer farmers, whose homes are often from twenty to fifty miles apart. The native inhabitants are largely Kaffirs, Hottentots and Bushmen.

All this time we have been traveling through Cape of Good Hope Province, but when we pass over the Orange River we cross into the Orange Free State. Here commences the highest and largest South African plateau, which extends across the Orange Free State, Bechuanaland and into the Transvaal, which adjoins Southern Rhodesia.

World's Richest Gold Field

West of Bechuanaland is the Kalahari Desert, which was once the home of vast herds of game, but is now a useless waste. The Kalahari stretches into the Southwest Africa Protectorate, a desolate region rich in minerals, lying between Angola and Cape of Good Hope Province. In the east of South Africa is a lofty range, the Drakensberg Mountains, and between them and the coast is the province of Natal.

Kimberley and Johannesburg are the two principal cities in South Africa from the point of view of wealth and industry. Kimberley is noted for its diamonds and Johannesburg lies in the richest gold belt in the world. In the gold mines, shafts several thousand feet deep have been sunk in the earth, and galleries have been driven out in all directions at the bottom in the search for gold, of which there seems to be a never-ending supply.

In 1835, as has been already stated, the Boers began to leave Cape Colony with their herds and flocks to settle in a land where they could live as they wished. To reach the Transvaal, where they founded a separate republic, these emigrants had to pass through the country of the Zulus, a warlike people who had conquered a large part of South Africa and possessed a vast army of trained warriors.

Boers Fight with the Zulus

One morning in the summer of 1836 it was reported that the Zulus were advancing to attack the emigrants. The Boers therefore formed their wagons into a square and piled branches between the wheels in order to prevent the natives from squeezing through. Then, with the women and children to load the rifles and prepare the ammunition, they waited for the black army to attack. This it soon did, opening out to right and left in the shape of two horns in order to encircle the wagons. The Zulus came on in thousands, seizing the wagons and trying to wrest them apart, ripping up the canvas covers with their broad-bladed spears and yelling their fierce war cries. But the Boer men and women fought with great determination and at last beat off the enemy. The Zulus, however, took away all their sheep and cattle and they would have starved but for the arrival of fresh parties who joined them in their northward trek.

Harvest Time Among the Matabele

The Matabele, who are a branch of the Zulu race, found in Southern Rhodesia, are among the best known of the South African tribes. They are tall, fine-looking people and live in round huts, with doors only some two feet in height. Their diet consists of meat, corn meal, milk and a form of native beer which they drink in large quantities. They have several festivals during the year, the chief of

PRESIDENT'S RESIDENCE THAT IS CALLED A BARN

This handsome building, so beautifully situated among the trees on the slope of a hill, is Groote Schuur—Great Barn—the old Dutch home of Cecil Rhodes at Rondebosch. It is now held in trust as the official residence of the President of the Union when he is at Cape Town, for it is only five miles from that city.

South African Govt.

HOW MAILS ARE CARRIED ON THE OUTSKIRTS OF THE KALAHARI

This is the post office of Mariental, in what was once German Southwest Africa. From the fact that camels are the mail-carriers we know it must be in desert country. Indeed, the great Kalahari Desert stretches eastward for wearisome miles. The coastal strip of Southwest Africa is also barren, but the central highlands are more habitable.

196

PIETERMARITZBURG IN AN AMPHITHEATRE OF HILLS

From the tower that surmounts the town hall we can here look down upon Pietermaritzburg and see the straight line of Church Street reaching away toward the surrounding hills. Pietermaritzburg, which has direct rail connections with the Transvaal, is the capital of Natal, a country of vast sugar and other plantations.

Nicholls

BOER HOUSEHOLD ON TREK: HOW A "REMOVAL" IS CARRIED OUT OVER THE SOUTH AFRICAN VELD

Seven yoke of bullocks seem a large number to draw one wagon, but when the wagon is loaded with all the household belongings of a farmer and with his wife and child, and when it has to travel not along hard, made roads but over the open veld, or, at best, over a rough, uneven, track, it does not seem too many. The farmer to whom this wagon belongs stands in the background, watching while it fords a narrow stream, ready with the long goad he carries over his shoulder to urge on any bullock that seems inclined to shirk a fair share of the hard pull.

WOOL CLIPPED FROM SOUTH AFRICAN SHEEP AWAITS SHIPMENT

Sheep are the most important stock animals in the Union of South Africa, and wool is one of the country's most important exports. Most of the baled wool is shipped out of Port Elizabeth on Algoa Bay and East London at the Buffalo River. The mild climate of South Africa and the extensive grassy plateaus make the country suitable for grazing sheep and cattle.

which comes at harvest time. On the great day, when the harvest has been a good one, all collect in a vast square in the village of the tribal chief. There may be as many as two or three thousand warriors formed in a semicircle eight or nine deep, each man with his assagai, or spear, and shield. They then begin to chant a song, keeping time with their feet; occasionally they beat with their assagais on their ox-hide shields, making a noise like thunder.

Now a man who has performed some great deed will spring out from among the warriors and execute a dance, thrusting with his assagai and otherwise showing how he would dispose of his enemies. Nearly all the warriors wear ostrich feathers stuck in their hair and have coats of the skins of different animals.

RICKSHAW BOYS WAITING FOR PASSENGERS, DURBAN

These two-wheeled, light vehicles, pulled by elaborately dressed young Zulus, prove fascinating to tourists in Durban. Located on the Bay of Natal just south of the Umgeni River, the city is one of South Africa's major seaports as well as a manufacturing and trading center. It is a popular seaside vacation resort with bathing facilities and sports grounds.

LOOKING OVER THE HOUSE-TOPS OF JOHANNESBURG

Johannesburg did not even exist until 1886 and the land, poor for farming, sold cheap. Suddenly gold was found at Witwatersrand (pronounced with a v). Ten years later two building plots were sold for about $100,000 apiece. The city is now the largest in South Africa. Cosmopolitan, energetic, it has become a bustling railroad and industrial centre.

The Bechuanas are another of the native races of South Africa and live in much the same way as the Matabele. They have the curious custom of adopting some animal as a sort of tribal mascot. Sometimes it is a crocodile, or it may be an antelope, a monkey or an elephant. Their dress is usually a cloak made from skins, and they are fond of ornaments in the shape of bracelets and anklets of beads, metal and the teeth of wild animals. For weapons they have assagais, small daggers and clubs called knobkerries, often beautifully carved.

The Bechuanas also are fond of dancing, and when several thousand of them perform together the scene is really splendid. Their marriage customs are similar to those of other South African tribes. The wife is acquired by purchase, her value varying according to her looks and her reputation as a housekeeper.

Rhodesia is named after Cecil Rhodes, a pioneer who in 1889 organized the British South African Company. It was also the land of Livingstone. We have pictured the country that he described, the waterfalls, which hamper water transportation, the herds of elephants, the rhinoceros and hippopotami in the rivers, and the lions lurking in the jungle. If

we go to Rhodesia to-day, however, we shall find that the elephants have largely disappeared, though lions are still to be found back in the bush. Rhodesia is a lofty tableland with a semi-tropical climate and beautiful scenery. It is rich in minerals, especially gold. On the Zambezi River, which flows through Rhodesia, are Victoria Falls, the mightiest falls in the world and a favorite with tourists, which we show in the chapter The Wonder of the Waterfall.

Southwest of Rhodesia lies the Kalahari Desert, where there is little rain and the precious springs are few and far between. The Kalahari is not like the usual desert, for it has small trees and bushes and occasional herds of antelope. Its inhabitants are a dwarf race known as Bushmen and Hottentots; their language is one of clicks, made by peculiar movements of the tongue inside the mouth. Each click has a certain meaning. These little brown people wander from place to place without settled habitation, sleeping under rocks or in the shelter of trees and bushes, with a rough lean-to of brushwood. Even in the old days they had no flocks or herds and lived from hand to mouth, existing on the game of the country, which they shot with their bows

THE UNIVERSITY OF CAPE TOWN IN A TRULY CLASSICAL SETTING

Devil's Peak (center) rises high above the buildings of the university. The grounds, in Rondesbosch outside Cape Town, were the gift of Cecil Rhodes, empire builder par excellence.

A BRIGHT DAY IN THE SUN AND SALT SPRAY AT DURBAN, NATAL

The broad beach on the Indian Ocean is close to the heart of the important city. Modern hotels, stores and apartment buildings line a beautiful esplanade beyond the embankment.

DIAMOND MINING IN SOUTH AFRICA

These miners are loading the rock in which diamonds are found into one of the 38 cars they fill each day. Africa, with its large deposits, is the most important producer of gem diamonds.

THE RESULT OF ONE DAY'S WORK

The diamonds shown are the "take" from the mines in one day—the work of many hundreds of men. The last bits of waste matter are sorted out by hand; only the diamonds are left.

A KRAAL OF THE ZULUS, A CRESCENT ENCLOSURE OF DOMED HUTS ABOUT A SMALLER CATTLE KRAAL

The Zulus, who once inhabited much of South Africa and violently and grain farmers. Their kraals, villages, dot the grasslands and bleak resisted the coming of the Europeans, now live at peace as herdsmen plateaus of the protected district, Zululand, in northeastern Natal.

and arrows. The bows they made from the branches of trees and the strings from the sinews of wild animals. For warfare they used arrows that were poisoned by being dipped in juice obtained from a plant or from a certain caterpillar. They still follow their old form of life, and when brought into touch with civilization they often pine away and die.

The Bushmen are especially interesting because their ancestors painted pictures of animals on rocks and in caves. These pictures are really amazing, considering that they were done by primitive men. They are finished with an accuracy that we cannot surpass today, and are still in a wonderful state of preservation. The Bushmen once occupied all South Africa from the Cape to the Zambezi, but they have gradually been driven before other and more powerful tribes, until now they inhabit only the Kalahari, Bechuanaland and Southwest Africa.

Living close to nature, they are wonderfully active and notice everything that is going on around them. They have a highly developed sense of direction and can find their way about on the darkest night. Though very small, they are incredible eaters. One man, it is said, will eat half a sheep at a sitting, and for him to dispose of forty to fifty bananas at a meal is nothing uncommon.

The Bushmen's homes are simple affairs. As the tribes are constantly on the move, their household goods consist of a few earthenware pots, spears and clubs for hunting and for use in warfare, ostrich eggs to carry water, tortoise-shells for holding food when in camp, and a few skins of wild animals to serve them as rugs and blankets. The Bushmen make excellent hunters; once an animal is wounded they follow it up until it is exhausted. Their powers of endurance are equal to those of the wild beasts, and they will run down a wounded antelope on the hottest day, keeping their quarry constantly on the move and allowing it no rest until it drops. A party of Bushmen once pursued a wounded giraffe for a distance of more than forty miles; then, when they had killed it, they went back the same

FORBIDDING RAMPART OF THE DRAKENSBERG MOUNTAINS ON THE WESTERN BORDER OF NATAL

Along the western frontier of Natal runs a range of mountains, the Drakensberg, which terminates suddenly in vast chasms and walls of rock. One of the peaks, the Giant's Castle, is eleven thousand feet in height, and several others rise to a considerable height. Natal occupies only one-thirteenth of the territory of the Union of South Africa, but it contains a greater variety of scenery than the other provinces. It might be termed the garden of that portion of Africa lying south of the Zambezi. The province supplies the whole of South Africa with sugar.

distance to bring up their families to indulge in the feast.

The Bushmen's knowledge of the habits of animals is probably unsurpassed. They seem to know exactly what an animal is going to do. They will watch a flight of bees high up in the skies where it is practically invisible to a white man. They will follow it until they reach the tree where the bees have their combs and steal the honey.

The Bushmen have many quaint beliefs. They say that when one of their number dies his spirit goes on a long journey until it arrives at a place where others have gone before, and that when they meet they share the hunting-grounds together. To them the wind, the dust, storms, lightning and all things in Nature are associated with spirits and are regarded with considerable fear.

They also believe that men and women can, in another existence, change themselves into animals. They regard natural phenomena as living things, but they do not worship either the sun or the moon. They remark, however, that the sun retires to bed each night and gets up in the morning like a human being.

Huge Hats of the Herrero Women

Southwest Africa, which was German territory until the end of World War I, is inhabited by the Herreros, a pastoral tribe whose dress is especially remarkable. The women wear huge caps made of skins, which terminate in three points like horns and from each of which hangs an ornament. The weight of this headdress is often great, yet, despite the heat and the discomfort, no Herrero woman would dream of appearing without her hat. In addition to this she has heavy metal ornaments, and her arms are covered with bracelets or what appear to be pieces of metal piping.

The customs of the Herreros are often cruel; for instance, those who are suffering from some disease which is believed to be incurable are left in a hut in the jungle until death or some wild animal makes an end of them. Old people are treated in the same way.

Hero of a Famous Duel

In Natal we find the Zulus and the Swazis, whose manners and customs are somewhat similar, as the Swazis fell under the dominion of the newly constituted Zulu nation in the early nineteenth century. Before the Zulu War in 1879 this tribe was organized into regiments and constantly engaged in wars and warlike preparations. They lived in large villages of huts, as they do now, and waged war on all the neighboring tribes, establishing such a reputation for ferocity that no tribe could oppose them.

When a Zulu army returned from any expedition, the men were paraded before the chief, who directed them to bring out any who had shown fright in warfare. These unfortunates were instantly killed as an example to the others. Much of the influence that Great Britain afterward acquired over the Zulus was due to a British subject, Colonel Johann Colenbrander, who lived for years among them.

He is said to be the only white man who has ever killed a Zulu warrior in single combat. The great duel took place on uneven ground, and just at the beginning of it the white man's weapon was rendered useless by a blow from the Zulu's battle-ax. The latter also carried an assagai. But the white man closed with him and after a desperate struggle actually succeeded in lifting the Zulu in the air, working his spear around him and impaling him on the weapon.

Plantation Coolies from India

Many of the native inhabitants of South Africa are employed as servants or farm laborers or in the gold and diamond mines and factories. They regard this work as being only temporary, and when they have earned sufficient money to buy a wife or some land they give it up.

Until immigration from India was prohibited in 1911, thousands of Indians came to South Africa. Today, in the districts where tea is grown, many of their descendants work on the plantations.

Sugar-cane has been planted successfully in South Africa. Indeed, large

TWO STICKS INSTEAD OF ASSAGAIS ARE CARRIED BY THIS ZULU

The Zulus, descendants of a race of warriors who were the overlords of the greater part of southeastern Africa, still retain their pride. If this powerfully built man were armed with assagais and had the ring of a proven warrior upon his head, he would be a counterpart of the Zulus of the nineteenth century who formed Chaka's regiments.

A YOUNG ZULU GIRL DISPLAYS HER MUSICAL SKILL

At an agricultural show in the Melmoth district of Natal, South Africa, a Zulu girl demonstrates a musical instrument that consists of one string and a bow. The Zulus are handsome and sturdy people. Once they were all-powerful in South Africa. The most important crop in this section is sugar-cane, and many Zulu families derive their living from it.

INDUSTRIALIZATION—THE ORDER OF THE DAY IN AFRICA

Visitors to Africa today are likely to find it very different from what they had anticipated. Vast areas are electrified and labor-saving devices that make for greater efficiency have been introduced. All types of home appliances are in use. The stove and the smaller mechanical items such as the percolators, toasters and grills above show the trend toward modernization.

areas are given over to sugar-growing. Here too we shall find Indian coolies extensively employed on the plantations; but if we go into a Natal sugar refinery we shall see "black boys" at work operating the machinery.

FROM CAPE TOWN TO THE ZAMBEZI: FACTS AND FIGURES

THE UNION OF SOUTH AFRICA

A sovereign state of the British Commonwealth, consisting of 4 provinces—Cape of Good Hope, Natal, Orange Free State and Transvaal—is bounded on the north by South-West Africa, Bechuanaland and Southern Rhodesia, on the east by Mozambique, Swaziland and the Indian Ocean, on the south by the Indian Ocean and on the west by the Atlantic. Area, 472,494 square miles; population, 12,646,000. A Governor-General is assisted by an Executive Council (Cabinet) which is headed by a Prime Minister. Parliament consists of a 44-member Senate and a 153-member House of Assembly. Principal crops are corn (mealies), wheat, potatoes, tobacco, tea, sugar and citrus fruits. Wool production is important. Industries include metal, food and chemical processing; construction; clothing-manufacture, and publishing. Mineral products include gold, diamonds, coal, copper, asbestos and manganese. Exports: wool, diamonds, base metals, fruits and nuts, coal, chemicals, footwear and beverages. Imports: food and drink, vehicles, textiles and machinery. Railways, 13,942 miles; roads, 25,000 miles; domestic and foreign air service; 415,518 telephones, and international radio-telephone connections. Christians predominate; there are Jews, Moslems and Hindus. There are a number of special schools; nearly 20,000 students in 9 universities, 2 are constituent colleges; 1,325,000 pupils in 9,110 primary and secondary schools. Population (European descent) of chief cities: Johannesburg, 332,000; Cape Town (legislative capital), 220,400; Pretoria (executive capital), 130,800; Durban, 130,200.

HIGH COMMISSION TERRITORIES

Basutoland, Bechuanaland and Swaziland are under executive and legislative control of a British High Commissioner. Supervision of each is vested in a Resident Commissioner.

Bechuanaland Protectorate. Bounded west and north by South-West Africa, east by Southern Rhodesia and Transvaal, and south and southwest by Cape Province; area, 275,000 square miles; population, 289,000. Resident Commissioner is at Mafeking, Cape Province. Chief exports are livestock and hides. Public and private schools, 170, and 1 teachers school.

Basutoland Protectorate. Bounded on the west and north by Orange Free State, on the east by Natal and on the south by Cape Province; area, 11,716 square miles and population, 574,000. Leading exports are wool, mohair, sorghum, corn and wheat. Motor roads, 523 miles. There are 1,018 schools with 91,000 pupils enrolled. Resident Commissioner is at Meseru.

Swaziland Protectorate. Bounded east by Mozambique and Natal and south, west and north by Transvaal; area, 6,705 square miles; population, 197,000. Resident Commissioner is at Mbabane. Chief exports are cattle, hides and skins, tobacco and butter. In 195 schools there are 13,800 pupils. Roads, 1,145 miles.

MOZAMBIQUE (Portuguese East Africa)

Bounded on the north by Tanganyika, on the east by the Indian Ocean, on the south by Natal and on the west by Swaziland, Transvaal, the Rhodesias and Nyasaland; area, 297,732 square miles, and population, 5,733,000. The Governor-General is assisted by a Council, made up of appointed and elected representatives of commercial classes. Chief products are sugar, corn, cotton, copra, sisal and minerals. Livestock, 1,197,000 head. Mineral deposits include gold, silver, samarskite, uranium and asbestos. Railways, 1,651 miles; roads, 18,068 miles; telegraph lines, 7,807 miles; 5,257 miles of telephone lines. There are 161,175 pupils in 1,150 schools. Population of chief towns: Lourenço Marques (capital), 70,000; Beira, 30,000.

MAURITIUS (British Colony and Dependencies)

Island and dependent groups in the Indian Ocean. Area of Mauritius, 720 square miles; population, 466,000; area of island dependencies —Rodrigues, Chagos (Oil) Islands, Agalega and St. Brandon Group—89 square miles; population, about 15,000. Under a Governor and Executive and Legislative councils. Leading exports are sugar, rum and aloe fibers. Railways, 116 miles; roads, 700 miles; telegraph lines, 218 miles; telephone lines, 7,118 miles. Hindus predominate; there are Roman Catholics and Protestants. There are 60,716 pupils in 179 schools as well as other primary schools and government colleges. Population of capital, Port Louis, 72,788.

FORMER MANDATED TERRITORY: FACTS AND FIGURES

SOUTH-WEST AFRICA

Bounded on the north by Angola and Northern Rhodesia, on the east by Bechuanaland, on the southeast and south by Cape Province and on the west by the Atlantic; area, 317,725 square miles and population, 430,000. Mandate, granted by League of Nations to Union of South Africa in 1920, has not yet been transferred to UN trusteeship. An Administrator, appointed by the Governor-General of the Union, is assisted by an Executive Committee and an 18-member Assembly. Leading exports are diamonds, lead-copper concentrates, zinc and vanadium. Railways, 1,133 miles; 17,326 miles of telephone and telegraph circuits. There are 174 schools. Population of capital, Windhoek, 23,500.

MYSTERIOUS MADAGASCAR

Interesting Island Detached From Africa

Ages ago Madagascar became a vast island, after having been a part of the continent of Africa. To-day a sweep of ocean ten thousand feet deep and 240 miles or more in width, the Mozambique Channel, lies between them. Yet the island contains not alone fossil remains of the African hippopotamus, but it has become the home of tribes of African origin—together with some of Malay extraction. Just how this came about, scientists are not sure. Some volcanic convulsion must have occurred which tore this huge piece from the southeastern coast of the continental land mass. All tribes are now united under the flag of France.

MADAGASCAR is an oval island, the largest in the Indian Ocean, with a coastline of three thousand miles little indented, though there are harbors at Tamatave, Majunga, Suarez, Diego and Tulear. Some of these ports, Tamatave especially, have been known to Europeans for several hundred years, but the interior, which rises in a hump of mountainous country, is still a mystery. Around the island with hardly a break, lies an almost impenetrable jungle forest from ten to forty miles deep. The coasts are marshy, and fully six-sevenths of Madagascar has tropic heat with a rainy season from November to April save on the east coast where, thanks to the vapor-laden southeast trade winds, it rains throughout the year. There are terrific thunderstorms, and residents of the coast often see water-spouts and hurricanes. In the high interior there is, however, a cool season when the nights actually approach the freezing point. The mountains include hundreds of extinct volcanic cones and there are occasional slight earthquake shocks.

It is possible that this great land mass, which lies off the southeasterly portion of the African continent—in places but 240 miles removed from the mainland—may at one time have connected Africa and Asia. At any rate, it appears to have been torn from East Africa by some geological upheaval in remote times.

The language of the island is said to be derived from the ancient Malay, and the Hovas, the leading people, trace their origin from the Malays. There are also Sanskrit words in the language which were brought in by Buddhist missionaries from India. There are Arabic phrases, for Arab merchants traded with Madagascar at least a thousand years ago. Both these Arabs and the Indian traders formed settlements on the coasts. Finally, on the west side of the island there are tribes showing Negro blood who are evidently descended from African settlers; and in the western forests there are the remains of a people called the Vazimba, supposed to have been the original natives of the island who were driven inland by the Malay conquerors. Added to all these there are traces of Melanesians (people from the South Pacific) but how they came is not known.

There are, according to a late census, about 3,800,000 people in Madagascar. The Hovas of the central province of Imerina are the most important. The word "hovs" really means the middle class of the tribe, as distinguished from the nobles and the slaves, and the correct name of these people is Merina or people of Imerina. They do not resemble Negroes in any way: except for their dark skins they might be Europeans, though their eyes are dark brown, their hair jet black and straight. Like other tribes of the central districts, they have been Christianized by various missionary societies.

The Bétsiléos, who live south of the Hovas, are larger and darker colored and their hair is curly. In the southeast are found the Baras, who are much more primitive. These people wear their hair in knobs done up with wax or fat and whitening. The middle knob is the size of a croquet ball, the others smaller. Each

211

Silree

ON THE WESTERN SLOPES OF MADAGASCAR'S MOUNTAINS: NATIVE HIDE-BEARERS TAKE A WELL-EARNED REST

Except for the forests that lie parallel to the coast, most of the western side of Madagascar is grassy prairie, over which roam great herds of humped cattle, some wild and some owned by the native tribes. The mammoth lozenge-shaped island has an important trade in raw hides, which, as there are next to no railways and few roads, have to be carried to the coast by native porters. The weighty ox skins are rolled tightly in bundles and tied, as shown in the photograph, to each end of a stout pole, which the men bear over their shoulders.

PREPARING THE GROUND FOR THE RICE PLANTS WHICH PROVIDE THE CHIEF FOOD OF MOST MALAGASIES

Silree

Rice is the most important crop of the central highlands and eastern Madagascar. Near the coast it is easy to grow, but elsewhere it is planted in terraces cut in the hollows of the hills to which water is conducted often from long distances. The ground is dug up by means of narrow, long-handled spades, and oxen are used to tread out the mud preparatory to transplanting. The rice is threshed by being beaten in bundles laid over stones set upright on the threshing-floor, and stored in rice-pits. The women pound the husks from the grain in wooden mortars.

Silree

WOMAN'S WORK IN THE PADDY FIELDS: TRANSPLANTING THE YOUNG RICE IN FIELDS OF SOFT MUD

Madagascar has between 1,000,000 and 1,500,000 acres planted to rice, and smaller areas to sugar, coffee, vanilla, cloves, manioc or cassava (from which tapioca is made), tobacco, cacao (used in making chocolate), cotton, rubber and the mulberries on which silkworms are fed. The Malagasies have many curious prohibitions which they call "fady" and which are very like the Polynesian "tapus." For instance, in one town of Imerina province it is fady for women to eat rice at all; in another place the unfortunate people may grow nothing else.

HOVA WOMEN, WITH GRACEFUL DIGNITY, DANCE TO THE ACCOMPANIMENT OF CLAPS FROM THEIR AUDIENCE

When Europeans first came to Madagascar they found that of all the native tribes the Hovas were by far the most civilized. They dressed elaborately in a pleasing costume that they still retain, although, as we see in the above photograph, European sleeved blouses are sometimes worn as well. The Hovas were the latest arrivals from Malaya. They dwell in Imerina province, in the central highlands, and when their queen, Ranavalona III, was overthrown by the French in 1895, they had been the dominant race in the island for fully a hundred years.

215

WHITE WATER FOAMS OVER THE BARRAGE (DAM) D'ANTELAMITA

Madagascar has splendid water-power possibilities. There are a number of rivers which flow down from the watershed formed by the central highlands. On the east the drop is very rapid. Here streams rush through gorges in a succession of magnificent cascades. A beginning has been made, with such dams as this, to harness the potential power.

knob is quite hard and on some heads you may count as many as one hundred of them. The Baras wear great wooden earrings and around their necks necklaces hung with charms. They love brass nails, and have dozens of them fixed into the butts of their guns, cartridge boxes and powder flasks. The head of each nail is the size of a quarter.

Along the western side of the island there are no fewer than twenty-five tribes, including the Betsimisárakas, the Tanalas, and the Sakalavas, who, before the Hovas rose to power, were the rulers of the whole island.

The natives make rather superior houses, with walls of red clay or planks and high-pitched, thatched roofs with pro-

jecting eaves which are ornamented with quaint wooden figures reminiscent of those used elsewhere on totem poles. The women are clever at plaiting straw and make sleeping mats, as well as wide hats of palm-leaf, and clothing of grass, cotton or tree bark the fibers of which they separate by beating it with wooden mallets. Unfortunately some of the younger set conceive it to be the height of fashion to stain every alternate tooth black. The Malagasy folk eat quantities of rice, which they grow on irrigated land and cultivate with a narrow-bladed spade. The Sakalavas, however, live largely on cassava and sweet potatoes.

In the old days the natives used the blow-pipe—one more way in which they

MALAGASY FISHER LADS WITH CURIOUS BASKET-LIKE HAND-NETS

With the baskets that will hold their catch upon their heads, these young men are ready to go fishing. The most notable fishermen of Madagascar are the Vezo, a tribe of the Sakalava race, who are as much at home in the water as on land, and the Antaizakas, whose name explains itself, since it is a Malagasy word meaning "hand-fishers."

217

THE ONLY KIND OF CARRIAGE KNOWN TO MANY MALAGASY FOLK

The scarcity of good roads in Madagascar means, of course, that there are few carts and fewer motor cars. Those who do not wish to walk must, therefore, take a "filanjana," which is something like the Eastern palanquin, or the European sedan-chair. On level ground four porters are needed, on rough ground and for crossing streams at least eight.

resembled the tribes of the Malay Archipelago. To-day, though, most of the men have guns, usually modern rifles, besides being sufficiently good metal-workers to forge the iron found on the island into spears and arrowheads, farm implements and knives.

The people keep sheep and cattle. The cattle are like the Indian zebus with a big hump behind the neck. No one knows where they came from, for when the Portuguese first landed on the island, cattle were, even then, the principal riches of the inhabitants. Most of the sheep are of the fat-tailed breed—creatures with black heads and very little wool, whose tails make choice eating, from the native point of view.

Malagasies make dug-outs from single tree trunks for use on the rivers, while the coast-dwellers build large boats made of planks literally sewed together with palm fibre. Some of these are fitted with outriggers like those of the craft used by the South Sea Islanders. The coast tribes are good at catching fish with nets and traps.

Even though Madagascar may have been at one time joined to Africa, it was separated so long ago that the wild life is now quite different from that of the continent. Most of the wild creatures of Madagascar are small and not particularly dangerous. The worst is the foussa, a brown civet-like beast about twice the size of a cat, with a small head, short legs with strong claws and a long tail. It is nocturnal and sometimes carries off lambs and kids, and when wounded defends itself with such ferocity that the natives believe it will attack a man.

Lemurs, monkey-like creatures of which there are many different sorts, are plentiful, and they are found in few other countries. The most puzzling animal is the aye-aye, a nocturnal lemur, about as large as a cat, with big bare ears, eyes which can see in the dark, rat-like teeth with which it cuts into tree trunks in search of the insects on which it feeds, and the most amazing, spidery-looking hands. The third finger of the right hand is as thin as wire, for it is used in picking out the grubs from the wood. It sleeps all day and feeds by night. Another queer animal is the tenrec, a spiny creature which lives chiefly on earthworms. It sleeps through the hot weather and wakes when it becomes cool.

Remains dug up in swampy places prove that there existed in Madagascar a huge, wingless bird which has been named Æpyornis. It would have made the biggest ostrich look small, for it was fourteen feet high, and its eggs, of which many have been found, are six times the size of ostrich eggs. It is believed to have been living up to a few centuries ago.

No fewer than two hundred and thirty-nine species of birds have been found. There are plovers, rails, herons and other familiar water-birds; also parrots, pigeons, crows, rollers, birds of prey and delightful little honey-eaters—creatures that look like humming-birds. The rivers hold two sorts of crocodile, of which one is peculiar to the island. Both grow to a great size and are dangerous to man and beast. A twenty-foot crocodile will pull

an ox into the water and drown and eat it. There are also poisonous snakes and swarms of stinging insects.

Madagascar, discovered in 1500 by the Portuguese, was for centuries an independent kingdom. The French established trading posts and began colonizing about 1700, and by the Anglo-French agreement of 1890 established a protectorate over the island, which six years later became a French colony. It was thought necessary to depose Queen Ranavalona III, who had succeeded to the throne in 1883, and eventually she was deported to Algiers. The French have, however, brought about such material improvements as the construction of railroads, the introduction of air service, the irrigation of dry lands and the conservation of valuable forest areas. To date they have constructed almost sixteen thousand miles of roads suitable for motor traffic, a railroad between the capital city, Tananarive, and the chief port, Tamatave, and one southward from the capital to the thermal springs at Ant-

DIEGO-SUAREZ HARBOR, ONE OF THE BEST IN THE INDIAN OCEAN

Diego-Suarez is at the northern end of Madagascar, on a bay of the same name. It has been a naval base for many years. The present town was laid out by the World War I hero Marshal Joffre. A Portuguese explorer, Diogo Soares, gave his name to the bay in 1543. It is also known as British Sound; and one may still hear the native name of Antsirane used.

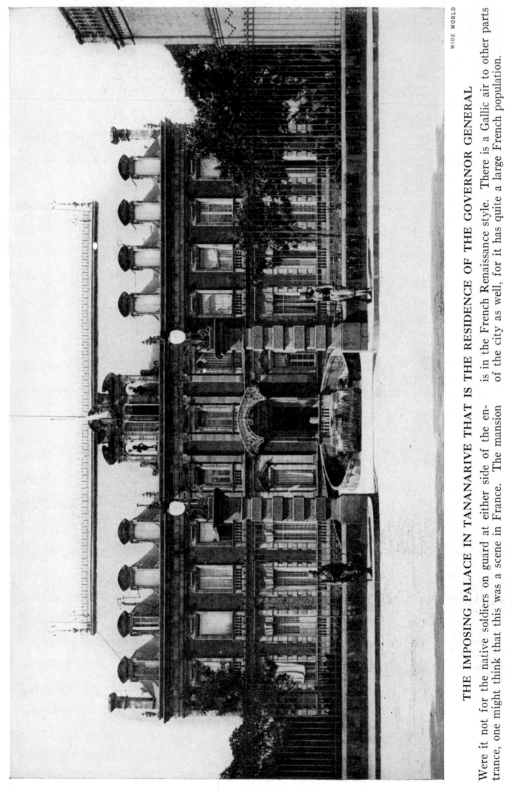

THE IMPOSING PALACE IN TANANARIVE THAT IS THE RESIDENCE OF THE GOVERNOR GENERAL

Were it not for the native soldiers on guard at either side of the entrance, one might think that this was a scene in France. The mansion is in the French Renaissance style. There is a Gallic air to other parts of the city as well, for it has quite a large French population.

WIDE WORLD

220

AN AUTORAIL CAR, A COMBINATION OF BUS AND TRAIN

There are only a few hundred miles of railways in Madagascar but almost three times as many miles of autorails. They provide quick and pleasant transportation between towns.

A POST OFFICE WITH A TROPICAL LOOK IN TANANARIVE

The lattice work walls let breezes sweep through the building—a welcome feature in a hot climate. Overhangs help to shield the interior from the intense glare of direct sunlight.

AN IMPORTANT ITEM IN THE DAY'S WORK OF A MALAGASY WOMAN

Mat-making is considered by most of the tribes of the island an important feminine accomplishment. Not only are the mats used to cover the walls and floors of their houses, but many are exported. Raffia and grasses are used, also a strong fibre found in the outer peel of a coarse sedge. The best mats are those made by the Sihanaka women.

MAKER OF HATS OF GENEROUS SIZE IN IMERINA PROVINCE

For a long time the people of Madagascar have woven straw, raffia and other plant fibres into hats, baskets and mats. The primitive appliances which this Hova hatter is using are the same as those which have been used for many generations. But since 1904 quicker methods of manufacture have been introduced by the French.

sirabe, besides two other lines, one running to the north of the island and one to the east coast. The motor bus service runs on a regular schedule along the main roads to the larger towns; and through the chain of lagoons on the east side a canal has been started which is adequate for small steamers. There is wireless communication with France, and French money is used. A Bank of Madagascar was established in 1925. The capital city is laid out with wide streets and other evidences of French influence.

From the steamy coastal plains rubber and vanilla are produced, and there were, by the latest statistics, some 1,400,000 acres sown to rice, the staple native food crop. While portions of the coast are desertlike, the great riches of the island are the coastal forests, which are full of such valuable timber as ebony, as well as gums and resins. But it will be many years before the forests can be extensively opened up, for the climate is deadly to white men. Cattle have been reared since the early days.

MADAGASCAR: FACTS AND FIGURES

THE COUNTRY

A large island in the Indian Ocean off the southeast coast of Africa, from which it is separated by the Mozambique Channel; the nearest distance between island and continent is 240 miles. Estimated area, 228,000 square miles; population is about 4,351,700.

GOVERNMENT

Administered as an overseas territory within the French Union. High Commissioner is assisted by a government council composed of the chiefs of the civil and military services and presidents of provincial assemblies, and a representative assembly of European and Madagascan members elected by the provincial assemblies.

COMMERCE AND INDUSTRIES

Cattle-breeding and agriculture are the chief occupations. Forests contain valuable woods as well as plants that yield rubber and resins, and dyeing, tanning and medicinal products. Leading crops are cassava, rice, corn, potatoes, coffee, haricot and French beans, sugar and tapioca. Livestock, 6,762,000 head. Industries include textile weaving, metal-working and hat-making as well as meat-packing and other food-processing. Graphite is the principal mineral; mica, gold and precious stones are also produced. Exports: coffee, tinned meat, cattle and crocodile hides, vanilla and cloves. Leading imports are cotton cloth, machinery, petroleum products, metalware, autos, clothing, silk and rayon cloth and jute bags.

COMMUNICATIONS

Regular coastwise steamer service between principal ports. Railways, 534 miles; motorcar service of 1,375 route miles; all-weather roads, 6,000 miles; telegraph lines, 10,383 miles; telephone lines, 10,018 miles. Air service between main towns and to foreign points.

RELIGION AND EDUCATION

Catholic and Protestant missionaries have Christianized many native tribes; there is a considerable Moslem population. Education is compulsory, for Europeans between 6 and 14 years of age and for natives between 8 and 14; secondary and higher-grade schools are also provided. Enrollment of 199,143 in public and private schools. There are college faculties and public service, technical, vocational and agricultural institutes and colleges.

CHIEF TOWNS

Population: Tananarive (capital), 174,000; Majunga, 32,000; Tamatave, 29,000; Diégo-Suarez, 24,000.

ISLAND DEPENDENCIES

Nosy-Bé (area, 130 square miles) off the northwest coast, and Sainte-Marie (64 square miles) off the east coast, as well as Europa, Juan de Nova, Barren, Bassas da India and Glorieuses, all in surrounding waters, are governed by the High Commissioner. Other dependencies, far to the south and east, are Crozet Islands (181 square miles), Amsterdam, St. Paul and Kerguelen islands (2,405 square miles) and Terre-Adélie, south of Australia in Antarctica.

COMORO

An archipelago between Madagascar and Africa in the Mozambique Channel; area, 838 square miles, and population, 168,890. It is an overseas territory with representation in the French Parliament and the French Union Assembly. Production of sugar, once the chief product, has declined; vanilla and sisal are the chief exports. Dzaoudzi, on Mayotte, is the capital.

REUNION

An island, 420 miles east of Madagascar; area 970 square miles, and population is about 255,000. It is an overseas department, under a prefect and an elected council of 36 members, with 3 Deputies and 2 Senators in French Parliament. Chief products and exports are sugar and rum. Other products include manioc, tapioca and vanilla. 33,557 pupils in lycée, primary and nursery schools; also a teachers' training course with 75 pupils. Roads, 400 miles; railways, 80 miles. Chief towns: Saint-Denis (capital), 36,096; Saint-Paul, 25,959.

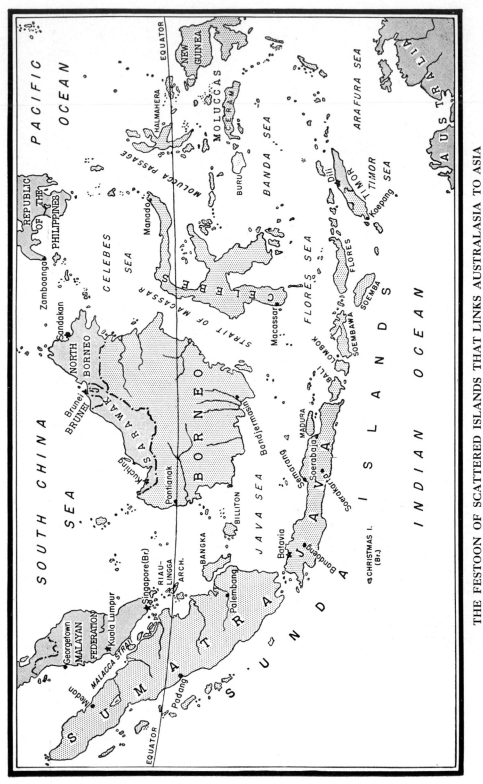

THE FESTOON OF SCATTERED ISLANDS THAT LINKS AUSTRALASIA TO ASIA

THROUGH TROPIC FAIRYLANDS

The Malays of the East Indies

Java, Sumatra, Celebes—to mention but a few of the islands in that huge group that makes up the East Indies—what a fascination even these names hold! These islands possess all the glamour of the East—princes and palaces, ancient temples, dark forests, impenetrable jungles—and though Java has become one of the chief sugar, rice, coffee and rubber-producing centers of the world, large portions of the other islands of this group remain unexplored. Tons of sugar are annually produced and there are many sugar factories. Every year many thousand steamers and sailing vessels touch these shores. Most of the people are of Malayan stock, who are peace-abiding, but some of the tribes still remain unsubdued and comparatively unknown. This chapter deals with Java, Bali, Sumatra, Madura and Celebes as they were under their Dutch conquerors. Since the end of the second World War, the islands have broken away from the Netherlands to form the Republic of Indonesia.

THE isles known as the East Indies, between the Malay Peninsula and Australia, are really the highest peaks of a vast, partly submerged volcanic mountain range. They consist of Java and Madura, Sumatra, a part of Borneo (which is dealt with in two other chapters) and Celebes, together with innumerable smaller islands—Bali and Lombok, the Moluccas, the Riau-Lingga and the Timor archipelagoes, Bangka and Billiton. Their area totals somewhat over 735,000 square miles and their combined population is over 76,000,000.

Java, the most important of these possessions, is a land of tropical rains, moist heat and equatorial lack of seasonal change, which makes the islands a naturalist's paradise. There are over five hundred species of orchids alone, and their perfume becomes poignant with the falling of the dew, while the evening sounds with the chirp, squeak, buzz and bumble of myriads of insects, including such strange ones as a musical worm and a bird-killing beetle. In the sun-starved jungle tangled with lantanas and silent with deep moss—that endless jungle which clothes the slopes of the extinct volcanoes—tigers and other big game prowl, rhinoceroses wear paths up the mountains and reptiles add their stench to the horrors of the unknown wilderness at night. But in the gardens of the beauty-loving natives and the luxurious European population, the tourist marvels at the sweetness of frangipani, the grace of pepper trees and the curiously twisted limbs of the gigantic figs that are planted for shade. Lotuses float upon the streams and ponds, and one finds vermilion fungi, tree-ferns, huge rasamalas (liquidambar trees), while the north coast of Java is fringed with mangroves.

Throughout Java, trees and shrubs grow to immense size, and the flowers and birds are of dazzling colors. More than four hundred bright-hued birds, including the peacock, are to be found in the islands. Indeed, some of the strange reptiles, insects, birds and flowers have not yet been given names. Botanists from all over the world come to Chibodas.

Many fruits grow plentifully. There are, for instance, over seven hundred varieties of bananas, ranging from little ones the size of a man's finger to those as long as his arm. The Javanese feed the big ones to their horses to make the animals have glossy coats. Mangoes, coconuts, pineapples and pears thrive equally.

The majority of the islands belong to the Republic of Indonesia. Of these, Java, which lies in the track of most of the winds of the Pacific and the Indian oceans, contains about two-thirds of the entire population of the East Indies. Jakarta (formerly Batavia) is the capital city.

Though Java does not look large on the map, it is actually nearly four times the size of the Netherlands. The population consists mainly of Javanese, though there are many Europeans, chiefly Dutch, and a half-million Chinese, besides Arabs.

225

PATIENTLY WAITING FOR A NIBBLE BY A ROADSIDE IN SUMATRA

A net attached to the four prongs of the rod hangs like a basket below the surface of the water so any fish that wander in cannot easily escape. The waters of Sumatra abound in marine life. Shell-fish are found in the rocks along the coast, and ponds and rivers yield a variety of other edible fish. This is a swamp between Soengei Gerong and Palembang.

Until the Malay inrush of the fifteenth century, the Hindus dominated the history of the island. The Portuguese came in 1520 and the Dutch toward the end of the sixteenth century, both in quest of the spice trade. The first Dutch settlement was that of a commercial company which for two centuries mishandled native affairs. In 1798 this company was broken up; and in 1816 the Dutch government took over the rule of Java, and wiser measures were put into effect. The Javanese did not yield to the Dutch without some trouble, however. The most serious outbreak in the early years of Dutch administration came in 1825. A native prince, Dipå Negårå, arose and he and his followers resisted Dutch rule for five years.

However, as the years went by, Dutch influence and power grew. They opened up previously unexplored regions and established great plantations where thousands of native workers were employed.

Between the two world wars, nevertheless, the Javanese began to show a desire for independence and their own government. When the Japanese occupied the island during the war, they fanned this desire into a vehement flame; and the Dutch returned in 1945 to find that the natives had established an Indonesian Republic. Fighting broke out between the Indonesians and the Dutch; and then there was an interval in which the Dutch seemed to be accepting the Republic as part of a proposed Netherlands Indonesian Union.

The United Nations intervened, but the conflict was not settled until late in 1949. Indonesia is now a republic.

Java is one of the most densely populated land masses in the world today. There are various reasons for this. For one thing, the land is immensely fertile, as we have seen. The fruits offered by nature and the cultivated products of the fields offer sustenance to an immense population. Timber trees, palm trees and bamboos provide ample building materials. Then, too, Java has a comparatively healthy climate. At times, indeed, the heat is excessive, but relief is often provided by brisk sea breezes. Though there are frequent thunderstorms near the high mountains, the island is not often subjected to storms which injure life or property.

The large plantations of Java are models of skillful planning and careful cultivation. Some of the land on which they are situated was once jungle, which had to be cleared away in order to make the soil available for agriculture. Even mountain slopes were leveled off for this same purpose. Today the well-drained mountainsides are covered with tea bushes, symmetrically laid out, and a model irrigation system has been planned for them. A variety of plants is grown, but the differing kinds of tea are due less to that fact than to the time and method of picking the leaves. The tea factories that are connected with the plantations are clean and airy buildings, in which modern machinery is employed.

A network of splendid railways, which has been made by European engineers,

AVA HAMILTON

JAVANESE WOMEN PRACTICE THE FINE ART OF MAKING BATIK

A pattern is first drawn on plain fabric, which may be linen. The pattern is then filled in with a waxlike liquid (the stage of the operation shown here). This is allowed to harden. When the material is dipped in dye, the wax repels the dye and only the background absorbs the color. Finally the entire fabric is boiled to remove the wax—and the result is batik.

A PLEASANT ROW OF HOUSES DESIGNED FOR HOT-CLIMATE LIVING

The dwellings are on Darmo Boulevard in Surabaya, Java. Wide windows let in air and steep roofs catch only slanting rays of the sun—cooling features for homes so near the equator.

PHOTOS, INFORMATION OFFICE, REPUBLIC OF INDONESIA

THE SPICK-AND-SPAN RAILWAY STATION IN WELTEVREDEN

"Taxis" await the traveler—sados, or pony-drawn carts. Weltevreden is an attractive suburb of Jakarta (which the Dutch once called Batavia), the capital of the Indonesian Republic.

A BATAK HOME ON SUMATRA WITH AN ELABORATE PEAKED ROOF

The Bataks build their houses on stilts and enter them by small staircases. They are large, often housing up to eight families. The upper story may be closed by a slatted screen (left).

229

Lewis

NEARING THE END OF THEIR WORK: COOLIES CARRYING THE DAY'S YIELD OF RUBBER TO THE FACTORY

Rubber is grown in Java. The precious latex, the milky sap of the trees, is obtained by making cuts spirally around the trunks and hanging pails beneath them. Besides plantation rubber, many tons of native rubber are annually obtained. The labor is performed with considerable skill by the Javanese, who are an industrious people. This procession wending its way among the young trees is bringing to the factory brimming pails of latex. The women carry them upon their heads, but the men hang one at either end of a pole across their shoulders.

A HARD-WORKING WOMAN OF JAVA

Rice is grown in Java at any time of the year, for there it is summer all year round. One field is harvested while the next is being sown; in another the paddy stands half grown, and in yet a fourth oxen wade knee-deep in watery mud, drawing wooden plows. This woman will be tired by night after her constant stoop to set out the young plants.

links up the plantations and towns. Wide roads, such as are seldom found in the East, make motoring delightful.

The natives, although small, are graceful, strong and well built. They are a branch of the Malay race and are intelligent and extremely polite. As the cultivated part of Java, which occupies more than one-third of the whole island, is covered with vast plantations of rice, coffee, sugar-cane, corn, cassava, sweet potatoes, groundnuts, soya beans, tobacco and lesser crops such as the Peruvian bark from which quinine is produced, the natives are nearly all agriculturists. They live in villages, or kampongs, and each village may contain from thirty to five hundred inhabitants, who live happily and peacefully tilling the land. Some work for hire on large estates, but the largest percentage of Indonesian land is owned by the individual farmers themselves. Though production of the staples, rice and corn, is plentiful, the population has increased with such rapidity that Indonesians have had difficulty raising all the food they need.

The villages are often surrounded by groves of palms, which sometimes quite hide the low huts. The houses are built of teak or bamboo, with thatched roofs, so that the native has nothing to fear from earthquakes, which in these volcanic regions are frequent. If his house gets

AGRICULTURAL STUDENTS IN JAKARTA REMOVING FISH FROM POND

Gadja Mada University at Jakarta, Java, has a fine agricultural college. These boys are students, working in rice fields that have been artificially flooded and stocked with carp. The fish fatten on the rice that drops into the water and so the fields are made to produce fish as well as grain. The boys are removing the carp from a pond that has been drained.

shaken down he soon builds a new one. Often each hut has a flower garden in front of it, which adds considerably to its picturesque appearance. Sometimes there are Chinese coolies in the villages, too, but they live by themselves. The beat of a drum made of a hollow log marks the passing hours, or warns the folk in case of an alarm.

The house of the better class native is made up of three separate structures which are often joined by corridors. There is the "oman," which contains the quarters of the family; then comes the "pandopo," where guests are received; and lastly the "pringitan," in which are the guests' sleeping quarters. These houses have no windows and no chimneys, but this does not really inconvenience the owners, as the Javanese pass a great deal of their time out of doors.

The poorer people live in huts made of bamboo, wood and rushes bound together with rattans. In western Java the floor is built some distance above the ground, so that cattle can be stabled underneath.

One of the best characteristics of the Javanese is his extreme affection for his family, which is generally a large one. The children have a happy time, as their fathers and mothers make much of them and seldom punish them. Little boys, with only a necklace for clothing, drive the tame buffaloes to their daily mud bath, or hunt for crickets, which they train to fight in imitation of their father's highly prized fighting cocks.

The Javanese marry at an early age, but only members of the rich or the upper classes have more than one wife. A wedding is an excuse for holding a feast and nearly everyone in the village gives some small gift of food. The dancing, feasting and merrymaking sometimes continue for days.

The chief food of the Javanese is rice, the cultivation of which is a laborious undertaking, though the climatic conditions are favorable. The people often work all day knee-deep in mud, which gives off evil gases and is the home of fierce insects. When they gather the harvest they are forced to work for days in a stooping position, cutting off the ears by hand one by one, for such an implement as a scythe is unknown.

WEAVING WHILE YOU WAIT

On her hand-fashioned loom, a native of Palembang, Sumatra, weaves a rattan mat. Palembang is the second largest city of Sumatra and is important as the port from which petroleum is exported. The Pladju refineries are close by. Palembang produces some native-grown rubber, and coal is mined near by. The city, with its own airport, can be reached by air, sea or rail.

KURKDJIAN

A SULTAN OF GOWA, at the southern tip of the four-fingured island of Celebes, wears a semi-European dress and has a retinue of but three body-guards. Of these, one shelters him beneath a pyong or state umbrella, the number of rings on which indicates the rank of the official. The retainer in epaulettes could defend him with the sword if need be.

A CARABAO, or water buffalo, quietly nibbles some grass along an Indonesian roadside. The animal carries a boy whose father carries a long, unwieldy plow — a curiously carved and painted affair. A furious beast when aroused, the carabao is, however, easily tamed and makes a docile draft animal. It is the Oriental farmer's most prized possession.

The Javanese love hunting and fishing. Sometimes a hunter may be so fortunate as to kill a tiger, for which he will receive a government bounty. He may sell the skin, but first of all he will pull out the teeth, claws and whiskers, which are considered to be powerful aids against evil spirits.

Some tigers may not be killed, because the people believe them to be friends who watch over their interests and frighten away other tigers. They think that the spirit of an ancestor resides in such a tiger. Wild pigs and deer are often to be seen; reptiles, including crocodiles, infest the swamps; and edible fish swarm in the rivers and coastal waters. With these sources of food at their disposal, the Javanese need not work hard to obtain a living, although they are gradually learning scientific methods.

Modern Industry Develops

While the chief occupations of the people on this enormously fertile island are in agriculture, industries spurted ahead during the ten years before the Japanese occupation. These included shipbuilding, automobile assembly, tires, glass and chemicals.

Most of the Javanese are Mohammedans. Among the many languages spoken in Indonesia, Javanese, Sundanese and Madurese are the most important. Malay is understood almost everywhere.

Jakarta, formerly Batavia, is the most important city in the East Indies. It is situated in one of the biggest sugar, rice and rubber-producing centers of the world. Part of the city, with its white stucco houses roofed with red tile, is quite modern. Thousands of miles of excellent railways run to all parts of the island, and a telegraph system has been in use since 1858. Indonesian has become the language of instruction in the schools, and Dutch-speaking professors at the university in Jakarta were given five years in which to learn Indonesian.

A Harbor Scented with Spices

Before Jakarta with its nearby port of Tandjong Priok is reached, we can smell the almost overpowering scent of spices that is wafted from the island. A train takes us from the harbor to the best part of the town, where there are good hotels, telephones and other modern comforts. Fine houses and offices, built in the Dutch style, are to be seen. There are well laid out squares and gardens, and wide roads, where Europeans in white, and Chinese, Malays and Javanese in their colored costumes add to the scene.

Many of the Javanese women living in the larger towns wear European dress, as do some of the men. The usual garment of the women, however, is the sarong— a wide piece of cloth fastened under the armpits and reaching nearly to the ground. When in public they also wear a short coat, with a scarf draped over the shoulders or tied around the waist. The women fasten their hair in a tight knot with pins; the men wear little turbans. Rings and bracelets are worn by both men and women, and the children frequently have anklets.

The old Dutch buildings, some of which were built in the seventeenth century, are well worth seeing. The city church is over two hundred years old, and has a fine pulpit and carvings. The imposing town hall dates from 1710. The Java Bank is housed in a fine modern building. A wide canal runs through the principal street and in it the Javanese bathe night and morning.

The city of Jakarta is actually divided into two parts. The new, modern part is a garden suburb known as Weltevreden. The tourist is delighted to find that it is one vast park checked off in mammoth public squares and gardens, fragrant with the perfume of orchids.

Old Section of the City

This portion of the city was known as old Batavia, famous for its sidewalk bazaars. Tourists enjoy the native banquets where rice is served with curry, chicken, peppers, fried fish and fried bananas, followed by wonderful coffee.

By the Tiger Canal live some thirty thousand Chinese—shopkeepers, hawkers and laborers—and here the buildings

OUTDOOR SPORT NEAR JAKARTA

It is all smooth sailing on the canals that connect Jakarta, Java's chief city, with the sea. The older part of the town is built on low, flat ground. The newer part—Batavia Centrum—is on higher land and is a beautiful, modern city. Near by is a fine harbor and an important airfield. Batavia Centrum used to be called Weltevreden, which is Dutch for "well satisfied."

and bazaars are Chinese joss houses, or temples, with their idols.

Semarang and Surabaya (Soerabaya) are also large towns. Surabaya is linked up east and west by good railways, and was the headquarters of the Dutch military authorities before World War II. Here are half-ruined fortifications which were built years ago by the Dutch.

Up until the early years of the twentieth century two strange states, called Jokja and Solo—short for Djokjakarta and Soerakarta—still existed in the center of Java. They were governed by a sultan and king respectively, and the old medieval forms of courtesy and court etiquette were still practiced. The tiny states seemed like kingdoms out of a fairy tale, complete with airy palaces and court nobles decked in gorgeous uniforms. There one could step into the long ago.

However, the king and sultan were rulers more in name than in reality. While

their states still existed, they had to obey Dutch officials.

At Jokja there are over a thousand temples, and strangely carved ruins add to the general picturesqueness. Here the chief industry is the weaving and dyeing of the beautiful cloth that is famous in Java. The cloth is woven without a loom and the wonderful patterns are tediously made by dyeing the cloth after the patterns have been covered with a wax that keeps out the dye. The work is known as "batik."

At Boro Budur, in the center of the island, are marvelous ruins dating back to the ninth century—relics of an ancient Hindu-Buddhist civilization that existed before the Arabs swept through the land in the fifteenth century. The ruins cover a small hill and are pyramidal in shape, mounting up the hillside in a series of terraces. There are five terraces and on them are the carvings that have made

237

LEWIS

THEIR TRAILING SARONGS, no less than their good features, show that these two young people of Bali are of high caste and that they are the aristocrats of their island. They live luxuriously in their richly decorated dwelling, waited upon by large retinues. The Balinese are of the same race as the Javanese, but they are of finer physique and taller.

LEWIS

ON BALI, a mountainous and volcanic island of the Sunda group, in the tail of the Malay Archipelago, rice is the leading crop. The grain is stored in thatched and painted wooden paddy-holders which stand by the roadsides. The one above rests on a pedestal of basalt, a volcanic rock of which the island is chiefly composed. The woman has a basket of rice.

239

CROP INSURANCE—A VIGILANT WATCHER KEEPS GUARD IN A TREE

So important are their crops to the Balinese that they take no chances on losing any part of them. From his vantage point atop a tall tree, a crop watcher keeps a sharp lookout.

SELF-SERVICE IN SUMATRA WHERE "PINCHING THE FRUIT" IS PERMITTED

Indonesian women shop for food at the *passar* (market) in Soengei Gerong, Sumatra. To leave her hands free, the young mother carries her plump baby in a sling, which looks comfortable.

241

LEWIS

IN THE PADDY FIELDS there is always work to be done—ploughing, sowing, planting out and reaping. This Javanese woman has come to that last stage in the year's work, and her labor is more exacting than the harvesting of more civilized people, for she has to cut every stem separately with her knife. Now she is carrying the sheaves home for storage.

BY A TEMPLE, time-worn and overgrown with moss and lichen, two men of Bali talk together, but not as equal to equal. He of the trailing sarong is a high-caste Hindu (Brahman); the other, of a lower caste. Hinduism spread throughout Indonesia in the early centuries of the Christian Era, but remained strong only in Bali. Most Indonesians are Mohammedans.

BALINESE DANCER—SMILING MASK AND LONG FINGERNAILS

The dance in Bali usually depicts some phase in the life of a native god. Like most Oriental dancing, it consists mainly of sinuous hand and arm movements, with very little foot movement.

Boro Buaur so famous. It has been estimated that there are three miles of carvings. The building of the temple must have been an even more stupendous task than the erection of the Great Pyramid in Egypt.

To the east of Java is a chain of islands, of which each one possesses strange and wonderful scenery. The largest and most important is the volcanic island of Bali, which is peopled by natives similar to those of Java, but bigger, stronger and more primitive. Here the natives, who are Hindus, not Mohammedans, are more religious, especially the women and children, who spend a great deal of their time praying and making offerings of spice, scent and flowers at the little temple courts seen all over the island.

Brass Drums and Fighting-cocks

It is a wonderful sight to see the women going to the temple with baskets of flowers balanced on their heads. Everything is peaceful, save when the brass drums resound. The men, in elaborate attire with flowers in their hair, bear their fighting-cocks against their chests or in ornate gold cages.

The villages of Bali, unlike those of Java, are enclosed by long, low mud walls, inside which the children play happily all day long. In the south are beautiful rice fields which rise up the hillsides in terraces. These terraces are very beautiful in Java, but in Bali they are even more wonderful. Among the most interesting sights to be seen in the island are the graceful dances performed by the young girls. The dancers are dressed like little goddesses and go through many elaborate poses, doubtless depicting the story of some Hindu god.

Bali is separated by a narrow but deep channel from the neighboring island of Lombok, yet the animal and vegetable life of the two islands is entirely different. The wild life of Bali is like that of Asia, but Lombok, with its marsupials and white cockatoos, resembles Australia. It really seems that the narrow channel between these two islands definitely divides one continent from the other.

A Vast Unexplored Region

Sumatra, astride the equator, is three times as large as Java and thirteen times the size of the Netherlands, but it is composed largely of unexplored jungles. The civilization of this island is probably of Hindu origin. There are Sanskrit words in the various native languages. And as in Java, the Mohammedans, then the Dutch came and their sovereignty was gradually but surely extended. The British acquired a foothold in Sumatra in 1685, but vacated in accordance with a treaty signed in 1824.

A vast range of mountains called the Barisans runs down its entire length like a spine. Although there are many rivers, those that flow west are too short for navigation. Huge lakes and swamps, containing crocodiles and crabs; dangerous and unexplored jungles inhabited by tigers and savages, all combine to make Sumatra a mysterious land.

The climate is similar to that of Java, but hotter. The inhabitants are a varied mixture of Malays, Hindus, Arabs and Chinese. The Malays include the Bataks, the Achinese and the Menangkabus. The Bataks are an interesting people—small but strong. They have known how to write since prehistoric days and their ancient books have pages of tree bark inscribed in brilliant ink. The Menangkabus are pure Malay. They live in the mountain regions of Padang which is believed by many to be the original seat of Malay stock. The Menangkabus must not be confused with the Orang-Kubus, a savage people who shun all contact.

With the exception of the Bataks, who are Christian, the inhabitants of Sumatra are mainly Mohammedans. Owing to the mixture of Arab blood, they are inclined to be stricter in their religious observances than the Javanese. Some make the long journey to Mecca, and on their return they are greatly honored by their friends and relatives.

Medan and the Rubber Plantations

Padang, the capital, is the chief town. Here we may see the results of European

LEWIS

A FAIR MAID OF BALI. Her dress and the tapestries behind her are from the looms of the island's skillful weavers. Like Bali itself, her costume is bright and highly ornate. In her hair are jewels in the form of tropical blossoms, and her earrings are heavy, golden whorls. As a mark of her high social standing, the nails of her left hand are uncut.

LEWIS

A CONSIDERABLE PERSONAGE, this Balinese chieftain displays both his wealth and his rank upon his person. Over his right shoulder we can see the jeweled hilt of his kris, a Malayan dagger that he wears in the back of his sash. The cultivated Balinese, like the Javanese, are an innately æsthetic people and delight in the vivid hues of the tropics.

VILLAGE ON STILTS, CELEBES

Celebes has an amazingly long coastline in comparison with its area, and much of its land is near the water. The equator passes through the island, the climate is torrid and the tropical vegetation is generally dense. Yet the islanders have learned how to take advantage of the sea and river breezes by building their towns near—or even in—the water.

"THE PLOWMAN HOMEWARD PLODS HIS WEARY WAY"

A villager of Gowa returns home from his fields in the early evening with his helpers—children and buffaloes. Coffee, indigo, cacao, sugar cane, the manioc root and tobacco are some of the crops raised in the rich soil of Celebes. Bamboo stems furnish material for housing, furniture, piping and utensils; and the leaves make good thatch for the roofs.

INTRICATE STONE SCULPTURE ON A BALINESE TEMPLE

The *pura* (temple) in Bali consists of three enclosed courts, the inner one containing the actual
temple building. Most Balinese are Hindus, and the temples are dedicated to the god Siva.

249

LEWIS

THE JAVANESE, with their expressive features, their punctilious courtesy and high intelligence, are termed "the flowers of the Malay race." For when, in the late fifteenth century, Mohammedanism became the religion of all the East India Islands except Bali and Lombok, it superseded a Hindu-Buddhist culture of unknown antiquity. That the older civilization was one more highly developed than that which followed is pretty well proven by the character of the ruins of temples, tombs and cities that lie buried in the jungle.

A DANCER OF BALI, just over ten years old, pauses—unmoving, delicate, graceful, under her towering headdress. She looks much like the statue of a Hindu goddess. Her costume is of gold-brocaded silk, and her collar, girdle, bracelets, rings and armlets are of gilded metal set with jewels. When she dances her whole being—from wide, expressive eyes to quick, sure feet—comes alive in uncanny harmony with the music of an orchestra that the Balinese call a gamelan. Balinese dancers start training almost from babyhood.

KAPOK MILL IN SUMATRA

This kapok mill near Palembang, Sumatra, was built by the Japanese when they occupied the island during World War II. After the war Sumatra joined other territory formerly under Dutch rule to form the Republic of Indonesia.

around the trunks in order to catch the thick, milky juice that oozes out. This is poured into cans and taken away to be prepared.

South of Achin, the northern part of Sumatra, live other Malay tribes, such as the Bataks, Korinchis and Jambis. The Bataks consist of six tribes who speak two different dialects. They are governed by hereditary chiefs who took over after their magician-king Singa Maharadja was killed in the hostilities against the Dutch in 1907. They have their own script and the upper classes can read and write. Much of their writing deals with magic and astrology. They are an agricultural people and, unlike many tribes, make use of the plow. Their main crop is rice. They also raise cattle and horses, and are skilled workers in metal. In spite of their relatively high degree of culture, there were some remnants of human sacrifice until the early twentieth century. However, many of their people are being gradually converted to Mohammedanism and Christianity.

The houses of the Bataks are built on poles. They have high roofs, and sometimes there are snakes carved above them to guard the owners. Little wooden staircases serve as entrances. The buildings are quite big, and often as many as eight families live together. One fire, which is never allowed to go out, is used for cooking by all of them, but each family has its own room.

occupation, though most of the island is still undeveloped. Medan is a new town, with cool, white buildings, and is surrounded by plantations where one finds the native Achinese and also numerous bands of Chinese coolies.

The rubber plantations are interesting. The rubber is procured from a beautiful tree, with strong, shiny leaves, and the trees stand in rows in gloomy forests where the sun can hardly penetrate. When the latex, or sap, is rising the trunks are notched, and cups are hung

The men and women wear cloth dyed with the indigo plant, and their fingers are always stained with this dye. Dogs and pigs run about in this village and act as scavengers. The pigs especially show that the people are not Mohammedans, as these animals are considered unclean by the members of that religion. Here, as in Java and other parts of Sumatra, the people are fond of dancing and give numerous displays. Nearly all the Bataks, as well as most of the other peoples of Sumatra, are farmers. The harrowing and plowing are done by buffaloes, who seem to understand the work. They pull the harrow between the young rice plants and never trample even one underfoot.

it looks somewhat like a starfish with an arm torn off the side that corresponds to the west coast of the island.

Here, perhaps, the scenery of the East Indies is to be seen at its best. Gorges and precipices abound in the south, and, when the walls of these project, a wonderful mass of vegetation, starred with gorgeous flowers, hangs down like a natural curtain. Most of the country is cov-

© Ernest Peterffy

COOLIES AT WORK ON THE COALING STATION IN MACASSAR HARBOR

The Dutch island of Celebes, compared to a star-fish because of its four protruding limbs, is separated from Borneo on the west by Macassar Strait. Macassar on the southwest coast is the chief town and ranks next to Batavia as a Dutch port; it has a lively trade, and its harbor possesses a government coaling station and two well ordered landing quays.

Little bamboo houses on poles may be seen under a palm or a banana grove near the fields. From these shelters lines, to which black tassels or bits of tin are attached, are stretched over the fields. The children manipulate the lines from the little lookout huts and so keep the beautiful but destructive paddy-bird away from their father's rice fields.

One of the four large Sunda Islands is Celebes, which is separated from the island of Borneo by the famous Strait of Macassar. Its outline is irregular and

ered with almost impenetrable forests, which we can cross only by the hardly noticeable paths leading to tiny villages.

A curious feature about Celebes is that it possesses animals and birds which are not found on any of the other islands. Only one hundred and sixty kinds of birds are found, but ninety of these do not exist anywhere else in the East Indies. The animals also are peculiar to the island, and even several species of its butterflies are unique.

Around the coast the natives dive for

LEWIS

THE VILLAGERS of Bali display the same love of gorgeous color as the high-caste Balinese of that brilliant, jungle-forested land. Caste is a very real thing in Bali, which has retained the older religion of the Hindus; though in Java, from which the island is separated by only a narrow strait, the people are Mohammedans and caste as such is disregarded.

THIS JAVANESE COUPLE from the east end of the island is typical of the East Indian branch of the Malay race, an amiable, agricultural people, unlike the indolent natives of Malaya in their capacity for hard work. They are extremely polite. The woman wears the native "sarong" and a sash; the man has a jacket as well and a strip of cloth worn turbanwise.

pearls and catch turtles for a living, but the products which come from the forests are the most important. The three principal Malayan tribes are the Macassars, the Mandars and the Bugis. The Macassars are fine men, well built and strong, and they love running, wrestling and hunting.

To the east of Celebes is that archipelago known as the Moluccas, which contains several large islands. There are Malay settlements around the coast of one of them, Buru, but the interior, which is largely dense forest, is peopled by strange tribes. These, though they are possibly of Papuan origin, are a yellowish-brown in color, of slight build and usually below medium height. They live in scattered communities and are almost untouched by civilization. Ceram, to the east of Buru, is a larger and more densely populated island, with Malay tribes on the coast, and the Alfoories (Alfuries), a far less civilized people, farther inland.

The end of World War II and the Japanese occupation did not mean the end of strife. To enlist the support of the Indonesians, the Japanese had encouraged the desire of the natives for self-government and fanned their resentment of the Dutch. The result was that when the Dutch returned to the islands after the war, they found a powerful group of Indonesians already setting up a Republic of Indonesia, including Java, Sumatra and Madura. Fighting broke out between the Indonesians and the Dutch, which continued off and on into 1949. On December 27, 1949, Indonesia (a republic since August 1950) received full independence; Irian (Western New Guinea) was still claimed by the Netherlands.

INDONESIA: FACTS AND FIGURES

THE COUNTRY

A group of islands in the Malay Archipelago lying along the equator between the North Pacific Ocean and the Indian Ocean. The total area is approximately 575,893 square miles and the population 76,500,000. (This includes Indonesian Borneo; for Borneo Facts and Figures, see page 270.)

Area and population (estimate) of principal groups of islands are: Java and Madura, 50,594 square miles, population, 41,614,000; Sumatra, 163,557 square miles, 12,000,000; Riouw and Lingga Archipelagos, 3,121 square miles, 107,700; Bangka, 4,611 square miles, 205,400; Billiton, 1,866 square miles, 73,400; Celebes, 69,277 square miles, 3,781,500; Bali and Lombok, 4,069 square miles, 1,776,200; Molucca Islands, 33,315 square miles, 525,600; Western New Guinea (also claimed by Indonesia), 159,375 square miles, 345,700; Timor Archipelago, 24,449 square miles, 1,657,400.

GOVERNMENT

A governor general represented the Netherlands in the East Indies until the United States of Indonesia received full independence in 1949. Indonesia became a republic in August 1950, and has a president, vice-president, Cabinet and a one-house legislature. The Republic is a single state with ten provinces.

COMMERCE AND INDUSTRIES

Agriculture constitutes the chief occupation of the bulk of the population, with large plantations being operated by foreign interests, as well as many, many small Indonesian farms. The chief products are: sugar, rubber, coffee, tea, rice, corn, cassava, tobacco, pepper, copra, kapok and cinchona (from which quinine is obtained). Fisheries are of considerable importance, and fish is an important part of the Indonesian diet. Native industries include the preparation of agricultural and forest products for export, weaving, dyeing and metal work. Tin is mined in Bangka, Billiton, Riau and Sumatra; coal in Borneo and Sumatra; petroleum found in Borneo, Sumatra and Java.

COMMUNICATIONS

Naturally there is considerable communication by water. Railway mileage, 4,611; road mileage, 43,700. Government owned telegraph, 4,573 miles; telephone, 16,921 miles; 129 radio stations. Air service.

RELIGION AND EDUCATION

Entire religious liberty; Protestant and Catholic missions; bulk of natives Mohammedans. Public and private elementary schools for Europeans, Chinese and natives; instruction in Indonesian and various dialects. There are about 27,500 elementary schools with around 5,500,000 pupils. There are professional, trade and technical training schools.

CHIEF TOWNS

Jakarta (formerly Batavia), capital, Java, 2,800,000; Surabaya (Soerabaja), Java, 800,000; Bandung, Java, 750,000; Jogjakarta (Djokjakarta), Java, 500,000; Solo (Surakarta), Java, 500,000; Medan, Sumatra, 500,000; Macassar, Celebes, 400,000; Palembang, Sumatra, 350,000; Padang, Sumatra, 150,000.

BORNEO THE ISLE OF SUMMER

Its Forest Folk and the Dayaks

To the extent that civilization demands a supply of rubber, every rubber-producing country is of interest. Borneo is one such country. It is a land of tropical jungle in which the mammoth orangutan and the gibbon, the python and the crocodile abound. Until comparatively recent times, Borneo was regarded as the home of the "wild men"—the head-hunting Dayaks. However, under the rule of the British (and of the Dutch, while they retained control of part of the island), piracy and head-hunting practically came to an end. This vast tropical area, which was under Japanese military occupation during World War II, has large sections that are still unexplored.

BORNEO is one of the two or three largest islands in the world. A part of the Malay Archipelago, it lies north of Java in the China Sea. As it rests on a submarine plateau, its coastal waters are not deep and there are few neighboring small islands, though Banguey and Labuan lie off the northwest coast and the Karimatas off the southwest.

The mainland rises in a hump of huge mountains densely forested, with some sixty kinds of timber which is extremely valuable but for the most part almost hopelessly inaccessible. Ferns, vines and exotic wild flowers add to the impenetrability of a jungle nourished by tropic warmth and bounteous rainfall. In Sarawak, in northwest Borneo, which is hemmed between the mountains and the sea, there is all of two hundred inches of rainfall per year, the heaviest of it during the northwest monsoon which blows from October to March, though there are thunderstorms and sometimes torrential downpours even during the southwest monsoon which controls the climate the rest of the year.

Vivid sunshine gives way to sudden wind squalls followed immediately by violent cloudbursts, while the rivers come cascading from the mountains till they can widen between wooded banks heavy with the pungency of rich black soil and wet foliage, or they become swirling rapids till at last they reach the fertile clearings of the plantations and the mangrove swamps of the coast. In other parts of Borneo the rainfall, though perhaps only half as abundant, still averages a hundred inches a year. As the equator passes through the island, there are no seasons. On the coastal swamps and plains it is always hot; at Sarawak it ranges from 70 to 90 degrees by day, but is cooler at night.

Borneo is a land of mystery and romance. Even in these days, when the darkest and most remote corners of the earth have yielded up their secrets to explorers, there are vast tracts of forest country in Borneo which are quite unknown. British and Malay settlements are situated around the coastal area, but the heart of the island is inhabited by savages who are primitive and wild. It is suspected that some of them are cannibals, and a few of them are undoubtedly still head-hunters.

Borneo is a land of mystery because there is so much still to be learned about its people and its natural resources. We know that in its forests there are valuable gutta-percha and rubber trees, coconut and sago palms, rattan canes and ironwood trees. It is rich, too, in orchids and all kinds of tropical flowering plants. In various districts there are coal, oil, gold, diamonds and other less important minerals.

Borneo is a land of romance because of its history. Of the original peoples who inhabited the island we know but little. When, centuries ago, it was overrun by Malays, these native tribes were driven inland. They still live in the heart of the forests—the Klemantans, Muruts, Kayans, Kenyahs and Punans—savages

A KLEMANTAN CHIEF, poised for battle, wears a war coat of the skin of a panther he has slain. His wooden shield, painted with tribal symbols, helps to ward off the spring of a cat, a tossed spear or the blows of an opponent's sword. Many such warriors have been coaxed out of the jungles to work in the mines and oil fields of the coastal settlements.

HOSE

AMONG THE KENYAHS, the warriors paint upon their shields conventional designs of human faces, then ornament these grotesque escutcheons with tufts of hair from the heads of their slaughtered enemies. Their chief weapons are the sword and spear. Under Western influence native warfare has, however, been reduced chiefly to the avenging of injuries.

259

whose principal weapon is the blow-pipe, whose chief occupations are hunting and fighting. A sixth and very numerous people of Borneo are the Ibans, or Sea Dayaks, or Dyaks, on the lower reaches of the main rivers of Sarawak, but also to be found in British North Borneo and the adjacent Indonesian territory. (This territory was controlled by the Dutch until 1949.)

Control of Borneo is divided between Britain and Indonesia, the Dutch having withdrawn after Indonesia was granted her independence. The Dutch established trading posts as early as 1604, but gained little authority for more than two hundred years. The natives were difficult to control and pirates were numerous. It was extremely dangerous for a white man to venture far from the fortified towns.

The first white man who gained any influence over the natives was an Englishman, James Brooke, who had served the East India Company before he determined to put down piracy and civilize the inhabitants of Borneo. His resolve was due to a voyage to China during which his vessel made its way among islands marvelous

AVA HAMILTON

THE LANGUR, OR HANUMAN, MONKEY OF INDIA, BORNEO AND SUMATRA

Langurs, distinguished by their long tails, beetling black eyebrows and general grayish color, are native to Indonesia as well as to India where they are free to roam the cities unrestricted.

BORNEO YOUNGSTERS ON RIVER RAFT "WATCH THE BIRDIE"

The somewhat surprising name of this river is the Sooengookween, a tributary of the Barito in southern Borneo. It flows past the town of Banjermasin, a port of more than 65,000 people.

HOSE

THESE YOUNG IBANS of the Sea Dayak group of Bornean tribes wear a gala dress rich with ivory, shell and silver and gay with gold-embroidered scarlet. For a hot climate the boy's attire, which conceals none of his splendid muscular development, would seem the more appropriate, though even his sword and turban are elaborate with trophies of the chase.

THIS DAYAK GIRL wears a corselet of rattan hoops covered with brass rings, above a skirt fringed with coins, to match those around her chest. Her shell necklaces are heavy with silver, as are her belt and bracelets, while the rings in her ears conceal little bells. Her comb is decorated with silver filigree and tinsel. No wonder she looks weighted down!

for their scenery but inhabited by savage tribes who were the scourge of the South Seas. Eventually the young man equipped a large yacht and trained a picked crew of twenty for the adventure of civilizing the wild men of Borneo and others equally barbarous. When he started, in 1838, he was but thirty-six years of age; but he was made of heroic stuff.

When he landed at Sarawak in 1839 he found several Dayak tribes, ferocious head-hunters, in revolt against the ruling Sultan. The Sultan's uncle, Rajah Muda Hassim, accepted Brooke's proffered aid; and the Englishman, with his small crew and some Javanese who had joined them, fought a winning battle. In view of this service the Rajah insisted upon abdicating in Brooke's favor, though the Sultan did not confirm the title till two years later.

Rajah Brooke and the Pirates

Brooke now determined to suppress piracy for the sake of developing the commerce of the archipelago; and to this end he first attempted negotiations with the chiefs of the most warlike tribes, but to no avail. He then made successive expeditions against the Dayaks, Malays and Arabs who had been making the most ferocious raids upon white traders, in the course of which large numbers of the pirates were slain. On his return to London in 1847 he received high honors and was made consul-general to Borneo. The name of Sir James (Rajah) Brooke became world famous. For over a generation he ruled wisely, suppressed most of the head-hunting in British Borneo and persuaded large numbers of Dayaks to take up agriculture.

Now the Chinese who had been working in the alluvial gold deposits in Upper Sarawak sacked Kuching in 1867, burned Brooke's house, and would have taken his life but that his nephew raised a force of the Malays and Dayaks of the district and suppressed the insurgency. This nephew succeeded Sir James in 1868 and the office of rajah became hereditary in their family. North Borneo is now governed like a crown colony as an independent State under the protection of Great Britain.

Plantations and Lumbering

Besides Sarawak, British Borneo (which became a protectorate in 1881, and which consists mainly of Mohammedan Malays, with a sprinkling of white men and Chinese) includes Brunei and North Borneo. All have huge coffee, coconut and tobacco plantations and important lumber companies.

Brunei is a tiny Mohammedan state and there are very few Europeans. The chief town, Brunei, is so subject to the rise and fall of the water level that the British Resident who conducts the administration had his house built upon piles at the end of the river, while the jungle-clad hills rise up about the town. The old native quarter is, indeed, built entirely over the river and some of the dwellings actually float upon the water. The market venders, usually women in wide straw hats, array their stalls with many brass and silver articles to tempt the purse of the traveler, and with cotton cloth and foodstuffs, each in a little boat anchored to the pile dwellings, and to these the purchasers make their way in other boats under a bombardment of native vociferation. The scene presents mingled odors of fresh-caught fish, rotting piles, and over-hot humanity, while toward evening a million frogs play bass in a symphony of bird and insect sounds—and mosquitoes and sometimes ants puncture one with fiery thrusts and from the nearest jungle one may sometimes hear the cries of a band of monkeys.

As to British North Borneo, it has a coastline of over nine hundred miles and in Sandakan, on the east coast, the one fine natural harbor of the island. At this point Borneo lies so near the Philippines that ships can make the crossing in less than a day. The tourists will find good hotel accommodations at Sandakan, with such touches of Western civilization as an automatic telephone service, a scentific society and a racing association.

Sultan Wore Huge Diamonds

The portion of the island formerly called Dutch Borneo is now Indonesian

TRADE CENTER IN WEST BORNEO

Natives discharge their wares in Pontianak, capital of the state of West Borneo, which is now part of the Republic of Indonesia. The city is the center of Chinese and native trade, and many of the boats have been en route for days and weeks before reaching Pontianak. Resident Chinese dealers buy from the native producers. The chief commodities are rubber and copra.

Borneo or Kalimantan. It is a part of the Republic of Indonesia. On the whole, it is very much less developed than British Borneo, partly because of the sparsity of its population which is confined to settlements along the rivers. It is under the jurisdiction of a governor who is appointed by and is responsible to the central Indonesian Government.

At one time, during Dutch administration, this part of Borneo was under a Sultan. The Sultan had a palace lighted by electricity and protected from the rains by a galvanized iron roof, which was his great pride. He wore incredibly large diamonds as part of his attire and kept fighting cocks. In those days the Sultan's subjects were addicted to piracy and head-hunting, and they are still somewhat wild. Today, however, there are Arabs and Chinese in the mines and fisheries and on the plantations. The Chinese conduct trade with their own country. Indonesian Borneo contains a wealth of minerals. There are big oil fields at Balik Papan, and new wells are continually being brought in. There are diamond fields, of which probably the richest lies at Martapura, and the timber (ironwood) and rubber industries are of considerable consequence because of the value of their products. In Martapura and several other districts of the southeastern division there is shipbuilding, iron-forging, diamond-polishing, gold and silver-smithery.

Borneo's location naturally directs her trade to China and Australia and to the Philippines. One expects her trading vessels to go forth laden with ironwood and rattan, rice, tobacco and spices, hemp, gums and resins. It is more surprising to find in their holds the gelantinous birds' nests found and collected in the vast sea caves of coastal regions, a Chinese delicacy, and *bêche-de-mer,* for the making of Chinese soup. There are also armadillo skins, seed pearls, gambier—a substance used in tanning and dyeing—camphor, and mineral oil from a rich field at Miri.

Need Roads and Railroads

One drawback to development in Borneo is the lack of good roads and railroads, though there are bridle paths and native trails. River boats connect the villages and coasting steamers ply from port to port.

Warring Tribes of the Interior

For the most part, as we have indicated, the dominant native population is Malay. More interesting as a matter of study are the savage races of the interior. Most of these tribes live in communities ruled by chiefs, but numbers of them wander about in the jungle, living on wild fruits and the flesh of wild animals. Being of different races and speaking languages that are unintelligible outside their own districts, they are constantly making warfare upon their neighbors. There is a good deal of sickness among the natives, due chiefly to lack of cleanliness about their persons and the food they consume.

In such a country as Borneo, with its thousands of miles of forest and jungle, the people of the interior are mainly dependent for their livng upon the wild creatures found there, though sago is cultivated in some places, just as rice is widely grown in the more civilized districts. Fortunately for the aborigines, deer, wild pigs, wild cattle and other animals are plentiful. These are snared in traps or are brought down by a poisoned dart.

The Hairy "Man of the Woods"

Monkeys, which are numerous, are killed and eaten; and here reference must be made to Borneo's distinctive wild animal—the orang-utan. This great ape, whose name means literally "man of the woods," grows to a height of over four feet; its hair is reddish in color; and the extraordinary length of its arms enables it to travel at an extraordinary pace by swinging itself from tree to tree. Elephants also are found, but only in North Borneo. The tarsier, a mouselike creature that lives on insects, but is really a primate, and thus belongs to the same order as do the apes, is also a native of Borneo. It lives in trees and is most active at night.

There are tapirs and ant-eaters, a monitor lizard, pythons and cobras. There are

NOT THE FAMILY WASHING, BUT FISH DRYING IN THE SUN

Just outside Kuching, capital of Sarawak, is a thriving community of Chinese fishermen who make their home there. After curing and drying their catch, they sell it in the Kuching market.

267

minas, birds that can be taught to speak. The honey-bear, by which is meant the little Malay bear, a lover of the stores of the wild bee of the jungle, is common in this land of queer creatures. There is also a mouse-deer or plandok, a dainty creature no longer than a rabbit and not nearly so heavy. A tender morsel for anyone or anything that can catch it, it goes leaping soundlessly through the brush, its big eyes seemingly round with fright.

Flying-frogs and "Pepper Ants"

At twilight the flying-foxes play by launching themselves parachute-like from the branches to the ground. There are even flying-frogs in the swamp lands. Less attractive wild swine, many with hornlike tusks, trot about in gluttonous herds, their little black eyes savage with hatred of the intruder. There are so-called Borneo ponies in British North Borneo; and if one is to enumerate several other living creatures that play a prominent rôle on this extraordinary island, one must name the fire ants and "pepper ants" with their painful bite, the sand-flies, the wood-leeches and in the marshes, the horse-leeches. The coastal waters are full of sharks. Scientists judge from the presence of a number of these species of animal life that the island may once have been connected with the continent of Asia.

Spiked Fruit and Pitcher Plants

Among other hazards of life in the jungle might be mentioned the durian, a large fruit covered with stout pyramidal spikes. When such an object falls from the top of a tall tree it really injures people. Its flesh is prized by the natives, though white men are appalled by its odor. Another strange thing found in Borneo is the pitcher plant, some of which are large enough to hold a quart of rain water.

Among the many interesting things to be seen in Borneo are the "long-houses," the wooden buildings in which communities generally dwell together. All the native tribes, with one exception, build these long-houses. The Punans, who wander from spot to spot, but usually inhabit the densest part of the jungle, do not lead any kind of village life. When some of them have been induced to settle, they have only been able to construct the rudest of houses, a poor imitation of those of their neighbors.

The long-houses of the various tribes differ only in size, in certain details of construction and in their decoration. One such house may be set up to accommodate fifty people; others will hold as many as three, and even five hundred. A long-house is built of wood and may be as much as four hundred yards in length with a long gallery, which serves as the village street, running along the front. The structure is divided into a number of rooms in which separate families lodge.

In a Kayan "Long-house"

If we were to peep into one of the rooms we should see that it was about twenty-five feet wide, that it contained several alcoves or sleeping-places screened off at the sides, and that in the centre of the mat-covered floor was a rough fireplace made of a slab of clay in a wooden frame. For ventilation and light, a trapdoor, opened and closed at will, is fixed in the roof.

In addition to the family fireplaces, the tenants of a long-house have access to other fires that are kindled at intervals along the outer gallery. Some of these are kept continually alight. Over one of these communal fireplaces—usually the one near the chief's quarters—is to be seen a row of dried human heads, together with various charms and war trophies.

All such native dwelling-houses are built along, or near, the water. This is because rivers are the great highways of Borneo. There are no roads except in those coastal settlements where towns have sprung up, and there are not even beaten tracks of any importance through the jungle. The long-houses are built upon piles because they thus offer better protection against marauding head-hunters; but the piles must be tall ones, for were the house not raised high from

WARRIORS OF THE QUARRELSOME SEA DAYAKS IN FULL DRESS

Muscular and graceful, these young men belong to the most warlike tribe in Borneo. Two of them have decorated their swords with tufts of human hair and all of them are wearing ivory armlets. The man on the right has a number of fibre wristlets which were once used as currency, a necklace of nuts, and, finally, earrings.

the ground, the sleeping inmates might be speared through the floor from below. We shall see that under the house are stored the boats that are not in actual use. Here, too, will be some of the livestock of the village—pigs, dogs, goats and fowls—all of which add to the unsanitary condition, however convenient the arrangement.

Of the native peoples mentioned, the Sea Dayaks, or Ibans, are the best known to white men. This is mainly because they are numerous in Sarawak. Stouter in build than his land brothers, the Sea Dayak has well proportioned limbs, his figure is neat and almost boyish, and he walks with an air that stamps him as a resolute fellow. Though he is not displeasing in countenance, his lips and teeth are usually discolored by the chewing of betel-nut.

The Sea Dayak is lively in disposition, often boastful and excitable, and always talkative and cheerful. His chief characteristic, however, is his restlessness. The darker side of the picture presents him as quarrelsome and treacherous, with little liking for discipline and with little loyalty to his chiefs. He is, moreover, an inveterate head-hunter.

The Kayans, who are found throughout central Borneo, are a warlike people, but they are less quarrelsome than the Dayaks. They excel above all things in various handicrafts. They are skilled in smelting iron and in the manufacture of swords. The Kayans are probably the best boat-builders on the island, and some of their decorative work on the boats and on the paddles is very striking.

Both the Kayans and the Kenyahs are fairer of skin than are the other tribes, and their physique is finer. The Kenyahs have the reputation of being the most intelligent and courageous of all Borneo's native tribes.

The Punans are the most primitive of all the tribes. They roam the forests in bands, supporting themselves as they travel on wild sago and other natural products, and by shooting game with their blow-pipes. For most manufactured articles, such as swords, spears and cloth, they are dependent upon others. Even to make their blow-pipes they must go to the iron-working Kayans, for the metal rods used in boring the long tubes.

BORNEO: FACTS AND FIGURES

GOVERNMENT

Great island in the Malay archipelago. Bounded on north and northwest by South China Sea, northeast by Sulu Sea, east by Celebes Sea and Strait of Macassar, south by Java Sea, and southwest by Karimata Strait. Area, 290,011 square miles; estimated population, 3,224,000. Politically Borneo is divided into (1) British North Borneo, (2) Brunei, (3) Sarawak and (4) Indonesian Borneo.

BRITISH NORTH BORNEO

Occupies extreme northeast section of the island. Area, 29,500; population (est.), 345,-000, chiefly Mohammedan settlers on the coast and aboriginal tribes in the interior. Administration was by the North Borneo Company until July 15, 1946, when administrative rights were transferred to the first Colonial Government. Products: timber, sago, rice, coconuts, gums, coffee, gutta percha, rubber, tobacco, coal. Exports: rubber, camphor, timber, spices, birds' nests, seed pearls, sago, coffee. Railway, 116 miles. Communication by telegraph, telephone and wireless. Protestant and Catholic missions. Capital, Jesselton, population, 12,000.

BRUNEI

Malayan Sultanate on northwest coast of island under British protection. General administration by British Resident. Area, 2,226; population, about 41,000, chiefly natives. Native industries: boat-building, cloth-weaving, brass foundries; chief products: mangrove extract, rubber, sago and timber. Imports: rice, tobacco, piece goods. There are 4 wireless stations; 25 vernacular schools with 2,000 pupils. Capital, Brunei, population, 10,600.

SARAWAK

Independent state on northwest coast of Borneo. Area, 50,000 square miles with 450 miles of coastline; estimated population, 550,-000. Under British protection; chief administrator a rajah. Products: sago, pepper, gold, rubber, gutta jelutong, gutta percha, cutch, crude oil and rattans. There are no railroads; 520 miles of roads; rivers used for internal transportation; 36 post offices; wireless stations; local government telephone system. Protestant and Catholic missions. Capital, Kuching, population 38,000.

INDONESIAN BORNEO (KALIMANTAN)

Central and southern section of the island, comprising nearly three-fourths the entire area. Two divisions: Western District, area, 56,664, population about 850,000; Southern and Eastern Districts, area, 151,621; population, 1,438,-000. Kalimantan is a province of the Republic of Indonesia and has a governor who is responsible to the central government in Jakarta, by which he is appointed. (See Indonesian Facts and Figures, page 256.) Chief occupations: mining, fishing, agriculture, spinning, weaving and dyeing, manufacture of iron implements, gold and diamond-polishing. Chief products: copra, petroleum, antimony, gold, diamonds, iron, mineral oils, timber, rice, pepper, tobacco, spices and coffee. Telephone, telegraph and radio communication. Entire religious liberty. Majority of natives Mohammedans. Protestant and Catholic missions. Government primary and secondary schools for all classes; instruction in native tongues and Dutch. Normal and technical schools. Capital, Banjermasin, population, 70,000.

THE MEN OF THE BLOW-PIPE

How the Bornean Savages Use This Peculiar Weapon

The blow-pipe is a mysterious weapon which deals death up to seventy yards; those most addicted to its use are perhaps the Borneans, though the blow-pipe is used in several other parts of the world. In the preceding chapter we have written about the Borneans themselves and the densely forested country in which they live. The pictures in this chapter show you how the "sumpitan," as the natives call the blow-pipe, is made from the wood of the jajang tree, how the pipe is tested and how the darts are tipped with the poisonous sap of the upas tree. Strange indeed that such a curious device should be used twelve thousand miles away, in Peru!

IT is green dusk in the forest. The tall palm and gutta-percha trees, with their interlacing branches and their masses of creepers, shut out almost all the sunlight. Down at their base the undergrowth of jungle is thick and at times impenetrable. It needs an ax to hack one's way through the mass of vegetation. In few other places in the world is the forest so dense and forbidding as it is here, in the heart of Borneo.

The humid heat is soporific. The ferny soil gives off a dank aroma that mingles with a faint perfume of wild orchids. High up in a tree a monkey begins to chatter. Soon others join in. The squabble, whatever its cause, becomes a noisy one. A score of monkeys are proclaiming their grievances to the world. Suddenly two dark-skinned native youths steal noiselessly into a little clearing between the trees. Each of them carries a long wooden rod with a slight curve in its lower end. This is the famous blow-pipe of the Borneans, a weapon of the most deadly character when used to propel one of the poisoned darts such as the natives carry in the quivers at their waists.

There is a moment's pause. Then a dart is slipped into the blow-pipe, the weapon is raised, aim is swiftly taken, and the chattering overhead breaks into confused cries of alarm as a monkey topples down, down through the leafy branches. The Bornean hunter has secured another of the tree-folk for his "bag."

And what is this blow-pipe, or "sumpitan," to use the native name—this death-dealer of savage devising? It is a weapon which, whether used in warfare or—as more commonly—in the chase, is the Bornean's typical instrument of destruction. In such a country as his, thickly covered with forest and matted jungle, a bow and arrow would be of little service. The blow-pipe has been fashioned to provide the forest-dweller with a weapon peculiarly suited to his surroundings.

For fighting, swords and spears are also employed by the native warriors, but the skill with which the blow-pipe and its deadly missile, the dart, can be utilized, makes it even more formidable. A Punan, it is stated, can kill his man at a distance of seventy yards.

The making of a sumpitan is an interesting process. First of all, a jajang tree is felled. From the hard, straight-grained wood are split strips of about eight feet, roughly, the length of the blow-pipe. One of these strips is then fashioned, by means of an adze, into a cylindrical form some two or three inches in diameter. But let us watch a native craftsman as he proceeds to turn out the finished article.

As one of our illustrations shows, the blow-pipe maker stands upon a platform several feet above the ground with the wooden rod set up vertically before him. This rod is strongly lashed to the platform and other supports during the process of boring that follows.

The operation is accomplished by means of a long, straight iron rod rather less in diameter than the bore desired for the pipe. One end of this rod is chisel-shaped with a keen edge. The Bornean makes his first incision with great care,

FIRST STEPS IN THE ART OF MAKING A BLOW-PIPE

Though the warriors of Borneo carry swords like the one here used as an adze, their most useful weapon is that amazing instrument, the blow-pipe. This Kayan is here shown cutting a length of a hard wood called "jajang" to the right diameter. In succeeding photographs he will be seen as he completes the making of his blow-pipe and uses it.

BORING A HOLE WITH NEITHER LATHE NOR BIT NOR BRACE

The pole of jajang wood is some eight feet long, and has here been whittled to a thickness of about two to three inches. The next process is to hollow it. To do this, the Kayan stands on a platform and hammers downward with an iron rod while a friend pours water from a bamboo vessel into the hole in order to float out the accumulation of chips.

THE CRAFTSMAN SEES THAT HIS LABOR IS GOOD

After the blow-pipe has been bored it is cut down to its final width of an inch at the mouth-piece, tapering to three-quarters at the muzzle. The central bore is then polished to a diameter of a third of an inch. Next the whole weapon is slightly bent, with the aid of heat, so that on looking through it only half of the hole at the farther end can be seen.

AT WORK ON THE SILENT DARTS OF DEATH

Finally comes the business of making the darts for the blow-pipe. These consist of two portions. The piercing part is a spike of tough wood about nine inches long. to the hinder end of which is attached a plug of hard pith. This must fit the pipe exactly for some of its length and then taper forward to lessen the air-resistance when in flight.

A DYAK TRIBESMAN DEMONSTRATES A FINISHED BLOW-PIPE

The blow-pipe in the hands of an expert is a truly deadly weapon. Made of ironwood, it may be from five to ten feet in length. A spearhead attached to the end gives it a secondary use as a lance. Darts dipped in ipoh, a deadly poison from the sap of the upas tree, are inserted in the hollow barrel. An experienced marksman can blow a dart through his gun with great force.

exactly in the center of the flattened end of the pole. He then continues to pierce the wood with downward blows. He turns the iron rod in his hands as he does so, and thus, inch by inch, a hollow is formed right through the tube. As the rod while being worked in this manner must be held exactly vertical, the blow-pipe maker fixes two or three forked sticks horizontally and at different levels above the platform. In these guides the metal rod slides easily up and down and is kept in the straight line required.

In the picture at which we have been looking there is a young assistant, to whom is allotted the task of pouring water from time to time into the steadily deepening hole. In this way the little chips of wood are washed out. As a rule, the work of boring through the whole of the pipe takes about six hours' continuous labor and unlimited patience.

The lower end of a blow-pipe is always slightly curved. This shape is produced by bending the pipe and binding it in position with rattan fiber for some time. The object of the curvature is to allow for the bending of the tube caused by the weight of a spear-head which is often fixed to the top. In this way the blow-pipe may be converted into a sort of bayonet.

Should the desired curvature not be secured by the means just described, the wooden tube is hung horizontally on loops, and heavy weights are then fastened to the muzzle end. When the craftsman peers through the bore, and sights only a half-circle of daylight, he knows that the precise degree of curving has been attained. He then heats the wood with torches so that when the tube has cooled it retains the curvature. Nothing now remains to be done but to finish off the blow-pipe by polishing. For

THE KAYAN GETS POISON FROM A RUBBER-LIKE TREE

A blow-pipe is deadly when used against small animals, and even against human foes; but this is solely due to the poison on its darts. The tree that furnishes the poison is the ipoh, more familiar under the name upas. Our Kayan has made deep cuts in the bark and is here collecting in a bamboo cup the milk-white sap that flows from the tree.

IIE PREPARES THE POISON AND TIPS THE DARTS

Before use the sap of the ipoh tree must be thickened by heating over a fire, a process which leaves it a dark paste. It is then thinned down again. It is now ready to tip the darts of the deadly blow-pipe. Many legends have grown up about the poisonous upas tree, such as that it kills all life around it for a great distance; but this is absurd.

smoothing the rough outside the best article to use is the dried skin of the sting-ray, a sea-fish which makes its way up the rivers. An extra surface is afterward given with the leaf of a certain shrub which forms a good substitute for emery paper. The inside—the bore itself—is polished by means of a long piece of rattan, a fibrous cane, which is pulled to and fro through the entire length until the blow-pipe maker is satisfied that the sides of the tube are really smooth.

Without its poisoned dart the sumpitan would of course have but little effect. The deadly little missile is made from the tough wood of the wild sago palm. It is only some nine inches in length and one-eighth of an inch in diameter. At one extremity is fitted a tapering pith cylinder an inch long the butt end of which is exactly equal in diameter to the bore of the pipe.

The poison which is applied to the dart is obtained from the ipoh tree. When the bark is cut a milky juice oozes therefrom, and this is collected and heated over a fire until it forms a dark brown paste. For the final application this paste is worked into a thinner consistency. In the meantime a circular groove has been cut around the shaft of the dart, at a distance of two inches from its tip. The poison is now rubbed in here and left to dry.

Such a poisoned dart as described is astoundingly effective if used against small game. But for human beings, for deer and pig and other larger creatures, it is necessary to employ a bigger dose of the ipoh poison. For this purpose a piece of metal, usually tin, is slipped into the shaft of the dart and the mixture spread upon its surface.

Although the tools employed by the native craftsman are rough, the blow-pipe is fashioned with considerable skill and artistry. Were this not the case it would be impossible for the Bornean warrior or hunter to attain precision of aim,

TWO BORNEO MARKSMEN OUT AFTER MONKEYS

To make the blow-pipe with such primitive tools is wonderful enough, but now let us watch the weapon in use. Light enough to be poised in one hand, it is roughly aimed while the dart is being inserted. Then comes the final aiming and—*puff!*—a monkey is dead. Within a range of seventy yards many of these marksmen are as accurate as a rifleman.

BACK AFTER A SUCCESSFUL DAY IN THE JUNGLE

Behold the spoils of the chase! Bigger game than monkeys can be killed with the blow-pipe, and our instructor in the art has captured a fine young forest pig for the cooking-pot. It will be noticed that just as rifles can have bayonets affixed to them, so the Borneo blow-pipe is given a second use by having a spear-point lashed to the muzzle end.

Must Use Iron Rod of Kayans

It is interesting to note in this connection that the Punan tribesman, who is one of the most expert users of the blow-pipe, cannot make his chosen weapon unassisted. He has no knowledge of working in metals. For the iron rod which is so necessary for the boring of the tube he has to go to his neighbor, the Kayan. At the present day the Kayans are the most skilled ironworkers on the island, and their swords and spears are rivaled only by those of the Kenyahs. Such iron as they use is mostly obtained from Malay and Chinese traders, but native ore is still smelted at some places in the far interior.

When not in use, the darts are kept in a quiver made of a section of bamboo fitted with a cap. This receptacle is attached to the belt by a wooden hook. As a general rule, the darts themselves are wrapped in a squirrel skin, while tied to the quiver is a small gourd in which is carried a supply of the piths used in the propulsion of the darts.

Like so many savage people the Bornean natives are steeped in superstition. They believe in magic, in spells and charms, and accordingly there will be a special charm attached to the quiver of a man's blow-pipe. This charm is often dipped in the blood of an animal that has been slain. The owner believes that the virtues of his mascot are thus greatly increased.

Death-tubes in Malaya and Peru

The fact that some of the inland tribes of Borneo were originally of Malayan stock, and also that the island was overrun by Malays centuries ago, accounts for the presence of the blow-pipe as a national weapon. For in the Malay States the sumpitan has been in regular use as long as history can record. In Perak, in the jungly hill country, some of the aboriginal inhabitants, such as the Sakais, still roam the woods with blow-pipes in hand. The Sakai makes his blow-pipe of a single joint of a rare species of bamboo; and he whittles darts as fine as knitting needles from the mid-rib of a certain palm leaf.

With these he can kill at thirty paces.

But if there is nothing extraordinary in the fact that the blow-pipe is common to the Malay States and Borneo, what shall we say when we learn that it is used by such far-distant a people as the natives of Peru, half the earth's circumference removed? Here is a seeming marvel. There can be no racial connection between the Indians of Peru and the several tribes of inland Borneo. It is not at all likely that any communication has been held between the two peoples in past times, and yet in each country the primitive savage forest-dweller has found out the secret of the blow-pipe's power to propel a poisoned dart from its mouth.

Make Use of Nature's Poison

We can but gather from this remarkable coincidence that the evolution of the blow-pipe from some earlier form of the weapon has resulted from similar conditions of life both in Borneo and in Peru.

In the swampy, jungly country east of that mighty chain of mountains, the Andes, whence the tributaries of the great Amazon flow, in the region known as the Montaña, the native Peruvian lives much the same kind of life as does his brown-skinned brother of the Punan, Klemantan, Kayan and other Bornean tribes. He hunts and faces his enemies in a dark forest world where no other weapon could possibly serve his purpose so well. The trees of his own land furnish the wood from which the indispensable blow-pipe is made.

The Peruvian Indian has also at hand the poison with which to anoint his darts. In place of the ipoh tree of Borneo, he resorts to a plant from which he can extract curari. This poisonous substance is deadly in its effect; it quickly causes paralysis and stops the heart's action. Like the juice of the ipoh, it is, of course, poisonous only if it finds its way into the blood directly through a wound. Otherwise game killed with it would not be fit for eating. In both South America and Borneo we thus see how the savage has turned to Nature to provide him with his surest weapons and means of securing his food.

PEARLS OF THE ORIENT

A Republic of Seven Thousand Islands

The first European to see the Philippines was a Portuguese navigator, Ferdinand Magellan, who had become a naturalized citizen of Spain. He landed on the islands in 1521 and claimed the entire group for Spain. Portugal also claimed the Philippines, but in 1565 the Spanish took possession and for more than three hundred years the islands remained under their control. The Spanish-American War resulted in the cession of the islands to the United States, and under American rule the Filipinos were allowed a large degree of self-government. Early in World War II the Japanese conquered the Philippines and held them until 1945. The following year, on July 4, the independent Republic of the Philippines was proclaimed.

THE Philippine Islands, if placed on the eastern United States, would extend from the Great Lakes to the Gulf of Mexico and from the Atlantic Ocean to the Mississippi River. Yet the area of the seven thousand islands is only two and one-third times that of the State of New York, or 114,000 square miles. From the northernmost island Formosa can be seen on a clear day, and from the southernmost Borneo is only a few miles distant. The nearest shore of Asia is five hundred miles away, and San Francisco seven thousand. Two-thirds the area of the archipelago is represented by the two islands, Luzon and Mindanao; other large islands include Samar, Negros, Panay, Palawan, Mindoro, Leyte, Cebu, Bohol and Masbate. The coastline is twice that of the United States.

Scientists tell us that the Philippines were once a part of continental Asia and that some of the islands have risen from the sea in recent geologic epochs. Being of volcanic origin, they have frequent earthquakes, and a dozen volcanoes are more or less active. Earthquakes have caused much loss of life and property in Manila, the capital, but most of the shocks are harmless. In 1911 an eruption of Taal Volcano, a low crater rising from Taal Lake, covered several small villages with hot mud, killing more than a thousand people. Mayon Volcano, 8,000 feet high, is perhaps the most perfect volcanic cone in the world, reminding one of Fujiyama, which is higher but not so symmetrical. Other volcanoes are Mt. Apo in southern Mindanao, 10,000 feet high and Mt. Canlaon in Negros, 8,200 feet.

The Philippines are mountainous or hilly with few broad plains or level valleys except in Luzon and Mindanao. The Central Luzon Plain extends from Manila Bay to Lingayen Gulf and through it flow the Pampanga and Agno rivers. This plain is the rice granary of the Islands. The Cagayan, Agusan and Mindanao rivers have broad valleys. Part of northern Mindanao is a plateau 2,000 feet high on which graze thousands of cattle. The coastal plains are narrow, and on many shores the mountains rise out of the sea. The coastline is irregular, but there are few good harbors on the eastern coast. Manila, Cebu, Iloilo, Davao, Legaspi, Zamboanga and Jolo are ports open to foreign steamers. Manila is on Manila Bay, entrance to which is guarded by the rocky fortress, Corregidor, and on the Pasig River which drains the largest lake, Laguna de Bay. Coral reefs extend along many shores. East of northern Mindanao is the greatest known ocean depth, 35,400 feet.

The mountains and much of the lower areas are covered with forests, practically all owned by the government which has title to five-sixths of the total area. Huge trees, some supported by flying-buttress roots, arise in a tangled growth of climbing bamboo, rattan and creepers of various sorts including the balete which finally kills the tree it encircles with its clinging arms. The tropical forests of the lowlands are dense, but in the high-

A REPUBLIC OF THOUSANDS OF ISLANDS

THE CITY OF LEGASPI AT THE FOOT OF MOUNT MAYON'S PERFECT CONE

Mayon Volcano in Southern Luzon is 8,000 feet high, and the base has a circumference of eighty miles. The cone is said to be more nearly symmetrical than any other in the world. The buildings in the foreground are a part of Legaspi, formerly known as Albay, one of the larger cities of the islands. Near by a ruined church tower is all that remains of Daraga, once a flourishing village, which was overwhelmed by an eruption more than a hundred years ago. The volcano is still alive, though there has been no violent eruption for a considerable period.

WHERE THE WATERS YIELD A PLENTIFUL HARVEST

Fishing is the occupation next to agriculture in importance. The waters teem with fish of many varieties, and there are many excellent food fish in the streams. Here a net placed in shallow water is being pulled. Many beautifully colored fish may be seen in the aquarium at Manila. Sometimes goldfish are fried for supper.

lands of Mountain Province there are open forests of a unique species of pine. The forests abound in woods valuable for cabinet work, veneering, and construction. Some logs are so heavy that bamboos are tied to them so they can be floated down the streams to market. Other forest products are rattan, rubber, gutta percha, gums, dyes and medicines. In usefulness the bamboo is pre-eminent. Though in reality a giant grass, some kinds grow taller than many species of trees. Of it houses are made from foundation to roof, although usually the thatch is nipa palm leaves or reeds. Of bamboo are made beds, tables, chairs, garden implements, harrows and rope. Indeed a house can be built and furnished and part of the farming and gardening implements made of it. Rice put with water in a green joint of bamboo thrust into a bamboo fire is nicely cooked before the flames burn through the joint.

Abaca, or Manila hemp, is hardly less important. These plants belong to the same family as the banana, and the fibre is extensively used for rope and twine. The finer fibres may be woven into delicate fabrics of great beauty. Very attractive hats are also made from the finer fibres.

The chief natural resources of the Philippines are fertile soil and seas teeming with hundreds of kinds of fish. Rice, sugar cane, coconut palms, hemp, corn, tobacco, sweet potatoes, coffee, peanuts and maguey are important products. The mining of gold, copper and iron has been carried on in a small way for centuries and still continues. Today valuable gold mines in Benguet and a few coal mines are in operation on a large scale. Sulphur, marble, gravel, sand and cement are also produced, the last by a government company. The fish include many game species like Spanish mackerel, pompano, sea bass, bonito and the curious climbing perch, which actually crosses fields and even climbs trees. Another remarkable fish that lives in deep waters uses an electric light to attract its prey. Giant rays are found in some waters and great clams, whose shells make good bath tubs for babies. Huge sea turtles are hunted for their flesh and shell. The shells of the pearl-bearing oyster of the Sulu Sea are made into buttons, and a flat translucent sea shell is cut to make small panes for windows and doors, lamp shades, screens and a variety of other useful articles.

In the Philippines the mean annual temperature (the average of all weather stations) is 26.9° C. or about 78° F. The variation in mean monthly temperature is slight—about 13° F. in northern Luzon and 5° F. in southern Mindanao. Though tropical, except in the higher plateaus and mountains, the temperature in the shade rarely reaches 100° F., and the nights are cooler than the summer nights in many temperate regions. The humidity is high, averaging about 80% with a variation from about 75% to about 80%. Baguio, the beautiful resort 175 miles from Manila in the mountains at nearly 5,000 feet elevation, has an average temperature of 17.9° C. or about 64° F. The cool nights make open fires welcome. In Manila the climate from November to February is delightful. April and May are warm and dry.

The average rainfall for the Islands is 82 inches, the variation being from less than 40 inches in some of the southern islands to 181 inches in Baguio. The latter claims the world's rainfall record for twenty-four hours, more than 46 inches, from noon July 14 to July 15, 1911. This deluge caused landslides that held back the Bued River until it was more than a hundred feet deep over the scenic road that follows its course to Baguio. Finally the dam gave way and steel bridges were swept away, twisted and torn asunder as if the steel beams were strips of paper.

The rainy season coincides with the

THE MANGO HARVEST IN THE PHILIPPINES

The Mango is one of the most delicious fruits known, and those grown in the Philippines have no superiors in quality. The only rival of the mango is the mangosteen. This picture is a reproduction of a painting by F. Amorsolo, a talented Filipino artist whose paintings have been exhibited in several cities of Europe and the United States.

occurrence of typhoons. These storms are great cyclones that originate as a rule east of the Philippines in the vicinity of Guam. They usually travel in a northwesterly direction; so Mindanao and the southern Visayan Islands very rarely feel their effects. Although they often raze buildings and damage crops, without them the western shores of the Islands would lack rain. From November to March the northeast trade winds bring abundant rain to the eastern coast.

In the forests are pythons thirty-five feet long. Poisonous snakes include the king cobra and other pit vipers and the deadly rice snake. But these dangerous reptiles are seldom met with and cause few deaths. Compared with Borneo and Java, there are few large animals. They include the wild carabao, or water buffalo, in a few places, the timarao, or antelope buffalo, confined to Mindoro, six species of deer, wild hogs, two species of monkeys, thirty varieties of bats, porcupines, civet cats, a few small rodents, crocodiles and lizards. Hunting wild carabao or timarao is not without danger, and crocodiles are numerous in some rivers.

In Rizal Hall at the University of the Philippines is an eighteen-foot crocodile killed by General Emilio Aguinaldo in the marshes along the northern shore of Manila Bay. Every house has its lizards, the small gekkos, which help keep the dwelling free of insects, and some have a house snake to keep away rats. These snakes are harmless and stay out of sight among the rafters.

Birds and Insects

Two-thirds of the three hundred land birds are peculiar to the Islands, on which fact scientists base their belief that the Philippines have been separated from Asia and the islands to the south for a comparatively long period. Game birds include ducks, snipe, plover, curlew and quail; others are hornbills, crows, martins, pigeons, doves and herons. The monkey-eating eagle has a fondness for small simians; there are no large ones in the Philippines. The Islands are especially noted for the great number of species of land

snails. Insects are many, but house flies few, for ants eat the larvae. Plagues of locusts have in the past, but not in recent years, troubled the Philippines—clouds of them so thick that they hid the sun and broke down the bamboos on which they rested. And such swarms left no blade of grass, no green leaf on rice or corn or sugar cane. Locusts are not only a pest but also an article of food, as they were with John the Baptist.

Flora Partly American

The flora of Manila and vicinity came in part from Mexico, as is shown by the Aztec names still applied to some of these importations. Such plants were brought on purpose in the yearly galleon that sailed from Acapulco in Mexico to Manila, or came by chance in the packing of articles and the fodder of horses. The plant life of the Islands as a whole resembles that of the East Indies, but there are many differences. Some forms are related to those of China; others are peculiar to the islands. Citrus fruits, mangoes, papayas, guavas, chicos, lanzones, duhats, bread fruits, jack fruits, custard apples and mangosteens are cultivated. Bananas are of many varieties and constitute an important element in the diet of the people. Vegetables include squashes, gourds and beans, cowpeas, melons, eggplant, tomatoes, radishes, pechay, mustard, onions, cabbage, sweet potatoes and carrots. Many vegetables from America have been introduced and have helped to diversify the diet. In Baguio are grown Irish potatoes, strawberries, cauliflower and other vegetables that need a cool climate.

A Cosmopolitan Population

The population of the Philippines has increased a great deal in recent years. In 1918 the population was 10,314,310. According to the 1948 census, the population had grown to 19,234,182. In addition to the native Filipinos, there are important communities of Chinese, Spanish and American residents. By far the largest percentage of the population lives on eleven islands. Only a small percentage of the population remains either pagan or Mo-

CARABAO CARTS AMBLING LEISURELY ALONG A ROAD NEAR MANILA

The carabao—the Philippine name for a water buffalo—is a useful draft animal. Its splay feet easily wade through swamps. Water buffaloes are common in warm parts of the Far East.

BUNDLES AND HANKS OF MANILA HEMP AWAITING SHIPMENT

The fibers are obtained from the stalks of abaca plants, which are stripped. Much of the production is exported. From Manila hemp, rope, twine and coarse fabrics are manufactured.

287

hammedan. Mountain Province has the largest group of pagans, and Mindanao and Sulu Archipelago contain practically all of the Mohammedans, commonly called Moros. Dr. H. Otley Beyer, the authority on Philippine ethnology and culture, divides the pagan population into three groups: the pygmies, the Indonesians and the Malays.

The Pygmies

The pygmies, the earliest inhabitants, now number only about thirty thousand, most of whom live in the mountains. By far the most numerous pygmy group is that of the Negritos, who walked to the islands when they were a part of the mainland of Asia. This theory is supported by the fact that they have no word for boat, nor do they use boats. They have a fear of water, and, from the bank, shoot fish with arrows to which are attached strings for retrieving the arrows—and the fish. The largest group of Negritos inhabit the Zambales Mountains, and the average height of adults in the group is four feet six inches. All have brown skin, curly hair and other negroid characteristics. Some live in small bands wandering in the deep forests and obtaining food by hunting, trapping and gathering wild forest products. Their only weapons are the bow and arrow, but they are good shots and kill many deer, wild hogs and birds. They build only rude shelters covered with leaves, and move frequently. They wear little clothing, and that made of bark cloth, and have few ornaments. Other Negritos, through contact with Filipino neighbors, have come to build more permanent houses, but it is their custom to leave a locality when a member of the group dies. They raise dry crops, such as beans and upland rice, but a sharp stick is usually the only implement used in cultivation. The ground is prepared for planting by cutting down all but the large trees and burning—the kaingin system. They also gather forest products and trade them for cloth, iron for arrow heads, salt and rice. The Negritos were driven back into the mountains by the later peoples migrating to the Philippines.

Their original speech has disappeared so far as is now known. They speak an archaic Malay just as some southern mountaineers speak Elizabethan English and some of the Canadians the French of Louis XIV.

After the Pygmies Came the Indonesians

In great contrast to the pygmies are the Indonesians, the tallest people in the Philippines, averaging five feet seven inches. When their migrations from southern Asia to the Philippines began is unknown. They took what lands they wanted and the pygmies, if in the way, retired. Some Indonesians built houses in trees for protection; others on the ground. They practiced a crude dry farming, but lived largely by hunting and trapping. They made no pottery, wove no cloth nor baskets, had practically no household utensils, and practiced tattooing. Their original language has largely disappeared but is a basic, though limited, element in Philippine languages today.

Missionary Effort Converting the Indonesian Pagans

Today the Indonesian groups evidence a much higher culture. Some are skillful irrigation engineers, their irrigated terraces equaling any in the world. They cherish Chinese pottery and other wares, some of which were imported six centuries ago. They weave good cloth and do skillful wood carving. They have elaborate codes of tribal law intricately related to their religious beliefs. Thousands have become Christians through the efforts of Catholic and Protestant missionaries. The Protestant Episcopal Church of America which limits its missionary activities in the Philippines to non-Catholic groups (the pagans, the Mohammedans and the Confucianists) has mission stations in Mountain Province.

As the pygmies were driven from the best lands by the Indonesians so the latter retired before immigrating groups of Malays. These early Malay immigrants also retired before later comers and are still pagans (the Igorots of Benguet and the Ifugaos), while the Bontoks and Tinggians are Indonesian-Malay mixtures. These and the Mohammedans (Moros) of Mindanao and the Sulu Archipelago are the only non-Christians of Malay stock.

The Moros are divided into several branches. The Sulus inhabit Jolo and neighboring islands, and the Sultan of Sulu until recent times was suzerain over a part of Borneo. The Samals were originally *Samal Laut* (sea folk) whose homes were their boats and some (the Bajaos) still are ocean nomads, but most of them now live in villages in the southern Sulu Archipelago. They were the most troublesome of all the Mohammedan pirates. The Magindanao Moros inhabit the island to which they gave their name, their two chief centers being the Mindanao Valley and the Lanao region.

The chief head-hunting groups are the pagans in Mountain Province, although some Mindanao pagans also practiced the art. The taking of heads has been so frowned upon by the government that it is now an infrequent occurrence, though a practice ages old naturally dies hard, especially when head-hunting had a religious and a social sanction. Formerly the taking of a head was the only road a young brave could take to a maiden's favor. Just as the American Indian buck must show his bravery and prowess by taking an enemy scalp or two, so the more heads the Bontok or Kalinga braves took, the greater their glory among the old men who ruled the village and among the maidens who ruled their hearts. The people of the next village inhabited by their own race (but not of their clan) might be the enemy, and village feuds existed as bitter as the family feuds among some of our own mountaineers in the Appalachians. Each spring the young man's fancy turned to head-hunting as a preliminary to love. So may it today,

UNDERWOOD & UNDERWOOD

THE FAMOUS IFUGAO RICE TERRACES

The Ifugaos, a people who live on the island of Luzon, are skilled farmers and irrigation engineers. Steep slopes do not daunt them, and water is brought long distances in canals or hollowed logs.

but wise administrators have taught him it is best to withhold his hand from the tempting head-axe. No more the distant hallo of the head-hunter returning victorious from the fray, nor the answering shouts of the village, including perhaps the glad outcry of the maiden who has selected him as her own.

The picturesque head-hunter and his strange customs have sometimes attracted so much attention that foreigners have lost sight of the fact that more than ninety per cent of the Filipinos are Christians living peaceful lives in villages, cultivating the soil, and practicing much the same arts and crafts as people in other Christian lands. But if the strange and unexpected appeal, what is more strange than that in the midst of Buddhists, Mohammedans, Shintoists, Confucianists, Taoists and pagans speaking an infinite variety of tongues there is a Christian people whose

MORO WARRIOR WITH SWORD AND SHIELD

The Moros are the Mohammedan Malays, who live in Mindanao and the Sulu Archipelago.
For three centuries they fought the Spaniards, making annual raids upon the islands of the
north. Stone watch towers, where a lookout for Moro raiders was kept, still stand on the
promontories along the west coast of northern Luzon.

Philippine Bureau of Science

A KALINGA WOMAN'S DRESS IS AN AMAZING MEDLEY OF COLOR

The Kalingas, whose ancestors were among the early arrivals on the island, live in the mountains of North Central Luzon. The Spaniards left the mountain people much to themselves, and head-hunting was prevalent. Now crimes of violence are very rare. These people are cleanly in their habits and are famed for the gaudiness of their dress.

common language is English? English is the language of instruction in the public schools, and now the "talkies" and radio programs in English are popular forms of entertainment. English has displaced Spanish as the common medium of communication except among the older generation, while the languages of the different groups are usually spoken in the home.

The Malay ancestors of the modern Filipinos came in many migrating waves from the Malay Peninsula and Sumatra, seeking adventure and new homes. The name of the boat in which a family or group of related families arrived was given to the settlement they formed (*barangay*) ; and the leader of the group, called *cabeza de barangay* in Spanish times, was for centuries the local ruler. These late comers occupied the land, the earlier comers of a less developed culture retiring before them. Skillful sailors, the Malays spread over the islands settling on bays or on rivers far enough from the sea to have some protection from pirates.

The writing of the early Filipinos was on bamboo or leaves, and no complete account of early history is possible. In the twelfth century Hindus from India founded in Java an empire called Majapahit, and the vast Boro Bodur ruins remain to testify of their culture. It is probable that for a period the Philippine Islands were subject to the Majapahit Empire. Hindu influence appears in the Sanskrit element in the language including place names as far north as Manila ; in the mythology, folklore and early literature ; and in political and social customs. Scholars say that the mythology and folklore of all Filipino groups except the pygmies is fundamentally the same and shows Hindu influence. The Hindu title "rajah" was still in use when the Spaniards arrived.

The Philippines had commercial relations with China also, and every year Chinese junks visited Manila, the Visayas,

THE ESCOLTA, A BUSY STREET IN MANILA'S BUSINESS SECTION

The Escolta is situated in the Binodo section of Manila, north of the Pasig River. It runs from the Plaza Moraga, and street and plaza constitute the business section of the city. To the south of the river lies the original walled city of Manila once known as Intramuros. Within its walls are narrow streets, Spanish-style houses and many old churches and convents.

northern Mindanao and Jolo. Chau Ju-Kua, who wrote about 1250, mentions this trade. Morga mentions trade with Siam and Cambodia, Malacca, India and Japan.

In the fifteenth century the Arabs conquered the Hindus in Java and Mohammedanism succeeded Buddhism. Before this event Islamism had reached Borneo and the Sulu Archipelago; then it spread to Mindanao, Mindoro, Manila Bay and other parts of Luzon. The arrival of the Spaniards with their proselyting zeal alone prevented the people of the Philippines from becoming Mohammedan. When the Spaniards took Manila it was from a Mohammedan rajah. Then began the long struggle between the Spaniards and the Mohammedan Malays, a struggle like the contest for the possession of southern Spain with the Mohammedan Moors; so the Spaniards called their new Mohammedan opponents Moros (Moors).

Magellan on the first voyage around the world saw the island of Samar on March 15, 1521. After visiting some of the smaller islands, he landed at Cebu where two thousand of the inhabitants were baptized. Magellan helped the Cebu ruler in an attack on the neighboring ruler of Mactan Island and was killed. One of his ships finally returned to Spain.

Three other Spanish expeditions made visits. One of their leaders named the islands *Las Filipinas* in honor of Philip II. Later Legaspi sailed from Mexico to the Islands and established a settlement at Cebu in 1565. Reinforcements from Mexico came, and in 1569 Panay was occupied. A year later Martin de Goiti and Juan de Salcedo took Manila which Legaspi made the capital. Due to the sparse population governed by rulers having authority over small areas, the skill of Salcedo and the eloquence of the missionary friars soon brought the greater part of the islands under Spanish authority.

The missionary friars by their devoted efforts led the people to accept Christian-

MAKING HATS OF SPLIT BAMBOO

These women are weaving fine bamboo fibres into hats. The block to shape the crown is between two hats that require only binding around the brims to be finished. The finest hats are woven in the early morning hours beside streams so that the dampness will make the delicate fibres pliable. You can pay a hundred dollars for a hat of the very best quality.

CIRCULAR RAFTS HEAPED WITH COCONUTS DRIFT DOWNRIVER

A very easy way to get coconuts to market is to pile them on simple rafts. On placid streams they float with the current, or they can be towed. The rafts are round so that they will not lodge against uneven, jungle-fringed banks, where roots of trees may extend out into the water. The meat of these coconuts will be dried to make copra, which yields coconut oil.

ity. Only the Moros refused; those who are now pagans did not come in contact with the Spainards till late in the Spanish regime. Today the impressive stone church in every town witnesses to the zeal of the missionary and the piety of the people. Some of these churches are very ornate, though the architecture does not generally compare with that of the Mission Churches in California and Southwestern United States.

Each year a Spanish galleon sailed from Manila to Acapulco, Mexico, carrying some Philippine products but mostly goods from India and China. On its return it brought new officials, articles for the Spanish inhabitants, and specie for the expenses of government. The galleons also introduced many new plants including tobacco, cotton and sugar cane.

The Spaniards paid little attention to elementary education, but the Royal and Pontifical University of Santo Tomás in Manila antedates Harvard. Some accounts fix the foundation at 1611, though some declare that 1619 is the real date. The historic university is still conducted by the Dominican friars.

In 1796 the Astrea from Salem, Massachusetts, sailed around Cape of Good Hope taking to Manila wine from Lisbon and Madeira and bringing back sugar, indigo and pepper. Nathaniel Bowditch was second mate and navigating officer and worked out the system of navigation that made the voyage notable for quickness. The American Practical Navigator which Bowditch later published is still the guide to navigation the world over.

American sailing ships visited Manila in increasing numbers and in the clipper ship era played a very important part in Philippine trade. About 1825 American firms were established in Manila and for a time they were dominating factors in the trade in sugar and important ones in that of hemp. Coconut products (copra, oil, copra cake, dessicated coconut) and tobacco were of no importance in Philippine-American trade until after the Spanish-American War. The establishment of British banks in Manila led to the failure of the American firms there, and steamers displaced sailing vessels largely; so American trade, though increasing in volume, was largely through British firms and in British ships. After the occupation of the Philippines, both American companies and American ships reappeared on the scene and became the largest factors in the import and export trade.

In 1842 Captain Wilkes of the United States Navy made a treaty with the Sultan of Sulu whereby American ships and sailors were given protection in passing through the Sulu Sea.

The Spaniards first divided the islands into districts, each of which together with its inhabitants was ruled by a Spaniard. However, this plan of control was opposed, and later provinces and military districts were established.

In the early years of Spanish rule, Spanish priests went into the interior of the islands. They learned the native dialects and converted the only large group of Asiatics that has ever become Christian. The Mohammedan Moros, however,

THE OLD WALLS FROM THE MANILA HOTEL ROOF

At the left is the old section of the city, known as Intramuros (between walls). It is still enclosed by walls built hundreds of years ago. The moat that once surrounded them has been filled and is a public park. Beyond the monument in honor of Legaspi and Urdaneta is an aquarium where fishes of brilliant coloring and strange shapes are on view.

FORT SANTIAGO, ONE OF THE OLDEST FORTS

The thick stone walls of old Fort Santiago were built by the Spaniards about three hundred years ago. Although the fort's bronze cannon are now museum pieces and no longer threaten the busy shipping in the Pasig River, they served a very useful purpose in former days when they helped to repel the frequent and savage raids by pirates on the city of Manila.

resisted Spanish church and government authorities to the end.

Foreign enemies also appeared. First the Portuguese, then the Dutch, came to contest Spanish supremacy. Mohammedan Malay pirates from the south ravaged the Visayas, and Chinese pirates from the north attacked Manila. During the French and Indian War, the British took and occupied Manila. Several times the Chinese colony in Manila was attacked and destroyed because of the belief that it was plotting to overthrow the government. At various times the Filipinos rose in revolt, the last time in 1896; and two years later, when Admiral Dewey destroyed the Spanish fleet in the battle of Manila Bay, the revolt had not been suppressed.

As a result of the Spanish-American War the United States received the Philippines upon payment of $20,000,000.00. But General Emilio Aguinaldo desired an independent status for his country and continued to oppose the Americans for several years until captured. For many years he took an active part in affairs of the new Commonwealth, established in 1935. Military government gave way to civil government under W. H.

Taft who, with his successors, set about making effective President McKinley's policy of administering the Philippines for the benefit of the Filipinos. Schools were conducted by soldiers before civil rule, and the employment of one thousand American teachers and supervisors was an early act of the Philippine Commission. The towering stone church fronting each town plaza testifies to Spanish Christian zeal. The concrete schoolhouse in its neatly kept and ample grounds testifies to American belief in public education.

During the period of American occupation illiteracy was greatly reduced. To-day public schools have been established everywhere, and the Republic has normal schools, agricultural schools, a nautical school, a school of commerce, and other specialized schools. At the top is the University of the Philippines, now a large institution which embraces a number of professional colleges.

Health agencies are organized and to-day the fear of epidemics of smallpox, cholera and plague is past, infant mortality is greatly reduced, and leprosy is being eradicated. The campaign against the last is aided by the $2,000,000.00

raised in the United States as a memorial to General Leonard Wood, late Governor General of the Philippines, who was deeply interested in its control. Good roads and railroads have been built, harbors dredged, piers and lighthouses constructed, and irrigation systems put in operation.

When the American occupation began, there were almost no good roads upon the islands, and many were only trails. Now there are thousands of miles of good roads over which the thirty thousand or more motor cars now registered can pass swiftly and safely. Some of the roads are scenic highways offering many beautiful views. However, among the mountains, and in the hill country, there are

CORREGIDOR ISLAND, TRAGIC BASTION OF WORLD WAR II

Corregidor, an island in the Philippines, two miles south of Bataan peninsula, is part of the inner line of defense of Manila. It is the site of Fort Mills, around which the American forces made their last desperate stand against the Japanese in World War II. They managed to hold out for twenty-eight days after the fall of Bataan, and finally surrendered on May 6, 1942.

BAMBOO is the most useful grass. It is of many kinds; some varieties grow to be thirty or more feet high. Of it a Filipino can build a comfortable house from foundation to ridge—posts, stairway, floor, partitions, windows, rafters, roof. The roof of a bamboo house is usually, though not always, built of the leaves of the nipa palm or of reeds.

298

HOUSES ON PILES are the usual thing in the Philippines, for they are more sanitary and in times of high water, essential to comfort. These houses are dry although the river has overflowed the site of the village. Many of the houses in the hills also stand on piles, high above the ground, following the old custom. We show one elsewhere.

PICTURE OF A FILIPINO GIRL

This picture of one of the attractive country-women was painted by a talented Filipino artist, F. Amorsolo, who has exhibited in Madrid, Paris and New York.

many miles of trails, which can be followed only on foot or on horseback.

In all movements toward either material or cultural development, the Filipinos have played important parts. Today only a few Americans remain among the civil service employees. Filipino teachers devotedly instruct boys and girls, Filipino engineers build roads and bridges, Filipino administrators and legislators actually govern the country.

Under American rule a great measure of self-government was allowed to the Filipinos. In 1935 the Philippine Commonwealth was created. The ordinance governing the relations between the United States and the Commonwealth lapsed on July 4, 1946 and, amid ceremonies, the Commonwealth took over full sovereignty and became the Republic of the Philippines. Japan's occupation of the islands during World War II required a rehabilitation program before the proclamation of independence.

The Walled City is the old Spanish residence and government district. Much of the old wall still stands. Formerly the walls were surrounded by a picturesque but ill-smelling moat, which has yielded to progress and is now the municipal golf course. Narrow streets lined with churches, government courts and administrative buildings, and houses with overhanging upper stories characterize the Walled City. Outwardly unattractive the houses often have charming gardens in interior courts.

Besides the churches, the visitor in Manila will visit the Yangco market to see products of Filipino handicraft; Bilibid Prison to see retreat; the canals, or *esteros,* which make Manila a Venice; to see the boats which are the homes of many; the Escolta to shop; the Ayuntamiento to view the medallions of the Spanish governors and the exhibit of Chinese wares taken from graves dating back to the twelfth century; a cigar factory where are made cigars that many prefer to Havanas.

Near Manila is Fort McKinley once a very large post of the United States Army, the ruins of the Guadalupe Convent, and the bamboo organ at Las Piñas made by Father Diego Cera more than a hundred years ago. Its seven hundred pipes are all made of bamboo, and it is still playable. Thousands of pilgrims yearly visit Antipolo to view the famous Virgin of Antipolo.

Street life in Manila is cosmopolitan. Europeans of almost all countries, Chinese and Japanese, Sikhs, Hindus, East Indians, Singalese, Turks, Arabians, and Christian, Mohammedan and other Filipinos tread its streets.

Baguio is a gem of a city set upon the hills five thousand feet above and one hundred seventy-five miles north of Manila. Cool climate, wonderful roads and trails, beautiful scenery, the scent of the pines, the glory of the sunset, the picturesqueness of the people, attract each year thousands of visitors from the lowlands and from most of the countries of the Far East. In an air that is as clear as the sky above is blue, people find delight in walking, riding and playing golf and tennis. Baguio is the playland of the Philippines, and the players are especially numerous from December to June. Then the public market is the meeting place alike of residents, visitors and strangely costumed mountain peoples. In the crowd are representatives of all the peoples who have formed the history of the Philippine Islands—the Negritos (the original inhabitants), the Indonesians who followed, the Malays who came next, the Spaniards, who first brought Western culture, and the Americans, who introduced the modern way of life.

The capital was moved from Manila in 1948 when construction of a large government center was begun in Quezon City, a suburb northeast of Manila. The new capital is named for Manuel Quezon, great patriot and statesman, first president of the Philippine Commonwealth.

The first permanent Spanish settlement in the archipelago was made at Cebu. It is now the second largest city of the Republic and an important trading center and port on the eastern coast of the island of Cebu. Magellan lost his life on Mactan, an island that forms the outer rim of Cebu harbor. Cebu city, divided into four sections, sprawls over a semicircular plain at the foot of the island's mountain chain. Factories produce and process sugar, tobacco, hemp, copra, potatoes, cement and textiles. The provincial capital building is outstanding.

On opposite shores of Guimares Strait are the next most important cities of the central Philippines—Bacolod on Negros and Iloilo on Panay. Both serve as centers of rich agricultural regions.

On opposite coasts of the southerly island of Mindanao are Zamboanga and Davao. Both are ports and both are in regions of dense hardwood forests.

PHILLIPINE REPUBLIC: FACTS AND FIGURES

THE COUNTRY

The largest group in the north Malay Archipelago; composed of 7,097 islands and islets. Bounded on the west and north by the China Sea, east by the Pacific Ocean, south by the Celebes Sea and the coastal waters of Borneo. Total land area, about 114,830 square miles. Luzon, the largest island, has an area of 40,420 square miles. The estimated total population is 19,234,182.

GOVERNMENT

Former insular possession of the U. S., now the Republic of the Philippines. The republic achieved its freedom in 1946. It has a constitutional form of government, with a President and a Vice-President elected for 4 years. The President may be reelected to office. He is assisted by a cabinet of 10 ministers and secretaries. There is an elected two-house Legislature consisting of the Senate with 24 members and the House of Representatives with 100 members. Both men and women citizens over 21 may vote, if they can read and write Spanish, English or a native dialect, and if they can conform to certain residential qualifications.

COMMERCE AND INDUSTRIES

Agriculture is the chief industry; principal products are rice, Manila hemp, coconuts, sugar cane, corn, tobacco and maguey. The Government owns 92.5% of the commercial forests furnishing cabinet woods, gums, resins, vegetable oils, bamboo, tan and dye barks. Livestock: hogs, carabaos, cattle. Gold is mined in commercial quantities. Considerable manufacturing (embroidering, weaving) in homes, but factories are increasing. Chief exports: sugar, hemp, coconut oil, copra, tobacco products, embroideries and shredded coconut. Chief imports: rice, wheat, dairy products, iron and steel manufactures (especially passenger cars and electric refrigerators), cigarettes and soap.

COMMUNICATIONS

Overseas trade carried mainly by American and British vessels. Road mileage, 14,933; railway mileage, 563; 419 radio and telegraph stations; 1,031 post offices; 6,917 telephones. Increasingly important in air travel. Coastwise trade by domestic vessels.

RELIGION AND EDUCATION

The dominant religion is Roman Catholic; 12,603,000 followers. Filipino Independent Church, 1,573,608; Protestants, 378,361; Mohammedans, mainly in Mindanao and Sulu, 677,900. Education is free and co-educational; more than 4,000,000 pupils in 21,100 public schools. There are also private, normal, trade, agricultural and nursing schools and numerous colleges as well as the University of the Philippines which has about 7,000 students.

CHIEF TOWNS

Population: Quezon City, capital (Luzon Island), 108,000; Manila (Luzon), 983,900; Cebu (Cebu), 167,500; Davao (Mindanao), 111,300; Iloilo (Panay), 110,100; Zamboanga (Mindanao), 103,300; Bacolod (Negros), 101,400.

ISLAND OF GUAM

A United States Naval Station; civilian governor, responsible to U. S. Department of Interior. Situated at the southern extremity of the Mariana Archipelago in the Pacific Ocean, east of the Philippine Islands. Total area, 206 square miles; population, 58,754.

THIS MANDAYA WARRIOR has a strange, gaudy costume. He comes from east central Mindanao. The Mandayas were noted fighters of the old days when taking a head was not a thing to be concealed from inquisitive constabulary officers. The various Mohammedan tribes which live in the southern islands are generally known as Moros.

THIS ILONGOT GIRL looks bashful but happy. Her good looks may fade early due to the hard life of these nomads who live in the forests and mountains of Nueva Vizcaya largely on game and forest products. There are only a few thousand of these people and they have not made as much progress as some of the other hill people.

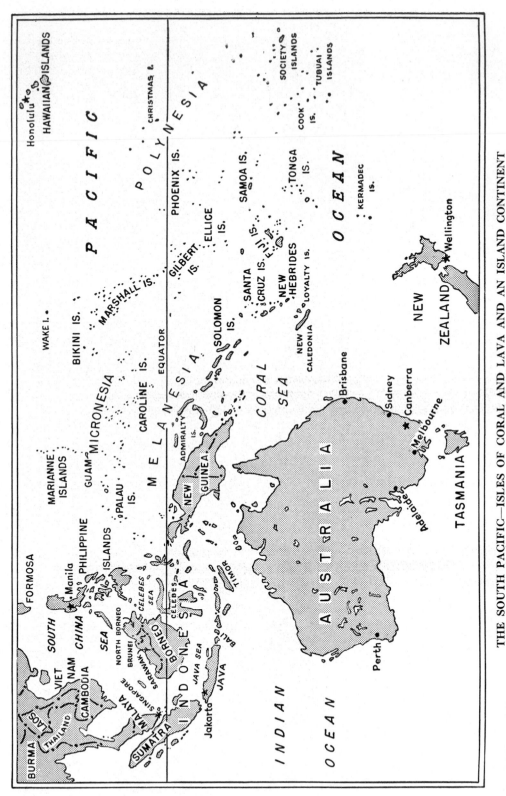

THE SOUTH PACIFIC—ISLES OF CORAL AND LAVA AND AN ISLAND CONTINENT

SUNSHINE ISLES AND SAVAGES

The Untamed Life of the South Seas

One is likely to think that where nature has provided sunshine and delightful scenery life must be at its best. But the human animal often degenerates in such surroundings. It is not the absence of any need to struggle for food and shelter that raises man above the beasts, but rather his need to employ brain and brawn devising means to subsistence. This law of life would account for the low state of the civilization of the South Sea Islands—Fiji, Samoa, Tahiti, Tonga and the Marquesas, Papua and less known ones.

THE Lotus Islands, the Islands of Delight—by these and other names the beautiful isles of the South Seas are widely known. And, certainly, no such description would seem to be too extravagant, for many of them are accounted to be among the loveliest spots on the face of the globe. Strung out across the Pacific Ocean, close to the Equator, they enjoy perpetual summer.

Of the principal groups of South Sea Islands there are two kinds. Some built up by volcanoes, like Tahiti, have mountains, rivers, waterfalls and grand and rugged scenery; others, such as the Paumotus, are of coral formation and very low-lying. While these lack the grandeur of the larger rocky islands they have a charm all their own. Viewed from a distance, only the waving tops of the palm trees greet the eye; then, as the vessel approaches, is seen the outline of the coral reef which forms the boundaries of the islet with its enclosed lagoon. Every traveler to these Eastern Pacific atolls tries to find a fresh phrase in which to convey their beauty.

For geographical purposes the South Sea Islands are classed in three groups: Polynesia ("many islands"), Melanesia ("black islands") and Micronesia ("small islands"). In the first named are included Fiji (north of New Zealand), Tonga, Samoa, Tahiti, the Paumotus, the Marquesas and Hawaii. (The last named will be treated in the same volume as the United States of America.) To the second belong New Guinea, or Papua, one of the two or three largest islands in the world, and the less civilized islands of the Bismarck Archipelago—New Britain,

New Ireland and the Admiralty Islands— the Solomons, the New Hebrides and the Loyalty Islands. In the third group we have the Caroline, the Marshall and the Gilbert Islands. While these names are useful enough, we may distinguish between the main groups in a simpler way.

Natives who are styled Polynesians are good-looking, often even handsome, with brown skins and either smooth or curly hair. Their Melanesian brothers, to the westward, are ugly in type, often repulsively so; they are of a darker color and have frizzy hair. It is to this last-mentioned feature that the Papuans owe their name. The native of New Guinea, the large island just north of Australia, boasts a head of hair that resembles a mop; the Malays christened him "papu-wah," which means "frizzled," and the name has clung to him.

The best known of these islands of the South Seas are perhaps the two hundred or more of the Fijis, though only eighty are inhabited. These offered themselves to the British government in 1874. They are among the most beautiful of all the South Sea Islands. They are further interesting because the Fijians themselves are of two races; indeed, they form a link between the Papuans and the Polynesians. Physically, they are a fine people, tall and strongly built. In color their skins are dark, and they usually have the frizzy hair of the Papuan, as may be seen by our picture of a Fijian belle combing her hair. In the case of children the heads are generally shaven, with just a few tufts of hair left growing.

That the islanders in former days were cannibals and had a reputation for fe-

T. J. MC MAHON

OCEAN ISLAND is one of the Gilbert group, which lies across the Equator and together with the Ellice Islands forms a colony under the rule of Great Britain. Like all South Sea Islanders, the inhabitants love to dance. Here their wide skirts, put on especially for the ceremony, are of palm leaves and their sugar-loaf hats of plaited grass, while feathers decorate their wands. The island—only six miles around—is yet a valuable possession because of the phosphate of lime it exports. This mineral is widely used as fertilizer for crops.

TAPPA AND KAVA are two native names connected with industries peculiar to many of the islands of the South Seas. "Tappa" is a cloth made from the bark of the paper-mulberry, and in the upper photograph we see it being beaten out on wooden blocks. "Kava" is a favorite drink made from the root of a pepper plant which these women are shredding.

rocity is only too true. Human sacrifices were frequent, for the savage mind believed that when a man was killed and eaten, such qualities of courage, strength and cunning as he possessed would pass into the bodies of those who partook of his horrid feast. The human flesh thus eaten was known as "long pig." Many victims were also slain on notable occasions through superstition. At the launching of a new war canoe such a sacrifice was held to bring good luck; on the death of a chief a number of slaves would be killed in order that he might be well served in the after life.

College for Fiji Islanders

With the coming of the missionaries these barbarous customs gradually ceased. From being a bloodthirsty savage the Fijian has become quite a reformed character. To-day he is a peaceable, if not actually gentle chap, with even a leaning toward foppishness in dress. His children attend school and many of the young people of the Fiji Islands go to distant colleges to be trained as teachers and clergymen. Nowhere in the South Pacific has there been such a complete and rapid change from barbarism to civilization as in these islands.

Missionary enterprise has, indeed, been active throughout the South Sea Islands. Ministers of all creeds have gone fearlessly among the wildest tribes to carry their message; many of them have suffered death at the hands of the natives. These workers in the mission field found that the native religion was based on what is known as animism; the people believed that all things, whether human beings, beasts, birds, or trees and stones, had souls which were in some way able to do them either friendly or unfriendly services.

Samoan Islands Divided

During the cotton famine that followed the Civil War, a Hamburg merchant sent men out to Samoa in the middle of the Pacific Ocean to start cotton plantations. But the United States had since 1839 enjoyed the exclusive right to maintain a naval base in the fjordlike harbor of Pago Pago, on the southern coast of Tutuila, besides which Australia and New Zealand were pursuing an important trade with the islands. Great Britain therefore conferred with Germany and the United States in 1880 and provided a government for the Kingdom of Samoa, but in 1889 they decided to divide the islands, and Tutuila and others fell to the lot of the United States, while Upolu and later Savaii went to Germany. Germany lost these islands after World War I. They now comprise a United Nations trusteeship under New Zealand administration.

It was a king of these islands, Malietoa, who befriended the missionary, John Williams. It was these gentle natives among whom Stevenson made his home and to whom he was Tusitala, "the story-teller," and a loved friend.

If we sail across from the Fijis, there will come a point, when we cross the 180th meridian, east longitude, where we will wake to find it the day before. We won't mind that, for we will be too eager to reach a land where we may sit beneath a palm tree and just watch the white-caps dancing across the blue sea, while behind us stretch jungle-clad hills. Tutuila has been built by volcanic action and lies ringed about with coral reefs. At low tide one can see the branches of pink coral rising above the green of shallow waters.

Grass Mats for House Walls

The natives play and bathe in the surf, eat the fruits that grow so abundantly and build their houses by weaving branches for a roof on four poles, then tie on grass mats which can be rolled to the ceiling. The floor is usually raised two feet and surrounded by a ditch to carry off the rain, then paved with stones and pebbles, and at night covered with sleeping-mats. Oranges, bananas, pineapples and breadfruit and of course coconuts grow luxuriantly. On Swain's Island, which was annexed in 1925, the natives pay their taxes usually in copra (dried coconut meat). The Tutuilans wave the Stars and Stripes on the Fourth of July, though the civil officers who are responsible for

FIJI ISLANDERS POUND ON DUGOUTS TO ANNOUNCE CHURCH SERVICES

Sections of ancient dugout canoes find some uses in the Fiji Islands. They are made into mortars for the preparation of food and are also used as drums to assemble the villagers.

the conduct of the island permit the native chiefs a show of doing the governing themselves. The American taste rather balks at kava, the drink of ceremony, for it is made from a root chewed by the prettiest girls to reduce it to a pulp, after which water is added and it becomes a beverage slightly intoxicating but tasting for all the world like soapsuds.

Robert Louis Stevenson has made a certain white villa famous, Vailima, which now is the official residence of Western Samoa. From there one climbs the steep mountain path, part of which the natives who built it call The Road of Loving Hearts, to the peak of Vaea where "R.L.S." lies buried. One finds on his tombstone the familiar verses ending:

> "Home is the sailor, home from the sea,
> And the hunter home from the hill."

AN ISLAND CHIEF in the Solomons wears with pompous pride a necklace of porpoise, shark
and dog teeth and upon his head a polished disk of tortoise shell.

SOLOMON ISLANDERS decorate their high-prowed war-canoes with mother-of-pearl and cowry shells and a carved figurehead designed to ward off danger.

A NURSERY FOR SEEDLINGS OF THE COCONUT PALM

The islands in the Pacific are the best places for the coconut palm, which prefers to grow near the sea. In cultivating a nursery the nuts are planted in mud, or sand and seaweed, and watered until a shoot appears. When this shoot has grown to about the size seen above the nut is transplanted. In about six years the tree begins to bear coconuts.

Tonga, or the Friendly Islands, is a Christian community. The natives are fine physical specimens, stalwart and good-looking, with skins of a bright copper brown and fair, curling hair. They are particularly fond of boxing and wrestling. About the end of the nineteenth century, these Tongans asked to be placed under British protection.

Of the three groups of Tonga Islands, one is of coral formation and one is high and mountainous, and there are active volcanoes on Tofua and Kao. A native queen has succeeded her father. Thanks to British and missionary efforts, there is a Tonga College, free dental and medical service, and at the capital, Nukualofa, a wireless station and a telephone system. About one ship in four weeks sails to New Zealand via Fiji and Samoa.

Eastward of Samoa lie the Society Islands, so named by their discoverer, Captain James Cook, in honor of the Royal Society which had sent him. Between 1768 and 1779 Cook made voyages of discovery which, broadly speaking, brought Polynesia and Micronesia to the knowledge of traders and explorers. He finally met his death in the Sandwich Islands, as Hawaii was formerly called. The principal of the Society Islands is Tahiti, a French possession, the Otaheite of the famous explorer. The natives are tall and robust, dark-skinned, with black curly hair; but they are not so fine to-day as their ancestors, those magnificent men who greeted Captain Cook on his first landing. For like so many Pacific people the Tahitians are decreasing in number, partly because of the diseases that too frequently make ravages among them.

Tahiti is a land of natural loveliness, richly feathered with palms and orange trees, its mountains covered with the umbrella fern and dense thickets of guava. This is "the Pearl of the Pacific," or, as a native bard once styled it, "Great Tahiti the Golden."

The Tahitian is a light-hearted, laughter-loving being with a fondness for dancing and singing. Parties of several hundred will assemble for "himenes" or native singing festivals in which their voices are really tuneful and pleasing. The Tahitian also loves to play some musical instrument. Says one unappreciative writer: "To see a great fellow, six feet high, sit down on the sand under the palms at high noon and go 'twangle, twangle' on a jew's-harp; to see half-a-dozen fo'c'sle hands on a small pearling schooner in a dead calm, sitting by the cookhouse and drinking strong black tea, while they make night hideous with long drawn-out wailings on an old wheezy concertina—such things are enough to make the gravest man crow with laughter."

Papeete, the chief town of Tahiti, is half French and possesses a good normal school. At its docks touch the steamships of the monthly service between San Francisco, Australia and New Zealand, and from its wharves the Society Islands export phosphates, copra and mother-of-pearl. Sailing boats also ply between Papeete and the various islands of the French establishments in Oceania.

Besides Tahiti, one must mention Moorea, the Paumotu group (which form two parallel ranges), Tubuai, and Rapa and the Leeward Islands (Iles sous le Vent). Under the French all of these have united to form one colony.

The Tahiti Islands (French Oceania) call to mind the story of a strange adventure. On Captain Cook's second voyage he had, as sailing-master of the Resolution, an English sailor, William Bligh, who because of his discovery of breadfruit was called "Breadfruit Bligh." He was later sent to take breadfruit trees from the South Sea Islands to the West Indies. The voyage involved a stop-over of six months at Otaheite which his men greatly enjoyed. When they set forth, in April, 1789, in the Bounty, a mutiny

C. W. Collinson

A SOLOMON ISLANDERS WAR-DANCE WITH BARBED SPEARS

War-dances keep the Solomon Islander happy when there is no one to fight. Each man paces forward and back, feints with his spear and guards with his shield, growling viciously all the time. The spear heads are made of the barbed and often poisoned bones of large fish. Under British rule there is now plenty of dancing, but very little real fighting.

v

broke out near the Friendly Islands and Bligh himself, with eighteen of his men, was set adrift in a launch. Day after day they tossed in an open boat, drenched by storms and tortured by hunger and thirst; but after four thousand miles of such progress they reached Timor in the Malay Archipelago. In the meantime the leader of the mutineers, Fletcher Christian, returned to Tahiti with twenty-five men; but the year following headed a party that included eight Englishmen, six Polynesian men and twelve native women and sailed to the sheer black lava cliffs of Pitcairn Island, then burned the Bounty.

Mutineers' Haven a Wireless Station

Here, a hundred miles south of the Paumotu Archipelago, someone found the survivors in 1800, by this time reduced to one white man, Alexander Smith, called John Adams, who was trying to train the half-breed people to the best of his ability. Later seamen who touched on these shores found a tiny colony of Seventh Day Adventists who cultivated beans, pumpkins and other produce and let their goats and chickens run wild. On its two square miles of area there is some timber, but no rivers though rain is abundant. The island had first been sighted in 1767 by a midshipman with Philip Carteret, and at that time was found to be uninhabited, though stone hatchets were found. This island has lately been chosen as a good location for a wireless station.

Still farther westward in the Pacific are found the Paumotus, the Pillar or Cloud Islands of early voyagers, the Drowned Archipelago of Captain Cook, variously called the Low Archipelago and the Dangerous Isles. Some eighty in number, these atolls, or coral islands, are not the least beautiful of natural phenomena in the southern ocean. The islands are low-lying, as has been said; the highest of them rises scarcely more than thirty feet above high water mark; but for quiet charm they are without a parallel. Some are circular in form, others are oval or of a horseshoe shape, but all boast the same feature: the blue lagoon encircled by a coral reef edged with tall palms. Indeed, the Paumotu atolls are a romance of Nature. They have slowly been built up by generations of coral polyps on the summits of submarine mountains.

Lone Traders in Atolls

Not all the Paumotus are inhabited. On more than half of them there is no life save that of sea birds and land crabs. Upon the larger islets a fairly deep soil has formed, and here the breadfruit tree, the coconut palm and the pandanus, together with the banana, flourish. From the dried coconut meat (copra) coconut oil is obtained. On many an atoll is to be found a lone white trader who employs scores of Paumotuans in collecting the nuts from the palm trees and chopping them open to dry.

It is the coconut palm which the robber land crab seeks out for his depredations. This native of the atoll is a monster crab, as much as two feet long. Its strength is remarkable, and it will bite off eight or ten nuts at each ascent of a palm. How the Paumotuan outwits this enemy is ingenious. When a native finds that a crab has made its way up a palm, he prepares a kind of wreath or girdle of clay and leaves or grass. With this he climbs some distance up the tree and plasters it firmly around the trunk. The crab comes down the tree backward, and when he feels the clay below him he takes it to be the solid earth. As a result he loosens his hold of the tree and falls to the ground below, where, if he be not already done for, he is quickly pounded to death, with a club.

Dive for Mother-of-pearl

For all that these South Sea atolls are so beautiful, the Paumotuan has a monotonous time of it upon his white coral beaches. His chief and often sole occupations are the collecting of copra and diving for pearl oysters. The latter, if they do not yield real pearls, provide the mother-of-pearl that is so valuable in commerce. The islanders are expert divers, scorn diving-suits and fearlessly descend into the clear, shark-haunted waters.

By nature the Paumotuan is quiet and serious-minded, very unlike the joyous-hearted Tahitian. This is the result of his surroundings. First, his range of food is small: the usual diet is coconuts and fish. Every lagoon is stocked with fish beyond number. In addition, at certain seasons, there is the fear of the cyclones which sometimes rage through this part of the ocean. Whole populations of islands have been wiped out at times by these awesome visitations and their houses and other possessions completely destroyed.

The Marquesas Islands are a Polynesian group which belongs to France, the largest of which is Nukahiva. Here the tropical trees and blossoming shrubs perfume the air. A plant peculiar to the Marquesas is the cassi, a bush bearing yellow flowers. This sweet-smelling shrub blooms every month of the year, and the fragrance of its pollen, which is blown far out to sea, can be smelled long before land is touched.

In 1842 France assumed a protectorate over the Marquesas, and in 1853 annexed the New Caledonia Islands with the idea of establishing a penal settlement.

It was in these islands that tattooing—an art practiced widely throughout the Pacific—reached its artistic height. The Marquesan has always been a splendid type of physical fitness. In times past he was among the most warlike of the islanders, even addicted to cannibalism, but to-day he lives peaceably with his neighbors. As a warrior he delighted to tattoo his body from head to toe, and nowhere else were such elaborate patterns devised.

The chief professors of the art, the

© Underwood & Underwood

SEA-PLANE AND FLYING BOAT ASTONISH A PAPUAN VILLAGE

Papua is the east or British portion of the great island of New Guinea, just north of Australia. Many of the villages are built on piles over lagoons. One day an exploring party visited the coast in an aeroplane with a motion picture camera. The natives were at first terrified, but curiosity soon mastered their fear, as is evident above.

"tuhukas," belonged to a guild of a most exclusive kind and ranked next to the chiefs. At festivals an assembly used to be held that was much in the nature of a country fair. People came in from great distances to feast and make merry, and be tattooed, or to have repairs done to their previously decorated skins. Often the full adornment of a man was not complete until his thirtieth year.

Under French rule, however, tattooing has been stopped.

In the Marquesas Islands the "tapu" convention has ever been strong. A tapu (from which we get our word "taboo") is a prohibition. For reasons often of mysterious origin, it was tapu for a woman to enter a canoe, to wear red or dark blue, to smoke inside a house or to carry a mat upon the head, and so on.

A STREET OF EXPORTERS AND IMPORTERS IN SUVA, FIJI ISLANDS

Suva, on the island of Viti Levu, is the capital of the colony and chief port. It has a fine harbor inside a barrier reef that forms a natural breakwater. Sugar is the main export.

A DUK-DUK OF NEW BRITAIN—HIDDEN IN LEAVES AND A MASK

The Duk-Duks are a secret society of men devoted to preserving ancient customs. They act as judges and pose as sorcerers. The grotesque costume seems to be designed to invoke fear.

Women might not eat in men's company. Certain animals and fish were tapu—that is, no one was allowed to kill and eat them. As a rule tapus were regarded as sacred, and few people were foolhardy enough to risk breaking one. In the case of the canoe tapu, this was ultimately set at defiance by some daring women, and the prohibition, once broken, was never put in force again. Similarly these brown-skinned suffragettes obtained the freedom to eat bananas and pork, neither of which had Marquesan women tasted for the past thousand years.

In that quarter of the Pacific known as Melanesia, where the natives are darker in hue and less civilized by contact with the white races, the two island groups of most consequence are New Guinea and the Solomons. New Guinea is a vast island, one of the several largest on the globe, a half of which belongs to the Dutch East Indies, treated in another article. By an agreement between Germany and England in 1884 these two countries divided the other half of New Guinea, and Australia administers British New Guinea (Papua), as well as the late German New Guinea which it seized in 1914.

Papua is the southeastern part of New Guinea. Here the tribes dwelling in the large settled areas have been induced by the missionaries to settle down and live peaceably with one another, and white planters raise coconuts, rubber and sisal hemp. A regulation strictly enforced obliges native land-holders to plant coconuts or other economically useful trees if the soil permits, and communal plantations have been established under European agricultural teachers. Native children are also obliged to attend schools where English is taught. Moreover, a government anthropologist is employed and a family bonus is paid to native mothers of four or more children under sixteen. Gold and copper-mining are important industries, and indications of oil have been found over a large area.

STEAMER IN HARBOR AT PAPEETE, TAHITI'S PORT OF ARRIVAL

The fourteen Society Islands are the most westerly of the French settlements in the South Seas. Of these, Tahiti, in the Windward (eastern) group, is the largest. Its chief town, the seaport of Papeete, is the seat of the administration of the French colony.

Horses and cattle are among the exports loaded every month on the steamer from Port Moresby to Sydney. The natives raise yams and taro for their own use and build long houses, sometimes on piles, especially along the coast, with often a community-house where gatherings are held and guests accommodated.

In remote portions of the mandated territory of northeastern New Guinea, cannibalism has not been entirely wiped out and blood feuds are sometimes carried on for generations. The high ranges of the interior are very little known, for the coastline presents few good harbors, the climate is hot and the rainfall excessive. Native children are recruited for the plantations. The missionaries and traders hope to civilize these people in time.

The British High Commissioner of the Western Pacific has jurisdiction over a number of islands, including the Southern Solomons and the small groups in Melanesia, Pitcairn Island (before described) and the Gilbert and Ellice Islands Colony

(with headquarters at Ocean Island), important because of its phosphates, which have been worked by a British company since 1921. The Gilbert and Ellice Islands Colony includes Christmas Island, discovered by Captain Cook in 1777, which possesses the distinction of being the largest atoll in the Pacific. It has a circumference of a hundred miles. Its population, however, like that of many of the bewildering number of South Sea Islands, consists of several white men and enough natives to work the coconut plantations.

The British Solomon Islands, a protectorate which covers a considerable area, includes Guadalcanal, Malaita, Ysabel, San Cristoval, New Georgia, Choiseul, Shortland, Mono (or Treasury), Vella Lavella, Ronongo, Gizo, Rendova, Russell, Florida, Ronnell and other individual islands, besides the Lord Howe Group or Ontong Java, the Santa Cruz Islands, Tucopia and Mitre Islands and the Duff or Wilson group. While rub-

Sir Basil Thomson

TURTLES FOR THE TABLE OUTSIDE A FIJIAN GRASS HOUSE

Great turtles swim in the seas around the islands of Fiji and come up on to the beaches to lay their eggs. Turtle meat is a favorite dish with the islanders. The best portions are the greenish jelly from the back and the yellowish-white flesh from the stomach.

ber grows well on many of the islands and the natives also collect ivory nuts, the seeds of certain palms which are so hard that buttons can be made of them, it is copra which provides them with the goods they cannot produce themselves.

In the past the Solomon Islanders had a reputation for being a fierce and warlike people. They upheld that reputation during World War II, when they served as scouts for the Allied forces in their struggle to drive the Japanese invaders from the Solomon Islands. While, like the Papuans, they wear little clothing, the Solomon natives are fond of ornaments. A chief, for instance, may wear a necklace composed of the teeth of sharks and dogs, earrings, bracelets and anklets, while with women tattooing is the height of fashion. Another characteristic of these islanders is their love of dancing.

The high-prowed canoes of the Solomon natives are distinctive and the special pride of their makers. Often the prows tower above a tall man's head and are decorated with an elaborately carved figurehead which is supposed to ward off danger. Beautiful designs are carved or set in shell along the crafts' sides.

The peoples of the New Hebrides, New Britain, New Ireland and the Loyalty, Marshall and Gilbert islands were once less friendly to strangers than were the Polynesians. Today, however, they are generally friendly and have a better understanding of the ways of white men. Nevertheless they still preserve many of their primitive customs. Since the end of the nineteenth century the New Hebrides have been divided between British and French rule. The larger of this group are Espiritu Santo, Malekula, Epi, Ambrym, Efate or Sandwich, Erromanga, Tanna and Aneityúm. There are active volcanoes on Tanna, Ambrym and Lopevi, and earthquake shocks are a fairly common occurrence. The New Hebrides Islands are all hilly and well wooded and their forests produce sandalwood and ebony. There are many large coconut plantations. The population of the islands is small; there are barely enough natives on all of them together to make up what we would call a goodsized town. However, Vila, the capital and principal seaport of the islands, is quite a busy port.

Nauru, twenty-six miles south of the Equator, finally, is a circular atoll surrounded by a reef of such forbidding character that there is no anchorage along its coast. But the plateau that rises inland is rich with high-grade deposits of phosphate which are worked by the British Phosphate Commissioners who maintain a plant upon the island.

ISLANDS OF THE PACIFIC: FACTS AND FIGURES

GREAT BRITAIN
Fiji Islands

Group of 322 islands (about 106 inhabited) in Melanesia. Total area, 7,056 square miles. The estimated population, 293,764. Area of Viti Levu (the largest island) is 4,010 square miles. The colony is administered by a governor, who is assisted by an Executive Council consisting of 9 members and a Legislative Council of 16 members with the governor as president. Chief exports: sugar, gold, copra, bananas and timber. Imports: textiles, flour, machinery, hardware and petroleum. There are government and mission schools. Population of Suva, the capital, is 11,398.

Western Pacific Islands, British

Includes the 5 territories of Tonga Islands, Gilbert and Ellice Islands, British Solomon Islands, Pitcairn Island, New Hebrides Islands Condominium and Caroline, Flint, Malden, Starbuck and Vostok of the Line Islands.

Tonga (Friendly) Islands. Three groups of islands in Polynesia; approximate area, 269 square miles; population, 48,250. British protectorate since 1900; monarch and Legislative Assembly of 21 members. Chief product and export is copra. Capital, Nukualofa.

Gilbert and Ellice Islands Colony. Micronesian and Polynesian coral islands with a total area of 375 square miles and population of 38,000. The colony is governed by Resident Commissioner at Tarawa in the Gilberts. It is composed of Gilbert Islands, Ellice Islands, Ocean Island, Phoenix Islands and Fanning, Washington and Christmas islands. Canton and Enderbury in the Phoenix group are controlled jointly by Britain and the United States. Chief exports are copra and phosphate.

British Solomon Islands Protectorate. Composed of the southern Solomons—San Christobal, Malaita, Guadalcanal, Tulagi, Florida, Santa

Ysabel, New Georgia, Choiseul, Vella Lavella and numerous small islands—and outlying Rennell, Santa Cruz and Ontong Java groups. Area, 14,600 square miles, and population, 100,000. Governed by Resident Commissioner. Copra, trochus shells and gold are leading products and exports.

Pitcairn Island Colony. Near Tropic of Capricorn 3,000 miles from South America; area, 2 square miles, and population, 130. Governed by an elected Chief Magistrate and council. Dependencies: Henderson, Ducie and Oeno islands.

New Hebrides. A group south of the Solomons governed as an Anglo-French Condominium. Main islands are Espiritu Santo, Malekula, Ambrym, Epi, Efate, Erromanga and Tanna; total area, 5,700 square miles, and population, 49,000. Principal exports are copra, cocoa, coffee and timber. The capital is Vila, on Efate.

AUSTRALIA

Papua. Consists of southeastern New Guinea, the D'Entrecasteaux, Louisiade, Trobriand and other near-by island groups; total area, 90,540 square miles, and population, 372,939. Administration was linked with that of New Guinea trusteeship territory and is under Administrator, appointed by Governor-General of Australia, and 2 councils, executive and legislative. Chief products and exports are copra, rubber, gold, manganese, coffee, shells and copal. Domestic and international air services. Port Moresby is the capital.

Other dependencies of Australia include Norfolk Island, 900 miles east of New South Wales, with area of 13 square miles and population of 1,148; the Territory of Ashmore and Cartier Islands; Cocos Islands, 700 miles southwest of Java with area of 1.5 square miles and population of 1,342; the Antarctic islands of Heard and MacDonald, and a section of Antarctica between 45 and 160 degrees east longitude with the exception of Terre-Adélie.

NEW ZEALAND

Cook Islands. A group in Polynesia; the most important are Rarotonga, Aitutaki, Mangaia and Atiu; area, 99 square miles; population, 15,031. Governed by Resident Commissioner and Legislative Council. Chief exports are citrus fruits, mother-of-pearl and copra.

Niue (Savage) Island. In the Cook group, administered separately by Resident Commissioner. Area, 100 square miles; population, 4,471. Chief product is copra.

Tokelau (Union) Islands. Atafu, Nukunono and Fakaofo atolls 300 miles north of Western Samoa; area, 4 square miles, with a population of 1,534.

FRANCE

New Caledonia and Dependencies. Overseas Territory comprising New Caledonia (area, 8,548 square miles), the near-by Loyalty Islands (800 square miles), Isle of Pines (58 square miles) and other minor islets and groups, as well as the outlying groups—Wallis Archipelago (40 square miles) and Futuna and Alofi (58 square miles). Total area, 9,401 square miles; population, 70,000. Governor is also French High Commissioner in the Pacific. He is assisted in New Caledonia by a Privy Council and Council-General. Farming, livestock raising, mining and manufacturing are carried on. Chief products are nickel, chromium, coffee and copra. Nouméa, the capital (population, 11,000), is an important sea and air port.

French Establishments in Oceania. Scattered islands in the eastern South Pacific administered by a Governor, Privy Council and representative assembly. Area, 1,543 square miles; population, 60,000; establishments are Society Islands, largest of which are Tahiti and Moorea; Marquesas Islands; Tuamotu Islands; Tubuai (Austral) Islands; Gambier Archipelago, and the distant island of Clipperton. Exports: copra and phosphate; mother-of-pearl and tropical fruits are also important. Population of capital and largest town, Papeete, on Tahiti, 12,500.

UNITED STATES

American Samoa. Includes the islands of Tutuila and Aunuu, Manua group and outlying Swains Island; area, 73 square miles; population, 18,937. U. S. Naval authority was transferred in 1951 to a civil governor under the Interior Department. Chief town is Pagopago.

TERRITORIES UNDER UNITED NATIONS TRUSTEESHIP: FACTS AND FIGURES

AUSTRALIA

New Guinea. Territory comprises northeastern New Guinea, Bismarck Archipelago (New Britain, New Ireland and Admiralty Islands) and northern Solomons (Bougainville, Buka and smaller islands). Area, 93,000 square miles; population, 1,071,000; administered with Territory of Papua. Exports: copra, gold and marine shells. Principal towns: Finschhafen and Lae, on New Guinea; Rabaul and Kokopo, on New Britain.

Nauru. Island near equator west of Gilberts; area, 8 square miles; population, 3,432. Authority granted to Britain, Australia and New Zealand; governed by Australia. Chief product is phosphate.

NEW ZEALAND

Western Samoa. Comprising Savaii, Opolu, Manono and Apolima islands and several islets north of the Tongas. Administered by Council of State and Legislative Assembly. Area, 1,130; population, 80,436. Principal products and exports: copra, cocoa and bananas. Roads, 263 miles; steamer and air service to Fijis and New Zealand. Chief town is Apia, on Opolu.

UNITED STATES

Pacific Islands. Consisting of Caroline, Mariana and Marshall groups; area, 829.7 square miles; population, 85,000. Formerly a Japanese mandate, since World War II under U. S. administration. Chief products: cotton, copra.

KOALAS—AUSTRALIAN COUSINS TO THE KANGAROO AND OPOSSUM

Australian native bears, or koalas, are not live "teddy bears" but tree dwellers that carry their young in pouches. Animal gourmets, they eat only the leaves of certain eucalyptus trees.

THE ISLAND CONTINENT

Home of the Australians

In the skies above Australia and in its flag gleam the stars of the Southern Cross, for Australia is the only continent that lies wholly south of the equator. People living to the north often call Australia the land "down under." Less than two hundred years ago, it was a mysterious place, almost unknown to the rest of the world and inhabited only by wandering tribes of primitive people. Today, it is a thriving, self-reliant nation of people who still bear the stamp of their pioneering ancestors. A loyal partner in the British Commonwealth of Nations, Australia is, at the same time, a separate country.

AUSTRALIA is the smallest continent and the largest island in the world. In fact, it is about twenty-five times the size of the British Isles. At its widest parts, it is about 2,400 miles from east to west, and about 2,000 miles from north to south. Including Tasmania, there are 12,210 miles of coast.

Australia is one of the oldest of the continents, formed at an early period in the earth's history. It is the most level in surface and the most regular in outline. There are no towering peaks—only the worn-down stumps of mountains that were high long ages ago. The chief mountain system is the Great Dividing Range. It runs like a giant fishbone down the whole length of the east coast, from the northern tip of Queensland to the southern part of Tasmania.

This range includes the beautiful Blue Mountains, in New South Wales, where Mount Kosciusko reaches the greatest height (7,328 feet) of any peak in Australia. Covered with snow in cold seasons, the Blue Mountains are a paradise for winter sports as well as for hunting and fishing.

Along the coast of eastern Australia, there are wide, deep valleys that long ago were carved out of high plateaus by swift rivers. This same process left spurs of cliffs at the edge of the coast, flanked by sandy beaches.

One of Australia's most fascinating features is the Great Barrier Reef, which skirts the coast of Queensland. The reef —actually a maze of reefs, shoals and islands—stretches for 1,270 miles and shelters a lagoon of 80,000 square miles. The strange plant and animal life here is of great interest to scientists, and the government of Queensland has a research station on Heron Island, in the heart of the lagoon. The reef is formed of coral—countless skeletons of tiny marine creatures called polyps. Flowerlike sea anemones wave their tentacles in the warm waters. Here live the dugong, or sea cow, and the mud skipper, a true fish, though if kept long under water it will drown. On many of the reef's islands there are cool, twilit forests of pisonia trees. Their sticky fruits are death traps for small birds, winged insects and spiders. Noddies and other terns nest in these trees, besides shearwaters (mutton-birds), gentle doves, kingfishers, noisy crow-shrikes and even sea eagles.

On the western side of the Great Dividing Range, there is a great plateau, which extends over practically half of the continent. The slopes of this plateau that ascend to the mountains are smooth and usually too steep for a plow. However, where they have been cleared of forest, they have become the world's chief merino wool-growing region.

In the heart of Australia is a great basin, usually dry. Here there are stony (gibber) plains, with little soil and practically no vegetation. The ground consists of limestone or quartzite. Beautiful opals, in which the fires of ages long past still shimmer, are found on these barren plains.

Australia was cut off from Asia at such an early period in the earth's history

THE "THREE SISTERS," RUGGED QUEENS OF THE BLUE MOUNTAIN RANGE

The jagged peaks of the Blue Mountains formed an impenetrable barrier to the first colonists of New South Wales. Today, they are a popular mountain retreat for the residents of Sydney.

WHERE FERNS GROW TO BE TREES

Australia lies in the temperate and tropic zones and has a vegetation as varied as its climate. Graceful "fern trees" flourish in the tropic gullies of the Black Spur ridges near Melbourne.

that animals survived on the island continent that died out elsewhere. It is the home of marsupials, animals that carry their young in pouches. The most famous marsupial is the kangaroo. With the tremendous strength of its tail and rear legs, it bounds across country in great leaps. Most endearing of the marsupials is the koala, which looks like a child's teddy bear though it is not a bear at all. Australia is also the home of perhaps the strangest mammal in the world, the platypus. Its four feet are webbed, and it has the bill of a duck, the tail of a beaver and the fur of a mole. The female lays eggs but suckles her young.

More than a third of Australia lies within the tropics, and the other two-thirds is within the southern temperate zone. Because of this position and the fact that Australia is an island and has no great land barriers, it has, on the whole, a more temperate climate than other regions of the same size in the same latitudes. Over the greater part of the continent the climate is similar to that of southern France or Italy. There are seldom any extreme degrees of heat or cold.

The winds that blow on Australia are the southeast trades and the prevailing westerlies. The southern limit of the southeast trades strikes Australia's east coast near the border of the states of New South Wales and Queensland. With a few exceptions, especially in Tasmania, the heaviest rains in Australia are along the east coast north of this point.

The westerly winds skirt the southern shores. They bring reliable, light to moderate rains to the southwestern parts of Western Australia, the agricultural parts of South Australia, to the greater part of Victoria and to the whole of Tasmania.

However, Australia has large areas of scant rainfall. In fact, nearly 40 per cent of the continent is, in effect, desert. Of this enormous area, 600,000 square miles is of practically no use to man and only

IS THIS CREATURE BIRD OR BEAST?

The platypus, native to Australia, is a duck-billed, web-footed mammal that lays eggs.

wandering tribes of aboriginies can eke out an existence in it. In some places, water has been found by boring very deep (artesian) wells, but the water is apt to contain too many minerals and is not enough to make up for the lack of rainfall.

The main Australian river system is that of the Murray (1,609 miles) and its tributaries—the Murrumbidgee, Lachlan

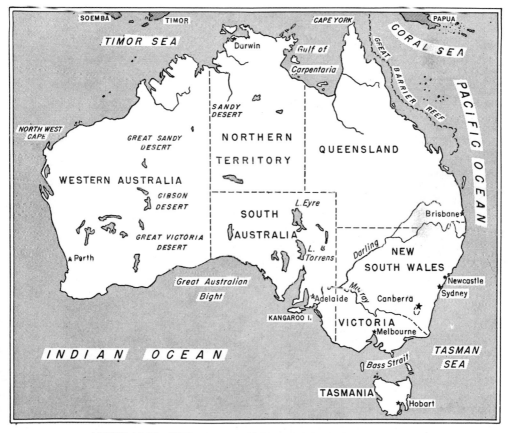

AUSTRALIA, THE FASCINATING ISLAND CONTINENT

325

THE CORAL SANDS AND SUNLIT WATERS OF THE GREAT BARRIER REEF

Australian vacationers have discovered the attractions of the coral islands of the Great Barrier Reef, which were once haunted chiefly by marine scientists and gaily colored fish.

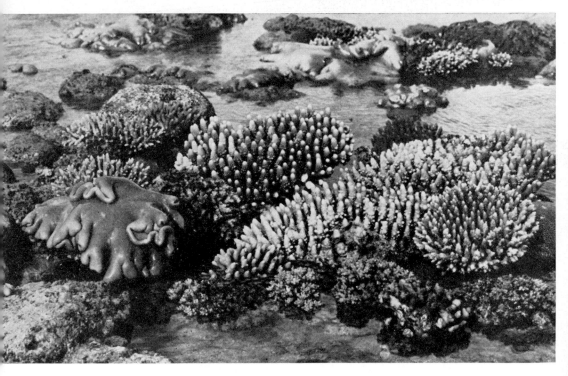

A BRIGHT CORAL GARDEN MORE THAN A THOUSAND MILES IN AREA

The Great Barrier Reef, a chain of islands north of Queensland, has been raised from the ocean floor by the action of microscopic coral animals working for many thousands of years.

and Darling. This system drains an area of 414,253 square miles, larger than the combined areas of France and Spain. The Murray and its branches rise in the Great Dividing Range and find their way to the sea through South Australia. On the eastern side of the Great Dividing Range, many short rivers run to the sea. So swift are their currents, however, that

corner of the continent. These forests are open and seem like parks. Both hardwoods and eucalypts are found in Western Australia. Here two of the chief timber trees are jarrah and karri. The karri is one of the handsomest trees in the world. It reaches up to 300 feet, seldom branching below 150 feet.

Beyond the eastern mountains are wide

A LOBSTER FISHERMAN PREPARES TO TRAP A SUCCULENT CRUSTACEAN

The export of frozen lobster tails is big business to the lobsterman. He buoys his wire pots with glass globes but, as in all fishing tales, some of the fish are carried away by the current.

few good harbors have been formed. Many of the rivers that run inland, north of the Murray system, are swallowed up in the dry sands of the interior.

In the tropical north are dense forests of cedar and other softwood trees. The famous evergreen eucalypt forests occur in the well-watered coastal regions of the eastern seaboard and in the southwest

belts of pine and more eucalypt trees. Farther inland there are savannas, where mulga and other acacias grow, and belts of mallee, a low-growing eucalypt. These areas are often well-grassed. Between the grassland zones and the desert regions are tracts of saltbush and bluebush. These are low, fleshy-leaved shrubs, which thrive in dry soil and are good

WHEN IT'S ROUND-UP TIME AT A NEW SOUTH WALES SHEEP STATION

At some Australian stations 70,000 sheep are sheared during the six-weeks shearing season. Here, a "jackeroo," Australian for young stockman, herds the sheep toward the shearing sheds.

sheep food. In fact, almost every plant in Australia may be eaten by sheep and cattle. For this reason, the wool and cattle industries are built more on herbage and scrub pasture than on improved grassland.

It was the American War of Independence that first turned Britain's eyes toward Australia. England's prisons were full and as the American colonies were closed to any more such exports of "undesirables," attention turned to Australia. Only a few years before, in 1770, Captain James Cook had discovered the east coast and had written about it with enthusiasm. So, in 1787, a fleet of eleven ships set sail for Australia with 1,500 persons— 800 of whom were convicts. In January 1788, after a wearisome voyage of eight months, this fleet reached Botany Bay, near where Australia's largest city, Sydney, now stands.

The early settlers had a hard time. There were few farmers or skilled workers among them. Sometimes it was many months between rains and the soft English wheat they had planted died. For a long time the settlers depended wholly upon supplies from England, including flour. When a ship was lost or delayed they went on hard rations of rice and salt pork. Too, the first settlement found itself hemmed in on a strip of land between two barriers—the vast Pacific Ocean and the wall of the Blue Mountains. Though not so high as the mountains of Europe, Asia and the Americas, these still presented a formidable obstacle to the further colonization of the Australian interior.

The land seemed anything but hospitable, and the establishment of permanent colonies was one of the toughest pioneering jobs ever undertaken. The outstanding names in early Australian history are not those of soldiers or statesmen but of explorers. These were the men who really developed Australia. They realized that they had to find better land than existed around the small settlement of Sydney, but it was twenty-five years before two men, named Wentworth and Blaxland, finally managed to find a way over the Blue Mountains. Once over the barrier, they saw great fertile plains that

GOING, GOING, GONE! BUYERS AT A MELBOURNE WOOL AUCTION

Bidding is a spirited but serious matter for these buyers from woolen mills the world over, who are competing for the best of the Australian crop at the Melbourne Wool Exchange auction.

GETTING WOOL OFF TO THE CITY MARKET FROM A SHEEP STATION

Heavy bales of wool are being dragged from the shearing sheds for transportation to the railheads. The bales are destined for Sydney, the biggest wool-shipping center in the world.

DRAY HORSES HAULING LOGS IN THE FORESTS OF QUEENSLAND

Machines cannot penetrate the dense interior of the Australian timberlands and horses and bullocks are still used. Queensland is noted for the fine quality of its cabinet-type woods.

REAPING AND SPREADING A FIELD OF FLAX

A mechanical reaper-spreader cuts and spreads a flax crop in South Australia. The fibers are then retted, or soaked, to separate them for linen. Flaxseeds yield linseed oil.

stretched westward, and their reports started other explorers on the westward trek. Colonists followed, who brought cattle and sheep with them. In some ways progress was similar to the early development of the West of North America. However, as the Australians drove farther westward, they found deserts instead of great fertile valleys and prairies.

Thereafter the population increased very slowly, for there was little to attract newcomers. Settlement might have continued at this slow pace, but chance and one man's alertness changed the course of Australian history almost overnight. In 1849, Edward Hargraves, an unsuccessful sheep farmer of New South Wales, went to California to join the gold rush. He had no luck, but he was a very observant man and he noticed that the countryside where the richest California finds were made looked very much like the countryside around his Australian home. With this in mind, he returned to Australia in

WHIRRING SPINDLES IN A LARGE COTTON FACTORY

Australian textile mills produce fine fabrics for the home trade and for export. These girls are tending the spinning frame in a cotton mill in Kilkenny, South Australia.

DREDGING THE BROWN COAL MINES FOR FUEL AND ELECTRIC POWER

The dredgers used in the open pits of the brown coal, or lignite, mines at Yallourn, Victoria, can dig ninety feet. The mineral is used to generate electricity and for fuel briquettes.

PRODUCING STEEL FOR THE HEAVY INDUSTRIES OF AUSTRALIA

A view of the steel works at Newcastle, New South Wales. Newcastle, the center of the steel and coal industry, has played an important part in the rapid industrialization of Australia.

1851 and, within a few weeks, he struck it rich around Lewis Ponds, New South Wales. Hargraves' good fortune was followed by strikes in Victoria and Western Australia. The word spread and people poured in from all quarters of the globe. In the next ten years, Australia's population jumped from 405,000 to 1,145,000. During this period, Australia produced more than $224,000,000 worth of gold. The discovery of gold also produced a social and economic revolution, for, prior to Hargraves' find, pastoralists, or squatters, had dominated the economic life and government of Australia. Though the country still rides "on the sheep's back" as far as overseas trade is concerned, the democratic ideas stirred up by the gold-mining days are now the accepted commonplaces of government.

The first Federal Convention, which prepared the draft constitution of the Federated States of Australia, was held in Sydney in 1891. The Commonwealth of Australia came into existence by an act of the British Parliament in July 1900, which took effect from January 1, 1901. The Constitution was worked out by Australia's own leaders and was established by democratic ballot taken among the Australian people. The first Prime Minister was Edmund Barton.

To understand Australia's Constitution, we must remember that it is a federal constitution. That is, the governments of the various states did not lose their separate identities. The state parliaments, under the Commonwealth Constitution, agreed to federate, or to hand over some of their government powers—but by no means all—to a central, Australia-wide government.

The spirit in which the task of drafting a federal government was approached was expressed by one speaker in these words: "I hold it to be a basic principle of this federation that we should take no power from the States which they could better exercise themselves; we should place no power in federation which is not abso-

ORE MORE PRECIOUS THAN GOLD

The atomic age has sent the world on a treasure hunt for uranium ore. Modern prospectors armed with Geiger counters seek new deposits of the rare metal in the Flinders Range.

lutely required for carrying out its purpose."

There are about 8,500,000 Australians. The national income of Australia was almost $7,000,000,000 in a recent year. The personal income of Australians in the same year was more than $6,530,000,000, of which more than $3,350,000,000 was received in wages and salaries by about 3,000,000 people. A further 600,000 worked on their own account.

Almost from the earliest days of settlement, Australia was a great primary producing country (agricultural products and basic raw materials), exporting large surpluses overseas. Today many persons abroad (and to some extent in Australia itself) are inclined to think of the average Australian as a man on the land. But although Australia retains her great primary industries, she has become one of the world's most highly industrialized nations, and the value of her production from industry is almost equal to that from the land.

It is interesting to note, however, that, in numbers, more than half of Australia's

A WESTERN AUSTRALIAN GOLD-DIGGER'S EQUIPMENT

The mechanical dryblower, at right, is used in the gold fields of Western Australia. As the tray shakes, dirt and dust are blown away, leaving any gold particles in the bottom.

THE FLARE OF THE WELDING TORCH AND THE RING OF THE HAMMER

At a gigantic New South Wales engineering plant, a welder seals the seam of a boiler. The man with the hammer hits the metal and the ringing sound tells him whether the metal is welded.

THE MAGNIFICENT HARBOR OF SYDNEY, AUSTRALIA

Sydney, the largest city and seaport of Australia and a famed industrial center, is the capital of New South Wales. It is the oldest Australian city, as well as the most populous, having been founded in 1788. In the foreground is seen one of the world's great steel arch bridges, the Sydney Harbor Bridge. It is 160 feet wide and has a span of 1,650 feet.

MANES FLOWING AND FEET FLYING, WILD STALLIONS SEEK FREEDOM

The brumby muster is a rough and exciting chase. Brumbies are Australian wild horses. A cowboy pursues the stallions toward the open country, away from the treacherous rocks.

ROUGH RIDING IN THE VAST CATTLE COUNTRY OF QUEENSLAND

Goondiwindi, Queensland, is the scene of the annual Bushman's Carnival. This cowgirl is competing in the camp drafting contest. In this event the task of the rider is to cut out a bullock from the herd and to drive the animal to a designated sector of the corral. The judges award points for the degree of horsemanship displayed by the hard-riding cowhands.

AN AERIAL VIEW OF THE FEDERAL PARLIAMENT HOUSE IN CANBERRA

Canberra, the capital of Australia, is a lovely tree-lined city situated at the foothills of the Australian Alps. The monument in the foreground is the King George V Memorial.

WAITING FOR THE GAME TO BEGIN AT THE MELBOURNE CRICKET GROUND

When Australia plays host to the "Battle of the Ashes," a series of championship cricket matches between England and Australia, the contest is held in this huge cricket ground.

338

industries are tertiary—that is, they provide services of various kinds. This means railways and roads, air lines, telephones, telegraph, radio and so on. The large proportion of such industries shows that Australians have a comparatively high standard of living.

Wool is Australia's greatest primary industry. In a recent year there were 116,000,000 sheep, and the value of the

Beef production runs to about 650,000 tons a year, and dairies produce about 165,000 tons of butter and 45,000 tons of cheese. Supplies of beef, mutton, lamb, butter and cheese are usually above the quantities needed at home, and the surpluses are exported, mainly to the British Isles.

Although Australia does not rank high as a wheat-producing country, she is one

EIGHTEEN-FOOTERS SKIM ACROSS THE WATERS OF SYDNEY HARBOR

Yatching is not a rich man's sport in Sydney, but a popular pastime. On regatta days, the eighteen-foot sailing yachts with ballooning spinnakers are the rulers of the big harbor.

total wool production was about $750,-000,000. With a normal annual clip of more than 1,000,000,000 pounds, Australia produces about 30 per cent of the world's wool and more than half of its merino wool. It produces 40 to 60 per cent of all wool and 70 per cent of all merino wool entering into world trade. Lamb and mutton (277,000 tons in a recent year) and sheep skins are important parts of the industry.

of the world's four principal wheat exporters. More than half the crop is shipped abroad. In a recent year the harvest from nearly 12,000,000 acres was 184,000,000 bushels.

There are important coal fields in the eastern mountains. In fact, the brown coal of Yallourn gives the state of Victoria most of its electricity. Early in the 1950's, uranium was discovered at Radium Hill, in South Australia.

A STATELY, MODERN HIGH SCHOOL BUILDING IN MELBOURNE

The Australian states support the primary and high schools in their areas. The Boys' High School at Forest Hills, a suburb of Melbourne, is one of the finest schools in Victoria state.

The majority of the Australians live in towns or in the capital cities of the six states. Largest of all is Sydney, capital of New South Wales. It has a magnificent harbor, spanned by one of the greatest steel arch bridges in the world. Sydney's George Street is the busiest thoroughfare in the whole of Australia.

Canberra, capital of the Australian Commonwealth, is in its own Federal Territory, not far from Sydney. Everywhere in Canberra there are avenues of trees—native gums (eucalypts), foreign oaks and flowering fruit trees. The location of the city is beautiful. To the south are the Australian Alps and to the north the Blue Mountains. In recent years, the population of Canberra has been growing at a rapid rate.

Darwin, once simply a lonely outpost on the northern coast, also has been growing at a swift pace since World War II, when it was the target for devastating bombing raids. The town is the chief trading center for the Northern Territory and a terminus for overseas air traffic.

The largest shipyards in Australia are at Whyalla, on the coast of South Australia. This town is becoming one of the country's most important industrial centers. Near by are Australia's chief iron-ore resources, and there are plants for

the manufacture of steel in Whyalla.

Australia is one of the most highly urbanized countries in the world. One reason for this is that settlement has been mainly on the fertile coastal strips. Also, Australian agriculture is highly mechanized, which means that large farms and livestock stations can be run with comparatively few hands. What is more, the growth of a big export trade has led to the development of the ports that, in most instances, are the state capitals.

In New South Wales, the railways radiate from Sydney like the spokes of a giant wheel. They also branch out from Melbourne, capital of Victoria, from Adelaide, capital of South Australia, and, to a lesser extent, from Brisbane, capital of Queensland, and from Perth, capital of Western Australia. In all there are some 28,000 miles of railways, which carry about 500,000,000 passengers a year.

Air transport is playing a big part in Australia, a land of immense distances. Air routes over the continent total 68,000 miles. By flying-boat, it is only a few days from London, by way of India, or from the western coast of North America. Today, Australia is a crossroads south of the equator of both air and sea routes.

Because of its special features, Australia has developed some novel educa-

ST. KILDA ROAD, ONE OF MELBOURNE'S TREE-LINED BOULEVARDS
In 1837 the city, founded two years before, was named in honor of Lord Melbourne, British
Prime Minister. It is laid out with wide thoroughfares and numerous parks and public
gardens. Between 1901 and 1927 the city was one of the temporary seats of the Australian
Government. The spired church at the left of this picture is St. Paul's Cathedral.

341

ESSENDON, MELBOURNE, AUSTRALIA'S BUSIEST AIRPORT

A passenger bus leaves Essendon Aerodrome for Melbourne, seven miles away. Air travel is one of the principal means of transportation between the widely scattered Australian cities.

tional systems. For children who live on sheep and cattle stations, long distances from any town, instruction is given by correspondence. In each of the state capitals there is a school with perhaps forty to eighty teachers and no visible pupils.

Tasmania was a pioneer in developing what are called "area" schools. Ten to fifty acres are set aside as a school estate. The children who attend receive class-room instruction and they also work on the estate in various activities related to their studies. They build barns, sow crops, care for livestock and so on.

The Australians are friendly people, who welcome visitors with open-handed hospitality. Descendants of pioneers who suffered great hardships, they are robust and independent-minded.

By Hartney Arthur

DARWIN, CAPITAL CITY OF THE TROPICAL NORTHERN TERRITORY

Darwin was badly damaged by Japanese bombing raids during World War II. The houses on this rebuilt road are especially designed for comfortable living in a tropical climate. Airy and louvered (using slanted boards to admit air and keep out rain) they are built on stilts for coolness and to keep out the wood-eating termites that infest the area.

HARNESSING THE WATERS OF THE MIGHTY MURRAY RIVER

The spillway of the Hume Dam, part of a vast irrigation project on the Murray River. The Murray, with headwaters in the snow-capped Australian Alps, wanders for 1,609 miles, forming the boundary between the states of Victoria and New South Wales. The great Hume Reservoir supplies water to irrigate the sun-drenched plains of central and northwest Victoria.

PREPARING TO STRIP THE BLUBBER FROM A HUMPBACK WHALE

Whales are brought from the catcher boats to the shore station at Babbage Island. They are then flensed—stripped of their skin and of the blubber, which is processed into meal and oil.

CARRYING IRON ORE TO THE BLAST FURNACES OF NEWCASTLE

The Iron Yampi is an Australian-built cargo ship which makes the run from the iron mines at Cockatoo Island to the steel workers at Newcastle and Port Kemblea, in New South Wales.

HIGH TENSION AT THE "HEAD" OF A GAME OF BOWLS

At the end of a game of bowls, the players often use a tape measure to determine which of the bowls is nearest to the "jack," the small white ball at the center of the photo.

TASMANIAN FISHERMEN READY THEIR BOATS IN HOBART HARBOR

Hobart, the capital city of the beautiful, heart-shaped island of Tasmania, smallest state in the the Commonwealth, is a thriving port with unsurpassed shipping facilities.

HOP-PICKING TIME IN THE BUSHY PARK-GLENORA AREA, TASMANIA

Each hop picker watches intently the vital business of weighing the bags of hops. The picker's wages are based on the weight and the number of bags he has picked in a day.

AUSTRALIA: FACTS AND FIGURES

THE COUNTRY

Australia, the smallest continent, is bounded on the north by Timor Sea, Arafura Sea and Torres Strait, on the east by Coral and Tasman seas, and on the south and west by the Indian Ocean. The island of Tasmania, to the southeast, is separated from Australia by Bass Strait. Area, including Tasmania, 2,974,581 square miles; population (1951 estimate), 8,380,207.

GOVERNMENT

A sovereign member of the British Commonwealth of Nations, it consists of 6 states—New South Wales, Victoria, Queensland, South Australia, Western Australia and Tasmania—and 2 territories—Northern Territory and Federal Capital Territory. Legislative power is vested in a Federal Parliament that consists of the Governor-General as representative of the British crown, a Senate and a House of Representatives. Executive power, formally vested in the Governor-General and an Executive Council, is actually exercised by a Prime Minister and Cabinet ministers who represent the majority party in parliament. For all citizens, male and female, over the age of 21, voting is compulsory; failure to vote is punishable by fine.

COMMERCE AND INDUSTRIES

Pastoral industries and agriculture are among the chief occupations. About 135,000,000 head of livestock. Chief crops are wheat, oats, barley, hay, potatoes, sugar and fruits. Coal, gold, silver, lead, copper, zinc and tin are the leading minerals. Manufactures include iron and steel, textiles, electrical and radio equipment, drugs, chemicals, paints, machinery and metal work. Leading exports: wool, wheat, meats, flour and butter. Imports: motor vehicles and parts, petroleum, textile piece goods, electrical and non-electrical power machinery.

COMMUNICATIONS

Government-owned railways, about 28,000 miles; 648 miles, privately owned. Hard-surfaced roads, about 125,000 miles. Regular air mail and passenger service. Telephone and telegraph systems, government-owned; number of telephone sets, 1,066,385; more than 9,500 telegraph stations; 148 radio transmitting stations.

RELIGION AND EDUCATION

No established church; nearly half of the people belong to the Church of England. The states control and finance public education. Total of primary and secondary, including privately endowed, schools, is 9,800; enrollment, 1,140,739. Each state has a university and a national university is under construction in Canberra.

CHIEF TOWNS

Canberra (capital) population, 19,000 (Federal Territory, 20,772). State capitals: Sydney (New South Wales), 1,549,590; Melbourne (Victoria), 1,288,000; Brisbane (Queensland), 429,530; Adelaide (South Australia), 416,000; Perth (Western Australia), 294,000; and Hobart (Tasmania), 83,600.

347

FISHING IN THE ANCIENT MANNER

Standing in his dugout canoe, the aborigine watches the water intently, his spear ready to pounce on the first passing fish. Eye and hand work in partnership with incredible speed.

AUSTRALIA'S ABORIGINES

The Original People of the Island Continent

The visitor from Toronto or London or Chicago will find the cities and towns of Australia familiar to him. But to meet the people who lived there for long centuries before the European settlers came, visitors must go far afield. For the Australian aborigines of pure descent have vanished from all but the most remote parts of the continent. The tribes that remain still have an intricate form of government and a religion involving magic, whose secrets have yet to be understood by outsiders. The Australian aborigines invented the boomerang and are among the most skillful of hunters and trackers.

THEIR origin shrouded by the mists of antiquity, the Australian aborigines form a race apart. They are wandering hunters and food-gatherers, without settled communities or knowledge of agriculture, even in their present comparatively civilized state. Yet they have complicated systems of tribal government, social organization and religious beliefs. Regarded in the old colonial days as being of the lowest intelligence and mere cumberers of the earth, they remained a despised people until the voices of those crying in the Wilderness of Indifference were heard and a better understanding of the aborigines spread among white Australians. Even then, governments were slow to act effectively for their welfare and only in more recent years have sincere and reasoned efforts been made to save the most interesting of all primitive races of man from the fate of the Tasmanian race, which became extinct in 1876 with the death of a romantic figure—the "Princess Truganini."

When Captain James Cook made his historic voyage along the east coast of Australia in 1770, it is estimated that there were about 300,000 aborigines. Today there are less than 50,000 of pure descent. We may well describe the decline of these primitive, hardy people as a tragedy.

The southern tribes are represented by only a few broken-up remnants. Decline has been rapid among natives of the central region and in the tropical north. The only exceptions to this are in Arnhem Land and the Kimberley country of the Nor'-west, where large numbers of aborigines are living as their ancestors lived before the coming of the white man to this island continent.

It was very early in human history when the aborigine arrived in Australia—perhaps more than 60,000 years ago. Whence he came we can only conjecture, but the evidence indicates that the ancestral Australians were a small band of venturesome people from southeastern Asia. It is probable that they were the first human beings to come to the land of the kangaroo. They brought with them a wild dog, the dingo, which increased rapidly and spread throughout the continent far in advance of its masters.

However, some authorities believe that, ages ago, Australia and Tasmania—which were not then separated from the mainland by Bass Strait—were occupied by a race of, probably, Negrito people. Perhaps members of a more advanced stock came at a later period and, intermarrying with the original inhabitants, produced a new people. The second of these two theories is disproved by the fact that the aborigines are of an extraordinarily pure stock. They definitely cannot be classed with the Negro, nor do they appear to be related to the Polynesians, the Melanesians or the Micronesians. Their dark brown hair, bushy, wavy or curly, and generally of coarse texture, resembles that of certain wild tribes of India, and distinguishes them at once from the woolly or frizzy-haired Melanesians and Negroes, and also from the lost Tasmanian people, who were certainly more primitive than the migrants from southeastern Asia.

A LONG WALK UP THE COCONUT PALM

Coconuts grow in a cluster at the tip of a palm tree, 80 to 100 feet high. The nut gatherers must literally walk straight up the tree; there are no branches to break the climb.

The boomerang has been described, by Lydekker, as "a very curious connection between the Australian aborigines and certain of the wild tribes of Southern India." It is a weapon unknown to any other peoples. The so-called boomerangs of India and of the ancient Egyptians are merely curved throwing sticks, of which the Australian aborigine has many. The true boomerang is an Australian invention, whose essential feature is its ability to hover or remain comparatively motionless in the air. The "return" boomerang, rarely used in hunting, except for throwing into a flock of birds, may be regarded as more or less a plaything. There are hunting boomerangs and fighting boomerangs. Both of these are longer and less curved than the "come-back" one, which can be thrown to travel distances of more than one hundred yards, sometimes making several loops.

The aborigine, although sometimes very closely approaching black, might be termed a brownskin, for, frequently, his skin is of a light brown color. The aboriginal infant is born cream-colored; but in a few days its skin darkens, only the palms of the hands and the soles of the feet remaining of a light hue throughout life. Among natives of the western Macdonnel Ranges, the newborn babies, in the majority of cases, have white or tow-colored hair, which darkens with age.

One peculiarity of the aborigine is found also in skulls of Neanderthal man of ancient Europe—an excessive prominence in the bony portion of the skull just above the orbits. This protects the eyes, which are usually dark brown. Very protuberant jaws are a Negrolike feature. The aborigine's nose, though generally broad and

ABORIGINES ARE BORN HORSEMEN

In Arnhem Land live 3,000 aborigines, nomads all. Sometimes they drop in at one of the isolated European missions. Above is a mission corral, with a casual visitor showing his equestrian skill.

flat, is sometimes distinctly aquiline, as in members of the so-called "Jewish" tribes of central Australia.

The women especially have a stately and graceful walk. They possess a natural dignity, which is apt to be hidden when they wear European clothes. Even partly civilized aborigines of the center and the far north wear but little clothing—the little children, none at all. Many, still living in

common articles of clothing worn by both men and women in wintertime. Summer dress for a man was an apron. Women of some south Australian tribes wore bark or skin cloaks over their backs. Bark-cloth capes were also the fashion among certain Queensland tribes.

Many of the girls are handsome; but all too soon they lose their young charms, becoming "old" women before middle age.

AN ANCIENT MYSTICAL RITE

The spear dance, a ritual during a corroboree, or sacred festival, has a secret meaning known only to an inner circle. Both men and women take part, their faces painted ceremoniously.

the Stone Age manner, go naked, except for girdles, or waist-belts, with a pendant of pearl-shell or a tassel made of fur. The women wear a bark belt, or a fringe. Human hair is the usual material for making waist-cords or girdles, which often are many yards in length. When tribes still lived in the south, of course, they needed some protection against the cold weather, and kangaroo and 'possum-skin rugs were

The young men of the tribes that have little or no contact with Europeans show the aborigine at his best. He is a natural man, fit subject for a sculptor. And the old men, who administer all tribal matters in their own favor, make a picturesque group sitting in secret council. The younger men are the hunters, but the choicer portions of the game they bring back to the mia mias (the tribal camps) go to the wise

MOTHER AND CHILD OF THE NULLARBOR PLAIN

Aborigines still roam a large, curious region of southern Australia that is perfectly flat. There
is not enough moisture to support trees, hence the name Nullarbor (no tree) Plain.

IN FULL PANOPLY OF WAR

Spears, boomerangs and firesticks are the weapons. Emu feathers make the ferocious-looking helmet. Morale is contributed by the war paint—white clay and red ochre—to terrify the enemy.

old fellows according to tribal law.

Although yams and other vegetables form a large proportion of the daily fare, the aboriginal menu includes many items curious, even repulsive, to other people. Witchetty grubs, for example, white ants (termites) and their larvae, caterpillars and clay. Animal tucker is as varied, ranging from kangaroos, wallabies, 'possums and bandicoots to flying foxes (fruit-bats) and wombats, sometimes even the dingo; birds, large and small; and snakes and lizards. On special occasions untamed tribes may be cannibalistic. Cannibalism was widespread before civilization modified or changed completely such savage customs as the eating of human flesh. Coastal tribes enjoy a far better standard of living than do those of the dry inland regions. At all seasons on the coast there is an abundance of food—fish, turtles and dugong and various kinds of shellfish. In the tropical north, wild pigs provide excellent pork.

The Medicine Man's Power

Although there are no kings or chiefs among the aborigines, a leading position may be held by some outstanding member of a tribe, often the medicine man, whose authority becomes supreme at all meetings of the council. He is recognized as the headman, whose decisions on any matter are unquestioned. The medicine man, apart from treating patients by various methods, including faith cures and mumbo jumbo, often is well paid to cause an enemy's death by pointing the bone. Any aborigine may point a death bone, but when the medicine man sings over one and performs the essential actions, the result is more certain. Unless powerful counter magic comes to his aid, an aborigine who knows that he has been "boned" sits down in despair, sickens and dies. This mysterious power has yet to be explained by modern science, although it is probably psychological.

One of the many strange customs rigidly observed by the aborigine is avoidance of the mother-in-law. Under dire penalty, no man may look at his wife's mother, nor may she look upon him.

It is harder for women than for men among these nomads. Each tribe wanders within the boundaries of its own territory, living in temporary camps; and the women bear the burdens when camp is shifted. Besides carrying heavy loads of household gear, spare weapons and so on, they must carry the fire-stick and keep it alight. As widows, their lot is harder still, for mourning customs include, not only wailing and shrieking by the lubras (women), but the gashing of their heads with stone knives. Heavy widows' caps, formed of kopai and burned lime or gypsum, were worn by the women of vanished Murray River tribes, and a ban of silence was placed upon the

luckless widows, a ban often lasting for months.

Aborigines living under the age-old tribal laws are a moral folk. The laws are strictly enforced, especially those governing marriage. Breaches of some of these laws are punishable by death. This social organization ranks the aborigines above some other primitive races. Not even scientists who study races fully understand the systems of tribal government and all the ceremonies and beliefs that make the aborigine almost a mystery man. While trained scientists have devoted years to the study of this primitive man's most intimate

ALL DRESSED UP IN EAGLES' DOWN

This headman is wearing his ritualistic adornment for the chicken and emu corroboree. Eagles' down is pasted to his body with blood. Chicken and emu are totems of the tribe.

life—which embraces cult totemism (a totem is an object or animal regarded as having blood relationships to a specific family), religious systems and beliefs, family, kinship and complicated marriage laws—it is admitted that these are still mysteries beyond the comprehension of the average person not an aborigine himself.

Many of their myths and legendary tales are as imaginative as those of much more advanced peoples. A selection of the bedtime stories told among the mia mias, with a little editing, would make a delightful book for children anywhere. The Alcheringa, or Dream Time of the World, when there were only spirits, who created the ancestral spirits of totem animals, groups of men and natural objects generally, is a complicated idea that could have been developed only by myth-makers gifted with intelligence as well as imagination.

Many vocabularies of the aborigines, more or less extensive, have been published. A patient student of the primitive forms of speech thus recorded will learn that the Australian language was general all over the mainland; certain root sounds are found everywhere. However, the numerous dialects show wide variations. An aborigine of the Daly River, say, would find it difficult to understand a native from the Darwin district, speaking in the Larrakia dialect. Such variations, of course,

must have developed through centuries.

There is no written Australian aboriginal language, though there are the "letter sticks," carried by official messengers and trading emissaries. These may be emblems of authority, aids to memory, or an invitation from the council of Old Men of a leading tribe to other tribes to attend some important gathering of a national character, such as an initiation ceremony. A letter stick relating to a ceremony bears markings that are readily understood by all headmen of the nation—a nation consists of a varying number of tribes.

The ceremonies of initiation into manhood are reasoned tests of endurance for the boys, apart from their tribal significance.

In their ceremonies, the aborigines are very serious, but they possess a sense of humor and are fond of rather rough fun. This is some relief from the fear of spirits and black magic and from the strictness of tribal laws. Aborigine youngsters may have as much fun as other children enjoy, but much of their play is training for the time when the boys will become hunters and warriors. Their playthings include little boomerangs and toy spears. They receive lessons in tracking both men and animals.

Corroborees and "Cat's Cradle"

Dances and games delight the grownups. The corroborees sometimes witnessed by outsiders are merely song-and-dance performances—a form of amusement, as the familiar word signifies (*corro,* to leap or jump; *boree,* to shout or yell). Western ballroom dances have been described as civilized corroborees. At "cat's-cradle" games the aborigines excel; they are highly accomplished artists in string. Even the girls and boys make, with ease, complicated designs beyond the skill of any other children.

A glance at the aborigine's manners and customs, amusements and achievements, at his daily life and his religious beliefs, reveals him as a deeply interesting human being, with both virtues and failings, like all other men.

By Charles Barrett, c.m.z.s.

THROWING A "COMEBACK" BOOMERANG

The aborigine can throw a boomerang so that it will hover briefly motionless. The "comeback" boomerang is not much more than a toy. Hunting and fighting sticks do not return.

A VICIOUS STING RAY SURRENDERS

Fishing becomes dangerously exciting when a sting ray swims past the dugout. These monsters have a whiplike tail armed with sharp spines that exude poison. The meat of some species is edible.

MOUNT COOK'S WHITE BONNET

In South Island snow-crowned Mount Cook looks upon Hooker River. It is the highest peak in New Zealand, 12,349 feet. It was named for Captain Cook. The aborigines called it Aorangi.

SOUTH-SEA ISLAND NATION

New Zealand and Its People

Most of New Zealand consists of two islands, called simply North Island and South Island. They are in the South Pacific Ocean, a thousand miles south of the Tropic of Capricorn and about twelve hundred miles southeast of Australia. There was a time when New Zealand seemed one of the most far-away places in the world, but airplanes, fast ships and radio have changed that idea considerably. In fact, this once remote country has become a leader in many ways. Its richest resource is its fertile soil. This has been used wisely and has helped to give New Zealand one of the highest standards of living anywhere.

IN its thousand miles from north to south, New Zealand contains an amazing diversity of physical features. Its scenic wonders equal and often surpass those of the rest of the world. It has mountain ranges of extreme grandeur; scores of beautiful lakes and fiords; the largest and most complex thermal (hot springs) region in the world; one of the world's highest waterfalls; and the most remarkable glow-worm cave yet discovered. The climate is pleasant, without extremes of heat or cold, and there are many days in the year when the sun shines brightly.

New Zealand, a self-governing member of the British Commonwealth, lies in the South Pacific, some 1,200 miles southeast of Australia. With a total area of 103,736 square miles in its two main islands, this little country is slightly larger than its motherland, Great Britain, 11,000 miles away. The bonds that link New Zealand with Great Britain are strong, and the loyalty of New Zealanders to the Crown is real. This was proved during two world wars and in the periods of peace that followed.

Remarkable development has taken place in New Zealand since about 1850. The passing years have seen the face of the land change from wild forest to highly productive pasture, until today New Zealand exports more farm produce than any other country. Tiny settlements of roughly built huts have grown into great cities and ports and important market towns. Roads and railways have thrust their way over rugged highlands; huge power dams have been built to harness rivers; universities, schools and other centers of culture have established fine records; daring experiments in social legislation have given the world a lead, which many countries have already followed.

Today the two million people who inhabit this lovely land look back on these years of progress with justifiable pride.

The Dutch navigator Abel Tasman received a hostile reception from the Maoris (the native Polynesian people) when he discovered New Zealand in 1642. He sailed away without gaining a real knowledge of the land. It was left to an Englishman, Captain James Cook, who made his first visit in 1769, to map the coastline thoroughly. He also came to know the Maoris and made friends with them.

Casual settlement began early in the nineteenth century, with whalers, adventurers and deserters from ships. This was soon followed by planned immigration. The permanent settlement of New Zealand was no haphazard affair. A Scottish venture, organized by the Church of Scotland, made its landfall in the southern province of Otago, the part of New Zealand nearest in natural features to Scotland itself. The Canterbury plains received settlers from the Anglican (Church of England) organization in the central counties of England. The Taranaki province, closely resembling Devonshire in many aspects, was founded by pioneers from the south of England. The newcomers were well educated, which had its effects in the establishment of New Zealand's fine system of schools.

Native chiefs ceded the islands to the British Crown by the signing of the

Treaty of Waitangi in 1840. The treaty recognized the rights of both the Maori and European inhabitants of the new colony.

New Zealand was granted a constitution in 1852, and a Parliament in 1854. This was, in fact, a series of parliaments, for in addition to the General Assembly, the provinces also had assemblies. These lasted until 1876. Maoris were given parliamentary representation in 1864. All men of adult age were given the vote in 1879, and women were given the vote —for the first time anywhere in the world —in 1893. Dominion status came in 1907.

Today, 98 per cent of the European population are of British stock, and most of the other 2 per cent are descended from French, Danish and Norwegian pioneers, who settled in communities that have left their mark in place names and in the surnames of their descendants. Foreign-born muster less than one per cent of the country's population, in spite of the several thousands brought to New Zealand under the plan of the International Refugee Organization. The balance of the people are the native Maoris, numbering some 120,000, or 6 per cent of the total population, with whom European New Zealanders— pakehas—live in friendship and on terms of equality.

This island country has a ruggedly beautiful coastline. Inland there are deep, swift rivers, which rush down from high mountains and flow through the greenest of pastures where well-fed sheep and sleek cattle graze. New Zealand's highest mountain, Mount Cook, in South Island, pierces the clouds to rise 12,-349 feet above sea level. In North Island there are two famous active volcanoes, Ngauruhoe and Ruapehu. It is not wise to venture too close to them, for now and then they discharge sulfurous fumes, ashes and even great rocks and hot

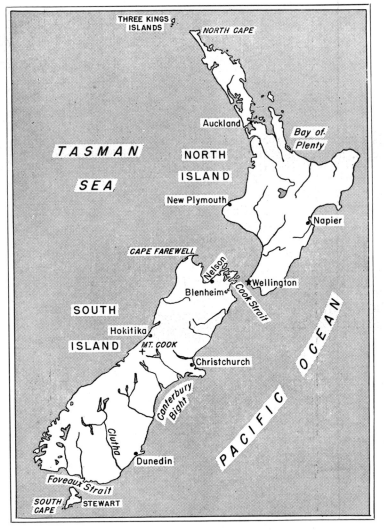

NEW ZEALAND'S TWO ISLANDS

PIX

DIPPING SHEEP, NEAR MASTERTON

The sheep swim down a trough that contains a solution of chemicals to kill vermin, and they are
thoroughly ducked en route. The scene is a large sheep station on North Island.

STALACTITES INCREDIBLY OLD

Stalactites and stalagmites merge in Aranui Cave, Waitomo, North Island. New Zealand is a geologist's paradise, with caves, hot lakes and thermal springs, volcanoes and geysers.

lava. Tongariro, beautiful Mount Egmont, often likened to Japan's famed Fujiyama, together with Tarawera—all in North Island—are extinct or quiet volcanoes. Mount Tarawera erupted last in 1886, destroying many villages as well as the beautiful pink and white terraces that had been one of the world's wonders.

In North Island is the world-famous Rotorua-Taupo area. This thermal region seems almost from another world. Freakish geysers shoot columns of steaming water into the air. The ground, vividly colored by minerals and in places hot and crumbling beneath the feet, is dotted with boiling springs and pools of hot mud. The Maoris living in the area have hot water for the asking at their back doors. They make good use of the hot pools for cooking and bathing.

The backbone of South Island is the Southern Alps, some of whose peaks are clad in eternal snow. On the west coast of this island are the famous glaciers called Franz Josef, Fox and Tasman, and wonderful fiords that rival in beauty those of Norway.

Man-Made Forests of Foreign Trees

New Zealand has no less than fourteen million acres of native forest, much of it state-owned. An adequate balance is maintained between timber needs and the conservation of scenery, water and soil. Vast man-made forests of timber trees introduced into New Zealand grow to maturity twice as quickly as they do in their native countries. They are already producing a large portion of the country's timber, and will provide the raw materials for New Zealand's pulp and paper making industry, which is being developed.

The land is the source of almost all the country's wealth. The natural advantages of climate and soil, stimulated by specialized farming techniques and scientific aid, have boosted the productivity of farmlands to a remarkable level. With electrification and the use of machines for farm operations, production per farm worker is the highest in the world—twice that of Britain, and three times that of Canada or the United States.

THIS IS THE WAY NEW ZEALAND FLAX GROWS

While European flax may grow to four or five feet, the New Zealand flax is gigantic. Long before
the white man's coming, the Maoris made linen cloth; it is still a favorite textile.

FISHERMAN'S LUCK—A RAINBOW BEAUTY

Trout are not native to New Zealand, but in 1868 some trout spawn were imported and the young
fish liberated in streams. Later salmon were introduced. Now there is fine fishing.

FOR DINNER TABLES HALFWAY ROUND THE WORLD

Meat constitutes about 20 per cent of New Zealand's exports, and most of it goes to Great Britain.
Modern methods of refrigeration are a boon to shippers and importers alike.

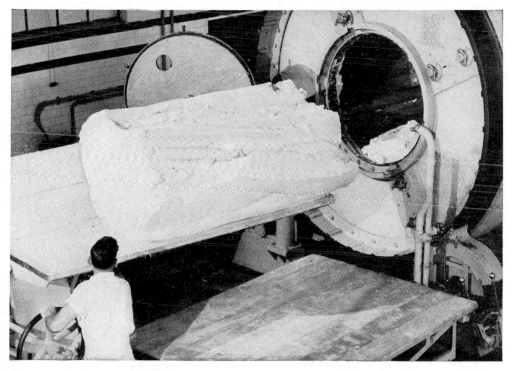

NO BUTTER FINGERS IN THIS MACHINE AGE

Annual butterfat production in New Zealand reaches about half a billion pounds, producing
almost 200,000 tons of butter, besides quantities of cheese and other milk products.

WELLINGTON ON ORIENTAL BAY

Wellington, on North Island, founded in 1840, was the first white settlement in New Zealand. It is situated on an inlet of Cook Strait, and commands the largest harbor in the Dominion.

POWER FROM RUNNING WATER

The Waikato River hydroelectric station, now completed, is one of a chain of stations that will add a million horse-power, trebling North Island's electrical production.

This small country is the world's biggest exporter of dairy produce, the second largest exporter of meat and the third largest exporter of wool. Butter, cheese and frozen meats fill the holds of the cargo ships bound for Britain. In a recent year, New Zealand was Britain's biggest supplier of dairy produce and meat.

Cattle Graze All Year Round

Dairy farming in New Zealand is unique, in that it is almost entirely grassland farming and can be carried on throughout the year without winter housing of stock. Farmers have made a close study of this pastoral farming and have developed a highly efficient technique. To raise the standard of their products and to secure the greatest returns from their land, they have made full use of agricultural research. Cows on most farms are milked by electrically driven machines. The average dairy herd is thirty cows, and the average farm is forty-eight to sixty acres, worked by the farmer and his family with no hired labor.

Sheep farming is efficient and scientific. There are three types of sheep farming— wool-growing, breeding and fat stock farming (for meat), but they merge into one another and the general aim is the production of good meat and good wool from dual-purpose sheep. The productivity of New Zealand farming lands has a direct bearing on the British standard of living. A "Food for Britain" campaign has intensified production, and the farmers, always interested—and successful— in increasing output, have been making special efforts to step up the volume of exports to the United Kingdom. Tangible evidence of their success lies in the fact that New Zealand now supplies 40 per cent of Britain's butter imports, 53 per cent of her cheese imports and a good 30 per cent of her meat imports. Smaller primary industries cover a wide range, producing cereals, fruit, hops, tobacco and flax, mainly for local needs.

In Westland and Southern Nelson, in South Island, are seams of the finest grade coal. At Greymouth and Westport there are large state-owned coal mines.

THE NATION REMEMBERS

The Cenotaph, in Wellington, erected to honor the New Zealanders who fought and died in World War I and who lie buried in foreign soil. The word "cenotaph" means empty tomb.

Since about 1935, manufacturing and other secondary industries have developed rapidly. Today, they employ one-third of the total labor force. In more than twenty thousand factories, the country processes almost all her own food, makes almost all her own clothing, boots and shoes, leather goods and furniture. Most heavy machinery is still imported, but there are well-established engineering works, iron and brass foundries, coach-building and motor-engineering works. Motor cars and trucks are assembled from imported parts. The manufacture of electrical goods, rubber goods, paint, glass, crockery and plastics is expanding rapidly.

Almost half of New Zealand's people live in cities of over 20,000 population, the largest of these being Auckland, in North Island, with 329,000. This city has grown rapidly in recent years. It offers a pleasant, warm climate, good beaches, and an excellent harbor for yachting. There are many beautiful

PLAYGROUND IN THE SKY

The Remarkable Mountains tower above Lake Wakatipu, South Island, offering a spacious playground to those who love to ski. Above, Coronet Peak (5,415 feet), one of the Remarkables.

homes, which perch on the hills or nestle in the bays, overlooking the harbor.

Nearly five hundred miles south of Auckland lies Wellington, the capital and seat of government. This city has a rugged beauty all its own and is set on one of the best land-locked harbors in the world, deep and wide enough to take the whole British fleet, if need be. Houses cling to the hills that lie behind the city. From the windows of many of these New Zealand homes, there are unsurpassed views of the harbor and city. A view of Wellington at night, with its myriad lights on harbor and hills, has been likened to night views of Hong Kong or Rio de Janeiro.

After crossing Cook Strait that divides North and South Islands and following the eastern coast of the latter for some distance, one arrives at Lyttelton, the port of Christchurch, now the second city in New Zealand. Christchurch is the chief manufacturing center of South Island. It is known as the most "English" city of the country. The pace of life is slower, and there is a restfulness about the tree-lined streets, the river Avon, with its weeping willows and grassy banks, the lovely churches, and attractive residential

suburbs with many gracious homes. For many English people it is the city in which they choose to live after retirement.

Farther south lies Dunedin, capital of Otago province and a university town, first settled by pioneers from Scotland.

The smaller towns have all the conveniences, on a lesser scale, of the cities, with well-paved streets, libraries, sports grounds and race courses. In most cases these smaller towns serve the surrounding farmlands.

The majority of New Zealand dwellings are bungalows, and most of the houses are wooden, though in parts of Auckland and in South Island one notices many brick and stone buildings. In 1951, nine houses were built for every 1,000 of population. The average number of people to every dwelling in the same year was 3.83.

An important factor in the rapid growth of secondary industries has been the development of hydroelectric power from New Zealand's ample water resources. It is the world's most electrified country, with 98 per cent of the homes supplied with electric power. The tremendous demand for power for industrial and domestic purposes has made necessary an ambitious plan for the extension of the country's generating capacity. A chain of ten hydroelectric stations is being built along the Waikato River. When complete, this will generate more than a million horsepower. New stations are also being built in South Island.

Because of its mountains and many rivers, New Zealand has been a difficult country in which to build roads and railways. Nevertheless, today it has well-developed road and rail systems that are being improved and extended continually to keep pace with the changing needs of modern transport. Owned and operated by the Government, the railway system of the country comprises a main trunk system through both islands, with cross-country lines feeding into it. The Government's policy now is to use electric locomotives as much as possible, and a general electrification program has begun.

There are 77,000 miles of roads and highways. Arterial roads—most of them state highways—provide a fast and safe means of motoring between main centers of population. The modern trend in the design of these state highways is toward the "motorway," to provide safe high-speed travel. On a population basis New Zealand is one of the world's most motorized countries.

Air services link the cities and the main provincial towns. The country is also served by the main international air lines. Air-transport time from Britain is three and a half days, and from Australia eight hours. There is a daily flying-boat service between Wellington and Sydney, and Auckland and Sydney, and a land-plane service between Christchurch and Melbourne.

The Government owns and operates the postal services, the internal airways and the broadcasting service.

In the course of a century, New Zealanders have developed their own national and individual characteristics, but their outlook remains predominantly British.

GRAND PARADE, JUNIOR STYLE

To the Agricultural and Pastoral Shows farmers bring their best stock and produce, and industries exhibit new models of all sorts. Young people have a part in the rodeos and other competitions.

LACE IN STONE, THE TOWER OF AUCKLAND UNIVERSITY COLLEGE

The graceful clock tower of Auckland University College presides over broad lawns shaded by palms and other trees. The college is a part of the University of New Zealand.

A VOLCANO OUTSIDE YOUR WINDOW

The Chateau, a hotel in Tongariro National Park, North Island, offers guests a remarkable view of Mount Ruapehu, a volcano more than nine thousand feet high. The park is in a volcanic area.

They refer to Britain as "home." The Maoris are friendly, hospitable, intelligent and adaptable descendants of the Polynesians, whose canoes were traversing the broad Pacific at a time when European seamen hesitated to venture far from sight of land. As a country, New Zealand is prosperous; it is a land of few extremes, and wealth is widely diffused.

New Zealanders know they need more people in their country, both for its further development and for adequate defense. Through the Government's immigration scheme, several thousand Britons have already been brought to the country to live and work. When it is in full operation, the scheme will provide free or assisted passage for ten thousand new settlers each year. This scheme also provides for a limited number of families from other countries to come to New Zealand. An agreement with the Netherlands Government provides for the immigration of two thousand settlers from Holland annually.

On purely physical standards New Zealand has attained a high level. In the population of European descent, death and infant mortality rates are almost the lowest in the world, and the expectancy of life is among the longest. From the prenatal level to the care of the aged, the aim to establish conditions of life that will ensure good health is strongly evident. In the practical education of mothers and expectant mothers the Plunket system has done a tremendous amount of good. Originated in 1907 by the late Sir Truby King, this system has spread from New Zealand throughout the world.

Health standards are closely connected with social welfare, the keystone of which is the Social Security Act. This ensures economic security to all who cannot earn because of age, sickness, or unemployment. Family benefits, medical, hospital and maternity benefits are also paid.

There is no unemployment in the country; in fact, there is a large number of job vacancies. Membership in unions is compulsory, and the working week is of forty hours, spread over five days. New Zea-

THE CATHEDRAL SQUARE, CHRISTCHURCH

Christchurch, on the eastern side of South Island, is laid out around this square. The city was founded by a group of Anglican churchmen; and it is the see of the primate of New Zealand.

land was the first country to adopt the principle of compulsory arbitration in industrial disputes. Minimum rates of wages and other working conditions are embodied in laws that are enforced.

New Zealand has an excellent educational system. The state provides free education for all children up to the age of nineteen. Children must remain at school until they are fifteen. All state primary schools are co-educational, and so, too, are the technical colleges, teachers' training colleges and some of the secondary schools. The Free Kindergarten movement is making rapid progress. In her educational policy New Zealand has aimed at providing facilities giving country children the same educational opportunities as city pupils. For children living in remote places and for invalids, an efficient Correspondence School provides tuition in all grades; radio is often used, and the children miss little except association with their fellows. New Zealand has four university colleges, two agricultural colleges and five teachers' training colleges. Parents who prefer to send their children to private schools have a wide choice. Most of these private schools, primary and secondary, are under church supervision. Many of them have boarding facilities, and all are subject to regular inspection by the Education Department of the Government.

The formal link with Britain is the Crown, represented in New Zealand by a governor-general.

New Zealand has its own legislature, or Parliament, which, until 1950, included a Legislative Council and a House of Representatives, the latter corresponding to the British House of Commons. The Legislative Council was abolished in December 1950. The House of Representatives has eighty members, elected every three years on universal adult franchise. Seventy-six members represent constituents of European descent and four are elected by Maori voters. The executive branch of the Government is headed by

RELAXING ON SUMNER BEACH, NEAR CHRISTCHURCH

No part of New Zealand is far from the sea. All the large cities are near the water, with fine
sandy beaches within easy reach. The scene above is near Christchurch, South Island.

the Executive Council, comprising the governor-general and members of the Ministry.

There are two main political parties in New Zealand, the National Party and the Labor Party. The Labor Party Government was defeated in the General Election of 1949 after fourteen years of continuous office. The 1952 composition of the House was: National Party 50 seats, Labor Party 30 seats.

Women are eligible for election to the House of Representatives, and they take an active part in political affairs. The 1952 Parliament included three women, one of them a Maori representative, and

another a Minister of the Crown.

In no other part of the world is the incentive to play in the open air greater than it is in New Zealand. Sport plays an important part in the national life. Organized games are only part of the ordinary New Zealander's sporting interests. Nearness to mountains, lakes, rivers and beaches gives unlimited opportunities for the enjoyment of individual sports such as swimming, tramping, shooting, skiing, angling and yachting. New Zealanders take full advantage of these opportunities; the effect is reflected in their general health and fitness.

BY N. E. DONOVAN

NEW ZEALAND: FACTS AND FIGURES

THE COUNTRY

A group of islands between the Tasman Sea and the South Pacific Ocean, 1,200 miles southeast of Australia; total area, 103,736 sq. mi. In addition to the main islands, North (44,281 square miles) and South (58,093 square miles), there are a number of others—Stewart (670 square miles), Chatham Islands (372 square miles) and minor islands (320 square miles). The population, including Maoris, 1,939,703.

GOVERNMENT

A sovereign state, it is a member of the Commonwealth of Nations. Executive authority is vested in a governor-general and an Executive Council, or Cabinet. The Cabinet, made up of a Prime Minister and 15 other ministers who represent the majority party in Parliament, carries on the government. Legislative power is vested in the House of Representatives; another chamber of Parliament, the Legislative Council, was abolished as of January 1, 1951. All adults, male and female, have the right to vote; Maoris have 4 seats in the House.

COMMERCE AND INDUSTRIES

Two-thirds of the land is suitable for farming and grazing. Principal crops are wheat, oats and barley. The country's principal industry is animal husbandry; livestock—4,723,000 cattle, 32,845,000 sheep—total of all kinds, 38,309,000 head; world's third largest producer of wool; one of the ten leading producers of meat. Leading manufactures are butter and cheese, preserved meats, clothing, prepared wood, auto bodies and parts, and fertilizers. Leading minerals are coal, gold, silver, silicon, serpentine, iron ore and petroleum. Chief exports are wool, butter, frozen meats, cheese, hides, skins and pelts. Imports include machinery, cotton piece goods, motor vehicles and parts, gasoline.

COMMUNICATIONS

Railway mileage in 1950 for North and South islands was 3,526, largely government-owned. Total mileage of roads and highways is about 77,000. Regular domestic and international air service. The telegraph and telephone systems are government-owned; number of telephone subscribers, 257,034. Number of radio transmitting stations, 31.

RELIGION AND EDUCATION

There is no established or aided religion; Church of England predominates; numerous other faiths are represented. Education is compulsory for ages 7 to 15 and free for regular public courses. There are 2,200 public and private primary schools with 276,659 pupils; 269 secondary schools with 51,623 pupils. 4 university and 2 agricultural colleges comprise the University of New Zealand; with 5 normal colleges there is a total enrollment in higher education of about 12,500. There are also rural, mission, village, special and technical schools and numerous correspondence students.

POPULATION OF CHIEF CITIES

(Provisional figures from the 1951 census) Auckland, 328,995; Christchurch, 174,100; Wellington (capital), 133,416; Dunedin, 95,309; Hutt City, 74,855; Hamilton, 33,138; Palmerston North, 32,800; Invercargill, 31,600.

ISLANDS

Chatham Islands, consisting of Chatham and Pitt islands, are 535 miles east of Christchurch and are administered as a county. Population of about 700 is occupied mostly in animal husbandry. Stewart Island, part of Southland district, is separated from South Island by Foveaux Strait. It is a tourist resort. Principal among the minor islands within geographical limits are Kermadec Islands and Campbell Island.

Outer possessions include Cook Islands, Niue Island and the Tokelau group. New Zealand administers the Western Samoas under a UN trusteeship (for Facts and Figures on these outlying territories see page 321).

THE MAORIS TODAY

New Zealand's Splendid Native People

In all too many areas where colonization has taken place in territory already inhabited by another and very different people, conflict has been the result. The relationship between the Maoris and the people of European descent in New Zealand is a shining exception. Here good neighbors live together on terms of mutual respect and complete equality. To be sure, the Maoris were already an advanced stock, highly gifted in the arts, before the Europeans ever came. Originally the Maoris, a Polynesian people, came from the central South Pacific islands, making the long voyage in outrigger canoes.

THE Maori people of New Zealand have been described as the leading Polynesian stock of the Pacific. It is a distinction amply justified by their intelligence, which is reflected in a wide and interesting variety of highly developed arts and crafts, handed down and improved through the centuries. The Maori has also endowed New Zealand with a wealth of mythology, traditions and legends, history and poetry, forming a rich store of material and inspiration for the writers, artists and poets of today.

By their own efforts, guided by their own outstanding leaders, and with the assistance of New Zealanders of European descent, the Maoris have raised themselves to a state of equality in every sphere of life. Today there is less evidence of a color bar in New Zealand than in any other part of the world. Maori development in recent years is no longer a progress toward equality, but one toward a closer partnership with the Europeans. There has been a sharing of civic and national responsibility since 1852, when the Constitution Act gave Maoris the same voting rights as Europeans. The Maoris exercise fully their right to return four mem bers of Parliament to represent them as a race.

In a population of 2,000,000 people, the Maoris number about 120,000, compared with 57,000 in 1921. The Maori birth rate has reached an average of 45 per 1,000, almost double that of the New Zealanders of European descent, and but for their higher death rate among children, the Maoris would be more numerous. If

the death and birth rates remain constant, there will be 547,000 Maoris by 2005; but there is every hope that they will number many more than that with the increasing number of Maori doctors, dentists, nurses and teachers working among their own people, and helping to break down the old reluctance to take advantage of modern treatment when ill.

The history of the Maori people in the last thousand years is marked by outstanding feats of navigation and seamanship across the vast spaces of the uncharted Pacific. A highly developed and closely knit tribal system, based on the family group, assured the Maoris of unity in times of danger or war. This system gave them courage, discipline and an ability to adapt themselves to new lands and conditions.

The discovery of Aotearoa (Long White Cloud), as New Zealand was named by the first Maori navigator, is attributed to their hero Kupe, who made one of the world's great sea voyages in a sturdy outrigger. He came to New Zealand by holding "a course to the left of the setting sun" according to Maori lore. When he reached the country, he sailed around both North and South Islands, giving to capes and bays and other features along the coast names that survive to this day. Kupe was followed 200 years later by Toi of Tahiti, using the sailing directions left by Kupe; and 600 years later by Captain Cook, who sailed around both islands in the same manner as Kupe had done, although at the time Captain Cook did not know of the great Maori sailor who had preceded him by several centuries. It was in the fourteenth century that the main Maori migration to New Zealand took place.

Scientists who study races and their cultures believe that the Maoris came to New Zealand from Hawaiki, subsequently identified as Raiatea, in the Society Islands. The history and migrations of the Maoris and their settlement of the island groups of the central and eastern Pacific are given in the late Sir Peter Buck's book, THE VIKINGS OF THE SUNRISE. Sir Peter, director of the Bishop Museum in Honolulu at the time of his death, late in 1951, and himself half Maori, was the best-qualified person to disentangle history from myth in the lore of his people, which was handed down only by word of mouth. He said that the Maoris entered the Pacific from somewhere in the Malay Archipelago, moving south by way of the Micronesian Islands, to the Caroline and Marshall groups, from where they spread: northeast to the Sandwich (present-day Hawaiian)

Islands; south to Samoa; southeast to the Society Islands; and then to New Zealand by way of the Cook Islands. Sir Peter came to the conclusion that the settlement of the group of islands in central Polynesia took place about the fifth century A.D.

Speaking on the origin of the Maoris, Sir Peter stated that in remote ages the ancestors of the Polynesians probably lived in some part of India, and worked east, but myths and legends do not reach back that far.

"They must have sojourned in Indonesia in order to reach the Pacific: the Polynesian language has affinities with Indonesian dialects," he said. "When the pressure of Mongoloid peoples, pouring in from the mainland, became oppressive, the Polynesian ancestors turned their gaze towards the eastern horizons, and embarked upon one of the greatest of all adventures." The same pressure of population, and also dissatisfaction with the

A KISS BY ANOTHER NAME

The Maori salutation, or welcome, is called "Hongi." It consists of a handclasp and touching of noses. These women of North Island have bobbed hair in the European manner.

THE ANCIENT ART OF WOOD CARVING

The center pole of the entrance to this Maori meeting house suggests, in its carving, the Indian totem poles. Most Maori patterns are in curves, straight lines being rare.

377

THE MEETING HOUSE AT GISBORNE

The Maori *pa*, or village, is usually built facing the *marae*, the open grassy space in front of the meeting house. Most meeting houses have a large social hall and kitchen attached.

THE SOLEMN CEREMONY OF TATTOOING

"Tattoo" (*tatu*) is a Polynesian word. The custom of tattooing, once widespread among the Polynesian peoples, is on the decline now. The Maoris developed the art to a high degree.

social order in the islands of the Pacific, led to the last great migration, which took the emigrants to New Zealand. By the time this happened, "Long White Cloud" was more than a legend to the Maori people. Kupe's discovery had been rediscovered, and the Maoris had all the necessary information to steer them to "the land full of birds," as Kupe put it.

The Little Fleet of Eight Canoes

The migratory party, with supplies of food, food plants, and seeds, set sail about 1350 A.D., in eight big outrigger canoes bearing the historic names of Tainui, Arawa, Takitimu, Aotea, Mataatua, Kurahaupo, Tokomaru and Horouta. Maoris today, as in the past, trace their descent to an ancestor who came in one of these canoes. "Coming over in the canoe" is to the Maori what "coming over in the Mayflower" is to Americans.

So the Maori settlement of New Zealand began. In South Island the new arrivals found the remnants of a race called the Moriori. These people, according to legend, had come to New Zealand in the last of a series of migratory waves from the Pacific Islands that had begun in the eighth century. This legend is supported by the fact that the Morioris also understood navigation. When the Morioris finally had to make way for the more vigorous Maori newcomers, they migrated to the Chatham Islands, some five hundred miles east of New Zealand. The last full-blooded Moriori died there about 1920; but some hundreds of Moriori descendants, partly of Maori or European stock, still live in the Chathams, where the main occupations are sheep-farming and fishing.

The Maori's settlement of New Zealand, looked at from any angle, was an outstanding success. He overcame all his formidable initial difficulties—a land vastly bigger than his previous island home; a colder climate, in which the kumara (sweet potato) was the only one of the many island food plants he brought with him that survived; and a climate that demanded much warmer clothing and housing.

The Maori prospered and multiplied. The nineteenth century saw the beginning of European settlement in New Zealand, but it was not until 1840 that ordered government was constituted. This followed the Treaty of Waitangi, under which New Zealand became a Crown Colony of Britain. The treaty was signed by Lieutenant-Governor Captain Hobson, representing the British Government, and by a majority of the Maori chiefs.

The Treaty of Waitangi comprises three short articles. In the first, the Maoris ceded "all rights and powers of sovereignty" to Queen Victoria. In the second, the Queen confirmed the chiefs and their families "in full, exclusive, and undisturbed possession of their lands and estates, forests, fisheries and other properties." However, the chiefs had to yield to the Crown the exclusive right of purchase over such lands as the proprietors were disposed to transfer. In the third article, the Queen gave to the Maoris all the rights and privileges of British subjects.

The Maori people have always been grateful for British protection and they are proud to be British subjects. During the

PIPING HOT WATER, BUT NO PIPES

Nature supplies the hot water for this young man's daily bath in the lake near his home. Around Rotorua, North Island, there are many hot-water pools and lakes and geysers.

second World War, their leader, the late Sir Apirana Ngata expressed that feeling when he declared:

"The protection enjoyed under the British flag was something no other nation could offer its peoples. Our war effort has been prompted by a full appreciation of the democratic principles, and by a desire to uphold the British Crown and Commonwealth and institutions, which guaranteed to all native peoples incorporated in the Empire, just and democratic treatment, such as native populations under other governments marvel at. To have failed to help at a time when the Empire and its principles were in deadly peril would have been an act of baseness. However, no one can accuse the Maori people of having failed in their duty."

Young Maoris to the Rescue

For fifty years after the arrival of the Europeans, the Maori population gradually decreased. A band of Maori intellectuals, known as the Young Maori Party, waged a battle for racial survival. They were led by Ngata, who had obtained the degrees of Master of Arts and Bachelor of Laws —he was the first member of his race to graduate. It was due to the devoted efforts of the Young Maoris that the decline in population was arrested. But the fight was uphill all the way. The battle was for better physical health, for improved educational opportunity, for understanding of the *pakeha's* (European's) way of life and adjustment of the Maori to it. The Maori moral code and age-old customs had to be adapted to Western civilization. The spiritual life of the race had to be refreshed and deepened. At the turn of the century, there began an astonishing resurgence, possibly without parallel in modern times.

This spectacular rise in the Maori population brought an economic problem—the problem of assuring a livelihood to the thousands of young Maori men and women of the present and future generations. No longer was the three million acres of reasonably good land, which was all that remained of the Maori ancestral holdings, able to maintain such a population.

More and more the young Maori had to seek a livelihood in the professions and industries of the cities and towns. This movement, which first became pronounced during the years of the first World War, presently received a new impetus as the result of an enlightened government policy. The keystone of this wise policy was the absence of racial barriers in the way of the Maori.

Today, Maori doctors, dentists, lawyers, accountants, school teachers (both men and women), nurses and dental nurses, skilled tradesmen and other Maori workers are playing a prominent part in New Zealand's economic and industrial life.

Two important government departments are administered by Maoris—one of them the Department of Maori Affairs, which is responsible for the vast development schemes of Maori-owned lands.

The whole field of education, from kindergarten to university, is now open to the Maori on exactly the same liberal terms as are enjoyed by the rest of the population. Much progress has been made in improving the standards of Maori housing and health.

Helping Maoris on the Land

All avenues of government employment, as well as private employment, are open to Maoris. There have been spectacular advances by which big areas of Maori-owned land lying fallow or underdeveloped for many years have been brought into production. The successful development scheme was initiated in 1929 by Sir Apirana Ngata, the most able administrator the Maori race has produced. In his capacity as Minister of Maori Affairs, he drafted legislation that laid the cornerstone for the enterprise which is today so lucrative for the Maori owners. The lands chosen for development are at first administered by the Department of Maori Affairs. During the development period, young Maoris are trained to be farmers, and when the land is ready these young men take it over.

Other Maori leaders who contributed to the renaissance of the race include the late Sir James Carroll, member of Parliament, and minister of the Crown; Sir

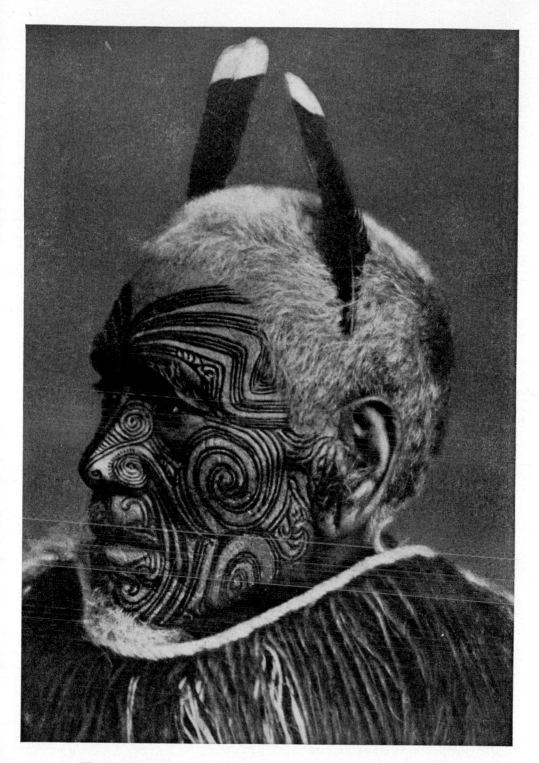

FEATHER CLOAK AND TATTOOING ONCE INDICATED RANK

The modern Maori chieftain no longer wears the traditional garb, a feathered cloak, nor is his face tattooed. He is a university man, trained for leadership in today's complex world.

PAPAKURA GEYSER, "A VOLCANO OF WATER"

At Whakarewarewa, North Island, geysers eject columns of water and steam at fixed intervals, to the accompaniment of underground rumblings or sharp reports. Papakura geyser is awe-inspiring.

A COMMUNITY LAUNDRY IN THE OPEN AIR

In the hot springs area of North Island, some pools and lakes are used for washing and different ones for cooking. There are pools of varying degrees of warmth in this astonishing district

ONE OF MOTHER NATURE'S COOKSTOVES

Yes, you can make a fricassee or cook cereal in this outdoor pool at Whakarewarewa. In past stages this whole area was a mass of spouting volcanoes. The activity has by no means died.

TRADITIONAL BEAUTY

Maori wood carving is a craft that has been handed down from father to son for generations. The work is done by hand, with slow and loving care. The art is encouraged by the Government.

Maui Pomare, the first Maori to become a doctor of medicine, and who later became Minister of Health; the late Sir Peter Buck, who represented the Maori race on the Executive Council, and was Director of Maori Hygiene, and later director of the Bishop Museum, in Honolulu. These men, and many others, spurred the race to effort after a period of decline that many thought would extinguish the Maori race forever.

These leaders were also conscious of their duties to the nation as a whole, as were their people. The Maori batallions raised to fight in two world wars were made up of volunteers, and their courage and enterprise on all the battlefields on which they fought is a cherished and glorious part of New Zealand's military record. The Maori, sensible of the reputation of his warrior ancestors, and displaying an inherent instinct for military tactics and strategy, covered himself with glory. One of them was the youthful Te Moana-Nui-a-kiwa-Ngarimu, a second lieutenant in the infantry. He won the Victoria Cross for outstanding leadership and courage in leading several charges against German positions in Tunisia, until he fell at the head of the last charge, which he commanded although already severely wounded.

The resurgence developed under the aegis of Ngata, Buck, Pomare and Carroll goes on uninterrupted. The preservation of Maori culture has manifested itself in the erection of many of the finely carved traditional meeting-houses, in a renewed interest in the arts and crafts and in the Maori language. In this work many New Zealanders of European descent are actively interested; and the Government has spent considerable sums of money to help the Maori race revive its culture.

There is much still to be done in this direction, but the main social and political obstacles, which would have made a cultural renaissance impossible, have long been removed. All the people of New Zealand may take pride in this achievement, by which a rich heritage has been preserved and is being fostered. The whole of the Maori outlook today is one of high hope and confidence.

BY GEORGE BRYANT

EDUCATION FOR TOMORROW

Maori youth are being educated in the sciences to take their place in the atomic age. Practically all Maori children and young people go to school, with European classmates.

INDEX FOR VOLUME V

COLOR PLATES IN VOLUME V

INDEX FOR VOLUME V

(General Index for entire work of 7 volumes may be found at the end of Volume 7)

A single star before a page number marks an illustration; two stars are placed before color-plates. The repetition of a page number, first without a star, and then with a star, shows that there is an illustration on the page, in addition to an important text reference.